It's Your Word Against Mine

How Words Express the Cultural Traditions of the US and Roebuck, St. Peter, Barbados

By Sylvester Carrington

Strategic Book Publishing and Rights Co.

Strategic Book Publishing and Rights Co., LLC
USA | Singapore
www.sbpra.com

For information about special discounts for bulk purchases, please contact Strategic Book Publishing and Rights Co., LLC Special Sales, at bookorder@sbpra.net.

ISBN: 978-1-62212-691-0

In Dedication
To Max and Aunt Gloria

CONTENTS

PROLOGUE

But words do matter. They provide life for our thoughts, our feelings, and our emotions.

When I first moved to the US mainland in 1980, I got into trouble numerous times when I opened my mouth to speak. Not that I cursed, was politically incorrect, or was verbally abusive to citizens of other cultures, religions, or countries of origin. I was not, and still am not, that kind of person. Many times, when I attempted to communicate in graduate school, in church, during polite and casual conversations, and in professional settings, I had to make a very deliberate effort to be sure that the message I was about to deliver, or that the response I was about to express was clear, and that it would be received without conflicting interpretations.

I was very aware of my deep, rich West Indian accent; Barbadian to be exact. Nobody knew better than I of the barriers my accent erected to block effective communication with others who were not of my imported culture. "Speak English," Grace Oliver, a teacher at Lookout Valley High School yelled at me one day as I addressed the staff. However, my accent was only one part of the two-tiered problem. A more troubling but humorous piece to the predicament was that some of the words I used, often caused quite a stir. These were simple words that meant one thing in my original culture but had a completely different meaning in my newly adopted way of life. This made for some very interesting times as one may imagine;

especially when Americans also used words that meant something vastly different from what they meant when I was growing up in Roebuck, Barbados.

One case in point. I was sitting in the bleachers with other parents at one of my son's Little League baseball games in Collegedale, Tennessee one afternoon, when a fly ball came our way. "Heads up," many warned as they protected their heads with their hands. I remember yelling "Look out!" while simultaneously taking evasive action. This was the only Barbadian warning I knew for such a circumstance.

Obviously, I was in the habit, and still am, of encountering similar experiences to the one mentioned above, and as time went on, the idea to record them in a book of some sort began to take root but it died a slow death as time passed. There was a rebirth several years ago while I was teaching a graduate class in multicultural education in Dade County, Georgia, for the University of Tennessee at Knoxville. While I kept the project at the forefront of my thinking since 1996, actual work on it remained dormant for quite a while.

The idea was given renewed thinking many summers ago while I was teaching a similar class at Southern Adventist University in Collegedale Tennessee. A friend was going to be away on leave and suggested that I submit an application to teach the class while she was absent. It was the best thing she could have done and the best invitation she could have extended. It was very early in the first meeting of the class that I decided once and for all that the book had to be written. But it is now several years since the final decision was made, and only now have I sat down at my computer to begin.

I must admit that with both graduate classes, I was not surprised at the first questions the students posed. I am forced to entertain them every time. "Where are you from?" "What language do you speak?" Some would be more direct and specific with their questioning. "Are you from Jamaica?" "Are you from Africa?" It is somewhat amazing that the same questions are asked of me by the students at the elementary, middle and high school levels where I have taught, or served as an administrator. They, like the older and more enlightened graduate students, seem to think that every black person with a foreign accent has got to be from Jamaica, or Africa. When I first came to the U.S, a similar episode like the one I just described would have upset me, however slightly. "Americans have got to realize that there are other places in the world apart from Jamaica and Africa," I would say. I have since discovered that their education consists almost entirely of movies and news briefs presented by the media; especially television.

I was quite aware that my accent was a huge hit among my graduate students as they often voiced that they loved to hear me speak, even though I had to repeat myself, sometimes too often, as I engaged them in heated discussions on several topics of culture and contemporary themes, ranging from religion to food to politics, and from racism to education, poverty, and sexuality. I was impressed with the quality of their oral and written assignments as intense debates raged from week to week. I especially looked forward to the cultural dishes that were weekly assignments, and the new vocabulary that accompanied them. In time, I surprised them with new and strange words of my own; words that sometimes entertained, baffled, and even confused them. I can't forget the time when I intentionally dropped words like *tot, buller* and *chopper* in context.

Encouragement to write the book also came from a foreign source. In 2001 I visited London with a group of teachers to observe the teaching of literacy in British schools. As it turned out, I was the only one in the group of a non-American descent and this made for some very interesting events. I vividly recall one large group meeting we had with one of the British hosts who was conducting a seminar on the teaching of reading and writing. At one point he mentioned these two words: *full stop*. Heads began to turn automatically as faces silently expressed the "I don't know what he is talking about" look — all, except mine, of course. I sat there proud as a peacock, confidently knowing that a full stop is the punctuation mark that comes at the end of a written sentence or statement. Americans refer to it as a *period.* I hate to think what would have transpired within that group had he mentioned *black lead* and *rubber,* or even *bonnet* or *pram.*

I spent all this time collecting and categorizing words and terms like these to include in the book, only to lay the project aside to write and publish *A Principal's Personal Journey,* a daily journal of my experiences for an entire year, while working as an assistant principal in an inner city elementary school in Chattanooga, Tennessee.

It's Your Word Against Mine is about words and word usage. It is simply a collection of words and terms that are commonly used in Roebuck, Barbados, where I grew up, that have a vastly different meaning in America; and some words that are commonly used in the US that have a completely different meaning in my native Roebuck. The book is written to inspire lighthearted and fun reading, while at the same time, transmitting knowledge about two cultures in a less formal and indirect way.

I have been a diligent student of words and word origins ever since my high school principal in Barbados, Mr. Lynch, told us one day that he did not want to see us *perambulating* the streets of Bridgetown when we should be in class. I did not immediately rush to consult my dictionary as to the meaning of that big new word. Contextual clues instantly provided its meaning. Additionally, my exposure to the study of Latin, French and Spanish in high school provided a helpful foundation in deciphering the origin and meanings of many English words. My interest in words and their origin still motivates me to enjoy numerous word games on the Game Show Network: Password, Super Password, Lingo, Pyramid and Chain Link, to mention only a few. Of course, the board game version of Scrabble is the grand daddy of all word games. I am also one that would sit and enjoy a boring televised spelling bee.

One of the obstacles that stood in my way as I worked on getting the project off the ground was my own self-doubt as a writer. Ironically, as an educator, I have always sought to encourage my students to write often and to think of themselves as authors. And it was encouraging to see the improvement some of them made over time, with regular practice. But when it came to self motivation to write, I found it difficult to take the same advice I had been giving to my students. As a matter of fact, my dilemma was not centered on a personal inability to write effectively.

Writing came fairly easily for me as a high school student at the Modern High School and later as a college student at Erdiston Teachers College, even though I never had a formal course in writing. Growing up in Barbados I was fortunate to be exposed to the British system of education, and as a result of the vast exposure to writing in every subject area, I became rather comfortable with the skill, and still consider my developmental level to be somewhere around the average level, or slightly above.

I was concerned about the nature of the content of this book. "Who would want to read about words used by people in Barbados?" I would ask myself. I fought hard to remove the self-doubt I had inflicted.

It became obvious quite early in the planning stages of the project that a mere collection of words and how their meanings and usage in Barbados differed in the U.S would not be sufficient to meaningfully engage readers for any length of time, or more significantly, on a level high enough that would maintain their interest. On the other hand, enough words had to be found that would provide enough material to include in the book. I needed to accumulate a list of words that had a completely different meaning in their usage here in America from the meanings to which I was accustomed when I grew up in Barbados; words like *biscuit, half bath*, *air* and t*ot*; to mention only a few.

To combat the issue of brevity, I had to be intentional about seeking input from as many people as possible, with a goal of significantly adding to the initial collection that was started earlier. One such meeting took place several years ago when I was visiting New York. My sisters and I happened to be meeting quite informally in Cousin Jenny's apartment in Brooklyn and we began to brainstorm the beginnings of a list of words that met the criteria for selection. Other sources along the way included my face to face conversations with several people, watching the news on television, as well as subsequent telephone conversations with my sisters.

Living in Ringgold, Georgia presented its own unique set of challenges. The opportunity to engage other Barbadians, even West Indians, in conversation is next to impossible, since the large majority of immigrants do not care to settle in areas that are less advantageous to their economic and educational growth. The metropolitan areas of Brooklyn, Miami, Atlanta and Toronto are more attractive by far; for obvious reasons.

This state of affairs was responsible for creating the, *if you don't use it, you will surely lose it* situation, as far as regular use of my Barbadian (Bajan) cultural words was concerned. This was compounded by the fact that by the time I had seriously begun to think about putting the book together, I had already left Barbados decades earlier and apart from the three years in Jamaica, where I enjoyed a close relationship with Randall Phillips, Lionel Lynch, Malcolm Clarke and Randy Skeete, four fellow students from Barbados, and later, following graduation, with Randall (Randy) and Lionel (Sammy) in the Virgin Islands, opportunity to practice my cultural craft was severely curtailed.

Thus, a feeling of inadequacy persisted; the feeling that I did not, and would never secure an enough material for a book of sufficient length. This too had its impact on the start of the project; again delaying its beginning for a brief time. When I finally began to write, I did so with the hope that more words would be discovered and that, most importantly, a strategy and format would magically emerge on the best way to present those ideas that would eventually begin to unfold.

Fortunately, as the manuscript developed, both wishes began to unfold simultaneously. The word bank grew significantly and a strategy and format on how to use them effectively to satisfy the purposes of the book were uncovered. However, it became quite evident that a mere listing of each word, with a corresponding description of its meaning and use in each culture would not be enough, and would be rightly perceived as being incomplete and even inadequate. Hence, the decision was made to formulate, as far as practical, a brief story around each word. In many instances, the stories are gleaned from my personal experiences, a decision that transforms some sections of the book into an autobiographical genre; an idea that was not even considered when the project was being considered in the early developmental stages.

As readers move through the early chapters, they will easily discover that the setting for the book is Roebuck, a small obscure country district in the northern parish of St. Peter, Barbados where I was born and raised. Even though the decision was made to focus on a specific locale, rather than on the island of Barbados in general, the cultural words that were selected for inclusion in the various narratives and the stories told throughout the book are applicable to many of the small agricultural districts across the island nation.

Something very exciting happened quite recently, just as I was preparing to submit the manuscript to the publishers. My wife, Hortense and I, along with my sisters, Elaine, Yvonne, Cheryl, Heather (Neats), Aunt Gloria and Cousin Jenny took a trip back to Barbados. We spent a great deal of time in Roebuck. While there, I welcomed the opportunity to reconnect with many of the people mentioned in the book and the chance to update and validate the stories that are included. Readers will be made aware of this as they progress through the book.

My hope is that readers everywhere, particularly those in the U.S, in Barbados, the Caribbean and beyond, will appreciate the project for the way it uses simple words to portray the differences, as well as the commonalities, between two cultures.

S.C.

CHAPTER ONE
They Said What?

In the final analysis, it is obvious that words play a prominent role in expressing the thoughts, and teaching the lessons of every culture.

The late Art Linkletter used to say a long time ago that "Kids say the darndest things." And how right he was! And Art might have also known that adults did say the darndest and most outrageous things as well. Similarly, I too have discovered that the most amusing words and sayings I have heard uttered by humans are not limited to the young of the species but that it is an equal opportunity condition that touches all age levels of the human spectrum.

When I hear language and word usage that sound different, I become alert and interested. While in the process of writing this particular chapter, my listening skills became much more acute as I listened most critically to news broadcasts, unintentionally eavesdropped on the private and personal conversations of others, and paid closer attention to the diction and grammar of my students, friends and colleagues; only to gather a collection of strange and invented words, or even those ordinary ones that were misplaced, misused, and even abused.

Suffice it to say, the following section that follows is not meant to demoralize individuals or groups. Rather, it is meant to draw light-hearted attention to cultural verbal differences; cultural differences unique to the US; those that I have encountered during my interactions with Americans since leaving Roebuck. Some I find

1

hilarious. Others are simply too far outside the realm of grammatical correctness. Yet, the cultural uniqueness of each situation described in the following narrative is simply that and nothing else — a cultural uniqueness.

As mentioned previously, I am always conscious of my unique accent and as I worked on this section of the project I was even more cognizant of that fact and would sometimes ask myself "Who am I, with my funny accent and strange pronunciation, to be poking fun at anyone when it comes to matters of the spoken word?" In my defense, I think my spoken language is excellent, but in this country other variables come into play. To tell the truth, I have become more than accustomed, and without being personally offended by "What did he say?" or, "Speak English" or "I didn't understand a word he said." Let's say that I have grown enormously since my initial arrival in America. Participating in graduate school discussions was difficult and daunting to say the least. Utter frustration, coupled with the fear of speaking, reduced me to silence for much of my graduate experience. But I was superior at getting my point across on paper, and not many could overshadow me in this regard. I well remember when the time finally rolled around for the oral defense of my doctoral dissertation. By that time I had already learned the art of controlling the rapidity of my speech in order to be understood. The accent, I could not change. As a matter of fact, I didn't want to. And I still don't. In reality, and in all honesty, I adore my accent. It is innate. It is who I am. It is me.

Before continuing, I am being overcome with the overwhelming feeling that somehow I was destined to write something about grammar, if only in a lighthearted way, as is presented in the following sections. I now remember with a chuckle, how focused I was on grammar after graduating from Erdiston Teachers' College. Somehow, a cadre of young college educated teachers that included Tony Jordan, Haynesley Benn, Francilla Haynes and Vasco Toppin, took it upon ourselves to act as protectors of the Queen's English, and anyone who dared to speak outside the boundaries of proper grammar was humorously ridiculed without mercy; as was the case with one of Haynesley's girlfriends, who responded with "I is not name so" after being called by another name. There is a lot more detail to the story but all I am going to say is that neither she nor Haynesly, nicknamed Czar, has been able to shake off the effects of that unfortunate grammatical declaration. It still has a way of popping up every now and then.

The sections that follow draw attention to several specific cases of misused words, cultural grammatical infringements and invented words and terms. Probably the best and most appropriate place to start is a place of familiarity for me — the school house. Of all places, the school house should be an example and dispenser of excellence in grammar, diction and other domains of literacy and language. But read on and be amused.

Back in 1991 I was newly hired as the assistant principal at Howard Elementary school in Chattanooga, Tennessee. One day, the principal was describing an incident to me that had happened between a teacher and a student. Her story had a line that went something like this. "… and the teacher *drugged* the student…" The first question that popped into my curious mind was, "Isn't it illegal for a teacher to drug a student?" Of course the teacher had done no such thing. The teacher was guilty of a much lesser offence; that of dragging the student. Not drugging the student.

Needless to say, I was absolutely certain that when used as a verb, drug simply meant *to affect with drugs*. Similarly, I also knew that drugged or drugging had nothing to do with the act of moving a person or thing from one place to another. It was the first time I had heard drug used in this form, but it was not to be the last because it kept coming up time after time, and each time I heard it I kept reminding myself that the people of Roebuck would have never abused drug in that way.

Some time had elapsed and I had again begun working on the

book in all earnestness. One evening I was watching the evening news on one of the major television networks when one news item resurrected the dragging issue, only this time it was perfectly stated. It was very refreshing to hear one Dan Satterberg, the King County Prosecutor from Carnation, Washington, in a press conference say that "The accused had dragged the dead body of the victim from its original location to another." I almost jumped up and down with glee, shouting "He got it right." But I didn't. Way to go Mr. Satterberg! You are a great example. But wait…

By this time the presidential campaign of 2008 was in full swing, and presidential candidate Mike Huckabee was involved in another drugging case. Commenting on the precipitous fall from grace of New York governor, Elliot Spitzer, Huckabee proclaimed on March 11, 2008 on Bill Oreilly's *The Factor* that "Spitzers's wife and daughters are going to be drugged through this." Drugged through this? I said to myself. Way to go Mr. Former Governor and aspiring president. This drugging business was worse than I had imagined.

Even men of the cloth need to ask forgiveness, for they too are guilty of drugging. And I have the evidence to prove my case. The highly regarded Joel Osteen, commander of the largest church in America, responding to a question on Sixty Minutes on June 8 about his parishioners, said in part "… they weren't drugged to come to church…" It is a good thing they were not. Who would have *thunk* it?

Speaking on the subject of thunk, I am realizing that it is quickly becoming an acceptable form of the verb to think. The first time I heard it I was sitting in church one day, enjoying a rather engaging sermon by a young minister, Mike Fulbright, when he suddenly sprung *thunk* on the sophisticated and highly educated congregation of the Collegedale Seventh-day Adventist Church. I did a quick look around to see how many heads were turning, or how many eyes were rolling but came up with a big fat zero, which quickly told me that thunk was acceptable. In Roebuck we never said thunk. We might have said *tink,* as in 'I tink so'. But never thunk.

And in Roebuck we never drugged anything, or anyone. We always dragged, as in this true and personal story I am about to tell.

One Sunday morning, I took out my sheep all by myself. Usually, my friend, Livingstone, and I would take out our sheep together to graze in Midfield, an open pasture, leaving them for the morning and returning around midday to *look for* them and *move* them to another grazing location before going back to take them home in the evening. We always said that we were going to look for the sheep. Not that any were missing or lost. That was the way we talked when caring for them.

Somehow, Livingstone, or Robin Hood, as he was nicknamed, went on without me on this particular morning and I was too scared to go all the way down Sedge Pond Hill to Midfield by myself. I was afraid the *heart man* would get me. So I took my little flock to a much closer location that was not as safe, and went back home, leaving my father to believe that I had taken them to Midfield. Around midday when I went back to look for them, one had become entangled in some bush and had hung itself. We always spoke of a sheep hanging itself when this happened. Without even thinking, I took the rope that was used to tie the sheep in place, and dragged my sheep all the way to Midfield, where it should have been in the first place. Dragging that sheep was a hard thing to do, but it was too heavy for me to lift and carry that far a distance. It was a big sheep.

Feeling good that I had covered my bases, I went back home, feeling quite sure that I would not be found out. I had already concocted a story in my mind to tell my father; that when I went to bring in the sheep for the evening, I had found one dead. It had hung itself. But before my scheme took shape, Ivan Worrell had already seen the dead sheep in the wrong location and had passed the news on to my father. I'll leave it up to your imagination to conclude what happened to me at the hands of my father that evening. But the point of the story is that I did not drug the sheep. There were no drugs in Roebuck in those days. I simply dragged the sheep.

But the situations mentioned above are not isolated ones. Not in the least. They fit perfectly into a pattern of bad grammatical behavior. I hate to be picking on schools, but I am confronted with the situation on a regular basis in which students, and even educators, find it difficult, or painful, to make use of the correct parts of some verbs, especially the irregular ones. I hold my profession to a much higher standard when it comes to the English language, especially grammar. Much higher than journalists, television anchors, preachers and politicians. But I must be fair and balanced (to borrow a phrase from Fox News) and interject that schools, students and teachers are just as guilty of butchering the English language. They, along with the general public, share some degree of culpability, especially in specific areas of grammar. It seems as if they are afraid to use participial phrases correctly. I often hear statements that go something like this: "The bell has *rang*." Or "the pencil is *broke*." Or "the car was *stole*." I sometimes wonder why it is so difficult for some to say broken or stolen. The disgraced politician John Edwards is a perfect example. In his concession speech in New Hampshire, I heard him say "I have spoke…" Let's go to the videotape, but I think I heard him correctly.

Only recently on the local evening news I heard someone say that he was *heartbroke* over some event he had experienced. My wife's comment to me was, "There is your word." We listened to another television lesson in grammar on September 3, 2013 while watching *Hollywood Game Night*. Jane Lynch, the hostess, described Britney Spears as all *growed* up. And about a week later, on September 9, I was working out at the gym and had a private laugh when I overheard one member say to another, "They have *froze* everything…"

I was in the gym earlier this evening, March 17, 2015, when I ran into one of the members who was working out without his usual workout buddy. "Where is your buddy tonight?" I asked. "His shoulder is *tore* up," he told me. I was tempted to do a Ms. Redman number on him but decided to hold my tongue. Ms. Redman was my primary school teacher who thought it was her duty to correct every incidence of bad grammar, written or spoken. She held us to a high standard and we were especially careful when communicating in her presence. I smile as I write this because years later, when we worshipped as members of the same congregation, I overheard her, more than once, quietly voicing a correction of inappropriate grammar coming from the pulpit.

After experiencing the examples mentioned above, I came to the conclusion that a grammatical oversight of this nature may be characteristically Southern. I spent four years in Michigan and California and never encountered the onslaught on verbs that I hear in these parts. I hope my friends in the South will not misinterpret my intentions, but will understand that my only intent is to view their grammatical gaffes as uniquely distinctive, indigenous, comical, and even cultural.

Interestingly, northerners like John McCain and Mitt Romney confirm my position. John McCain, while participating in a Republican presidential forum, described social security as being *broken*. And Mitt Romney, debating on the same program on Fox News on January 6, referred to Washington as being "fundamentally broken" instead of being fundamentally broke. I didn't expect less of him anyway. However, the Reverend Al Sharpton appeared not to have received the memo from his fellow northerners. He was heard saying on his own show, *Politics Nation* on MSNBC on August 27, 2013 that "… even a broke clock is right twice a day." And he said it again tonight, March 17, 2015, when he was making a comment about Rudy Giuliani. I could not believe my ears. And what is more disturbing is the fact that he appears not to know better.

I also learned that it has become quite trendy among Southerners to use *brung* instead of brought as the past tense of the verb to bring. So let's conjugate the verb to bring in the past tense: "*I brung, you brung, he brung, etc.* At three years old, my grandson, Max, who usually uses perfect grammar, and is known for correcting himself, fell into the *brung* trap only recently and did not seem to understand his mistake when corrected. Maybe we should take a closer look at the verb to bring.

This next one is off the charts. I had to include it because it almost made me burst into laughter but I managed to contain myself. I hate to relate tales about my students outside the walls of the school but at least my moral code expects me to conceal the name in order to protect the guilty. Here is the story.

I was sitting in my office one afternoon when a teacher handed me a discipline referral. She had written up two girls for writing some curse words that were directed towards a third student. It was my practice to handle office referrals expeditiously, so I walked down the hallway to pick up the two second graders from their room for a talk back in my office. Neither of the girls would admit to writing the nasty note, with perfect spelling and grammar. We went back and forth for a while, trying to decide on the guilty party. I had only two alternatives left. I would deliver a consequence to both girls, or I would exact a sample — a writing sample. I settled on the latter. I hastily grabbed two sheets from a yellow pad on my desk, along with pencils and clipboards, and instructed both girls to copy word for word from the dirty note. I would come to a conclusion by comparing the penmanship of the samples provided by the two youngsters. To my astonishment, before even one word was recorded by either of the accused, the guilty student confessed. "I *wrute* it," she volunteered. "Wrote" I corrected. "I *wrute* it" she insisted. I thanked her for her honesty and struggled to keep a straight face as I dismissed her innocent classmate.

Some time after the incident mentioned above, another student showed up in the office one afternoon, and I quickly determined that my second grader was not feeling very well. The office staff was quite busy at the time so I decided to help. "What can I do for you?" I inquired. Her response was "I need my temperature *tooken*." I dared not make fun of a serious situation, but I grabbed a pen and recorded the entry on a post-it note and deposited it in my pocket for future use.

These are common infractions that have been allowed to become part of the vernacular and everyday lingo, and students and adults alike, find it difficult to separate the casual from the official and the formal. Although these are broken academic and grammatical rules that need *fixing*, they are precious and comical, and should be preserved for moments such as these.

My mention of the word *fixing* above is not coincidental, or accidental. Its introduction was carefully planned as a way to set the scene for a story I am about to share about an experience I had many years ago. In Roebuck, fixing had only one meaning — to repair, or to make right. We were good at fixing a *fly stick*, self-made scooters and *tots*. We were good at fixing the toy *lorries* we made from tin cans and scraps of wood. Very soon after arriving in the Chattanooga area from California in August of 1987, I learned that fixing had a Southern twist to it. Like the situations described above, this one is to be preserved and protected. Not to be corrected. It is one of those original cultural keepsakes that I find both hysterical and amusing. Here is the story.

I was just about to finish my first week as principal of Avondale Seventh-day Adventist School, a small private Christian school. It was a Friday afternoon and the school secretary, armed with money bags full of tuition, looked at me and said, "I am fixing to go to the bank." She understood immediately from the "what is she talking about?" look on my face, that she had not only completely and humorously baffled me; she had also enlightened me. "I am getting ready to go to the bank," she explained with a chuckle. Later, I wondered, after a moment of recovery, what she would have said to me when she returned from the bank and had not seen me before she had left. "I fixed to go to the bank, but you were not around?" I would have exploded in uncontrollable laughter, and even tears.

Since then, I have grown to love fixing. Even presidential contender Rick Perry, would use fixing years later in a debate on October 18, 2011 when dismissing Herman Cain's 999 tax plan. He mentioned that he was fixing to do something, the details of which I am not able to recall. But can you imagine Mr. Perry as president in a summit meeting with Putin, or Gordon Brown, or with Prime Minister Fruendel Stewart of Barbados mentioning that he was fixing to propose new policies on nuclear disarmament, or education, immigration, or race relations? What's even more disturbing is Mr. Perry's inability to switch to formal speech when the situation demanded. In the same debate he charged that Mitt Romney's decision to hire illegal aliens to work on his lawn was "the *hith (height)* of hypocrisy." My superintendent, Rick Smith, was also fixing when he addressed us in an administrative workshop on July 24, 2014.

I am trying really hard to move away from the school environment but I am finding it impossible. The two stories that follow, though indirectly related to education, had their setting in the school I mentioned earlier. I find them terribly entertaining. I was in a school board meeting one evening and the treasurer introduced this new word — *stiphen*. She announced that she was paying somebody a *stiphen*. A *stiphen*? No heads turned but mine, telling me that it was business as usual in these parts. It would have been a whole lot better if she were planning on paying a stipend. Sitting in that same meeting was the chairman of the Board who had mentioned something to me one day earlier about her dish *warsher*. Dish Warsher? We didn't have dish washers in Roebuck but I doubt that we would have called them *warshers* if they were a staple in my Roebuck culture.

That exchange brought back memories of a story my friends Sammy and Randy had shared with me when we were students in Jamaica. Professor Green had made reference to a *hot water heater* in his lecture in their business class that day. "Why would one need a hot water heater if the water is already hot?" they joked. I had to agree. My only explanation is that Professor Green knew that my school board chairman could not use her *warsher* if she did not have a hot water heater. Years later, on October 20, 2011 a serviceman came to my home to do some minor work. I chuckled inside when he asked, "Where is your hot water heater?"

When I first came to live in the US I usually wondered why the news media hardly drew attention to cases of bad grammar made by politicians and other people of importance; like they always do in cases of political missteps and scandalous behavior. That was until I came to realize that media personalities are just as guilty when it comes to grammar, diction and word usage. As time passed I grew to admire Katie Couric. Whether she was anchoring the news or taking the lead in her long-running morning show, I was a fan. For a long time Katie was America's sweetheart and I felt then, that she was deserving of the many accolades she received. However, she should have known better when she said on the CBS Evening News that Barry Bonds will always have an *asterik* beside his name in the baseball record books. In Katie's defense, she is not the only high profile personality to replace the asterisk with the asterik, but she gets paid too much money to be allowed to go without rebuke. But Mike Allen from Politico.com got it exactly correct on Hannity and Colmes on July 7, 2008. He actually said asterisk during a conversation with the hosts of that once popular television program. Recently, I was in a math class conducting a teacher observation. She too was in support of the *asterik,* asking the students to place one beside an entry they had made in their notebooks. I was tempted to bring up the *asterik* in her post observation conference but decided against it.

I always thought that presidential candidates, talk show hosts, and high profile politicians should be better role models as far as correct word usage is concerned but I soon found out how wrong my assumption had been. Mike Huckabee gave his endorsement to a bad word, *pundant.* I heard him with my own ears on Sean Hanitty's radio program while I was driving home from work on January 2, 2008. He said in part "… there are lots of political *pundants*…" No one should be allowed to be president if he or she cannot tell the difference between a pundit and a pundant. And Neal Boortz was not to be outdone. The conservative radio talk show host confidently announced on Hannity and Colmes on February 12, 2008 that "The pundants are demagoging the fair tax."

I have not always agreed with President George W. Bush's policies and decisions, so it is no surprise that I am not pleased with his treatment of the word nuclear. In case you haven't noticed, President Bush has recreated a perfectly normal and regular word into a non word that is even more difficult to spell, or write — *nucalar.* That's my wife's rendition of the president's literary contribution to the English language. She is an English teacher so I am not going to argue with her inventive spelling. I have often wondered why he and numerous others had to mess with the word and damage it in the way that they have. My only conclusion is that the president and those who took it upon themselves to effect the change from nuclear to *nucular,* may have determined that a *nucular* bomb is not as potent as a nuclear one. Interestingly enough, it has been a long time since I wrote this paragraph about President Bush. Now it is February, 18, 2015, and earlier today I happened to be watching Jeb Bush deliver a major foreign policy speech in Chicago in which he said in part "I love my brother and I love my father … but I am my own man." I had to laugh to myself when he could not help himself when he, like his brother before him, went *nucular.* So much for being "my own man." On the other hand, it was quite refreshing to hear President Obama remain consistent throughout the recent negotiations with Iran. In his public statements, he always provided the proper pronunciation — nuclear. This says a lot in favor of the man who was supposedly born in Kenya.

While we are talking about President Bush, I think it is quite appropriate at this juncture to talk about his former secretary of state, Colin Powell. I sit idly by and simultaneously fume with a mild form of anger mixed with disgust every time I hear a simple name like his being butchered in the media, by his colleagues, and by the civilian population. The secretary's name is Colin, pronounced *Kahlin*. Not Colon. It doesn't have to take a Biology major like myself, to know that the colon is the scientific name for the large intestine, the bowel (rhymes with Powell). It is rather unjust to associate the secretary's name with that part of the human body that is well known for its anatomical function. But the Secretary is a very dignified gentleman, who I am sure, gave up a long time ago trying to right the pronunciation of his name in political circles, as well as in the everyday and mundane aspects of his life. Knowing Jamaicans as I do, I am surprised that there has not been a public outcry against those that continue to defame the name of Colin Powell, whose roots originate on the island. Jamaicans may be more forgiving than was once thought.

By the way, Colin has had a good reputation in Roebuck and in all of Barbados. Not Colin Powell but Colin Blades. And not Colon Blades either. Colin Blades, who now resides in Bermuda, used to be a household name (before he migrated) with expertise in cricket and track and field, with a specialty in the high jump. There was also a Colin from Indian Ground, a district *butt and bound* with Roebuck. Colin was a real character and a folk hero of some sort. To us he was Colins. The addition of the s may be a result of a Roebuck (and Indian Ground) tradition, but it is still not half as bad as Colon.

In the final analysis, it is obvious that words play a prominent role in expressing the thoughts, and teaching the lessons of every culture. This is a book about words — simple words. Common words that tell a story and teach lessons about two cultures that are as far apart and as foreign to each other as the geographical distance that separates them. One is America, (Ringgold, Georgia to be exact) my adopted home. The other, deep in the heart of Barbados, in an obscure village called Roebuck, where I grew up loving every moment. The former is a small, thriving metropolis. The latter, a small intimate district, steeped in agriculture, farming and plantation life.

The two are so culturally different that even the mere mention of the simplest agricultural terms present opportunities for informal lessons in cultural awareness: like *taking out the sheep* for example. As a boy I took out our flock of sheep, as did other boys in Roebuck. Taking out the sheep meant that we took them out from their pens early in the morning; sometimes close to *foreday morning,* to graze in an open field called Midfield on Sedgepond Plantation. We never used the word flock in Roebuck, even though some of us had a rather large number of sheep. We went back around mid-day to *look for* the sheep. Not that they were lost, or that they were sick. But we also went to *look for* people when they were sick, just like we do in America. Looking for the sheep meant that we went to see how they were doing, and *move* them to a new place to graze. I remember my mother telling me to go and move the sheep around midday. We went back to get them in the evening to bring them in. My mother would tell me to go and *bring in* the sheep. Once again the narrow road was filled with my sheep, Michael's sheep, Livingstone's sheep, and other boys' sheep coming home for the night. The vocabulary concerning our sheep was very specific; very cultural to Roebuck. We took out our sheep. In America, boys *take out* girls, like on a date. In Roebuck we took out sheep — To graze; to eat grass.

My responsibilities were not limited to taking care of the family's sheep. We had of *fowls* and I had to look after them as well. We didn't call them chickens. The only time we called them chickens was when they were newly hatched, and were cute, fluffy and yellow. In Roebuck, chickens grew into fowls and our back yard was always littered with *fowl down.* In America they call them chickens, no matter how big they get. We didn't eat chicken in Roebuck. We ate fowl. We would catch them, cut their necks, and throw them in boiling water and pluck the feathers.

One of my jobs was to *feel* the fowls for eggs. My mother would remind me to feel the fowls and I knew exactly what she meant. I would catch the *hens* one by one while they *pecked* on *scratch grain* and gently enter my little finger into their *pooch.* If I encountered a hard egg, that particular fowl would be kept in the *fowl house* or in the *run* until she laid her egg. She would *cackle* excitedly when she was done; a signal to us that she had delivered. The *cocks* were not put through the feeling process. They did not lay eggs; only the hens did.

Oftentimes some of the hens would escape us and secretly lay eggs in a *fowl nest,* made in the security of a nearby bush, or under the house, sitting on them until the eggs hatched, proudly strutting out later to reveal their new yellow family, provided that the always vigilant *mongoose* did not spoil the plan. In Roebuck, our fowls and ducks were like collectables; so cherished because of the contribution they made to the economic stability of our families. Not only did they satisfy our need for fresh eggs on a regular basis, they were the major source of protein in our Sunday dinners, *out-ings,* sponsored by The Roebuck New Testament Church of God, and other not so special occasions. Even at such festive times we did not refer to fowl meat as chicken. Surprisingly, it became chicken when we went to Speighstown to buy frozen *chicken back* from Elmer's Supermarket. Chicken back soup was popular in those days. Sometimes we added chicken neck and chicken feet. *Steppers,* I once heard someone refer to them as such. In any case, I don't think *steppers* was a Roebuck word.

Sometimes, as kids we would grab a fowl or duck and cook it for dinner when it was our turn to cook. While this was meant to be a pleasant gesture for our parents when they came home from work, it was sometimes a dangerous decision to make unilaterally and without prior approval from our parents. Jenlyn was to experience this firsthand, even though the incident was quite accidental. I held on to my own version of the story for years but was pleasantly surprised by even more first-hand details when we visited Roebuck recently, and even after we returned to the States, a conversation with Jenlyn filled in the missing facts to corroborate the story.

One weekend, Sylvie Morris, Jenlyn's mother, killed and cooked one of two *drake* ducks for the family dinner, leaving the remaining drake to fill one distinct role — to service the hens. Some time later, Jenlyn was feeding the family's brood of ducklings when the surviving drake repeatedly used his size and seniority to monopolize the food. Jenlyn, meaning no harm whatever, grabbed the *coo-coo stick* and released a *lash* in the direction of the drake with the intention of chasing him away so that the younger birds could have access to the food. Unfortunately, the cuckoo stick connected with the drake's head and he *cocked up* dead. A frightened Jenny went into quick action, cutting off the neck, throwing a pot of boiling water on the bird to make plucking the feathers possible, and did what else she had to do to prepare the drake for dinner. Apparently, my sister, Cheryl, not only witnessed the accident but stayed around to enjoy a *share* of the finished duck dinner. On her way home she happened to run into Ms. Morris coming down the *line*. "Ms. Morris," Cheryl blurted, "Jenny killed your duck and cooked it for dinner." To which the shocked Ms. Morris responded "Uh don't want nuh duck. Uh want muh duck." (I don't want any duck. I want my duck).

I mentioned *feel* previously in one context but in Roebuck, the term *feel* took on another meaning, especially when combined with up, as in *feel up*, a term I do not feel comfortable discussing due to the connotation it conjures up as far as girls are concerned. That being said, boys usually spoke of feeling up their girl friends. In Roebuck we never spoke of necking, or petting; only feeling up. But to be fair, it appears that women did, and still do their share of feeling up. My friend, Hal, was telling me of a recent encounter he had with a woman in the produce section of a food store in Atlanta, Georgia. She, like many women, was feeling up some fruit, putting it back, feeling up some more and putting it back on the shelf until she was satisfied she had the right one before making her purchase. "Why are you feeling up the fruit?" he asked her. "And where in Barbados are you from?" she replied.

I seldom go shopping with Hortense but each time I do, she puts the fruits and vegetables through a similar interrogation process, sometimes so intense and time consuming that I usually show my impatience and vow never to go shopping with her again. She and I had a feeling up experience when we were in Barbados recently. We stopped by a roadside food stand to purchase a loaf of sweet bread. Hortense took up a loaf, and in her usual shopping mode, began inspecting it and handling it as if to detect its firmness. The vendor became quite irate, "Don't feel it up," she warned. I laughed inside and did not realize that the feel up comment had registered with Hortense until we laughed about it later while doing some editing of the book.

The obvious conclusion from that exchange has to be that both sexes in Barbados, and from Roebuck specifically, are guilty of feeling up. Pushing the feeling up idea a little farther reminds me that *feeling up* usually leads to something else. Americans call it *sleeping together,* or *going to bed together.* The first time I heard someone in the US say that he slept with someone, I was completely surprised at the choice of words, even though I understood the meaning he was trying to convey. In Roebuck we slept together all the time but it had nothing to do with sex. The truth is that boys slept with their sisters for years, meaning that they went to bed together; meaning that they slept in the same bed or bedroom because that was the only practical arrangement. Boys and girls did not have their own room…at least not in my house.

CHAPTER TWO

Air

His request showed me how much I had changed, and how much of my own cultural roots I had readjusted since coming to America.

Some time ago, my good friend, Floyd, came to visit me in America. At the time my family was living in Tennessee and Floyd had flown from Barbados to Nashville to attend a conference there. I had not seen him in years and obviously I was delighted to see him after such a long time. I drove to Nashville to pick him up to spend a few days with us in Chattanooga before he returned home. Naturally, we stayed up late that first night catching up on the years that had separated us. We were tight friends as boys, engaging in all manner of mischief. Our friendship continued into adulthood. We both left Barbados in 1973 to attend college. He to Trinidad. I chose Jamaica. We had not seen each other since then, except for one weekend when I attended his wedding in Trinidad.

The next morning we got up early. It was not my choice. Floyd has always been an early riser, even to this day. He now lives in Washington State while I live in Ringgold, Georgia. Even with the three- hour time difference he sometimes calls me just to talk, at times when I think he should be still in bed. He is that kind of friend. When he moved to Washington several years ago I visited him to serve as best man at his second wedding. He and his wife Shirley have made it a tradition of spending Thanksgiving with us in Ringgold. We still talk several times a week, sometimes more

19

often, depending on the current news, or on topics that may be of interest or concern to both of us. But we call each other every weekend for sure. There has been some talk about the two of us authoring a book about our conversations.

Since this is a book about culture, permit me to take you on a short cultural detour before getting back to Floyd. I had no doubt that my wife, Hortense, had plans to prepare a big breakfast for us to enjoy that particular morning. She is a great hostess and goes to extra lengths to make sure that visitors to our home are treated with warmth and kindness. I honestly believe that she has been gifted with the ministry of hospitality. She is a great cook, who can have a four course meal ready in minimal time, and without the need to consult a recipe. Whenever I attempt to cook something big, I have to go shopping the week before the event, and subsequently follow a recipe religiously to the very end. Even then the results are suspect. Hortense doesn't do that. She throws in her own personal touch here and there, and the end product is always the same — simply delicious. I have seen her, on more than one occasion, come up with a full meal that she skillfully pulled together from odds and ends, so to speak. She continues to amaze me with the ease with which she does it. Weekends are her favorite times to occupy the kitchen. This is when she puts her hospitality to work by entertaining friends from church, and most importantly by providing a home-cooked meal on a regular basis for some of the students studying far away from home at near by Southern Adventist University.

Her practice of making up her own recipes has been responsible for more than a few tense moments when she has tried to explain one of her creations to others who ask. One such incident happened in my presence not so long ago. One night I was eavesdropping with great interest on a conversation Hortense was having with a friend from Texas. Previously, I had mentioned to Anysia about this casserole that Hortense makes using potatoes, sour cream, and eggs. She also has a *salt fish* version of the same recipe. I am sure that some seasoning is involved but those are the main ingredients. I had mentioned to Anysia that it was a very scrumptious dish and how much I enjoy feasting on it, even though a large serving is not in my best interest because of the high starch content. I believed that I had done a very effective commercial in advertising the casserole because Anysia felt impressed to call and ask Hortense for the recipe. From the conversation I could tell that Hortense was having a difficult time explaining the process in a way that was simple to Anysia, simply because it was a special dish from Hortense's culinary and creative mind. In a subsequent conversation I asked Anysia if she had tried the recipe and how it had turned out for her. She was hysterical. "It was a wreck" was her exact response. She continued by saying that she discovered where she went wrong, and that she was willing to try again. She had cooked the potato far too long, but would get it right in the next try.

This cultural way of life is so ingrained in West Indian behavior that I think it is fitting to highlight one aspect that is especially strong and common among women like Hortense and other West Indian women. The art of cooking is one that is definitely and intentionally passed down from mother to daughter and from generation to generation. It is an art that is taught, observed, and practiced from youth, with mothers making sure that their daughters and sons know their way around the kitchen. I can think of only a few West Indian women that can't cook. On the other hand, I know of several who boast with gratitude that when they were girls living at home, they were expected to practice their culinary skills until they were perfected. That expectation was also standard in our home in Roebuck. My sisters were cooking from a very tender age; cooking for the entire family at that, and without the aid of cook books and recipes. Every summer when school was out, my sister, Elaine, would cook lunch for my mother, who worked on the plantation. My job was to take the food to her when she *knocked off for lunch* at 12:00. My sisters still cook a lot today, and delight in preparing a feast ever so often. I recently spoke with them by telephone as they were preparing for their annual fish fry, which I am sure would be attended by a cross section of West Indians living in their Brooklyn neighborhood.

It goes without saying that there are marked differences among the islands in methods of preparing peas and rice (or rice and peas), *roti, fish soup* and *conkies* but it is safe to conclude that most West Indian women know how to cook. And West Indian men appreciate that qualification in their women, since we are not too keen on eating out night after night. That's not cultural. Very often I run across young American women, and older ones as well, who proudly declare that "I can't cook." My response is always "How can this be?"

Before I get back to Floyd, I must tell a story that supports the virtues of Hortense's cooking; a story that rightfully relegates my cooking to its rightful place when compared to hers. One day, when our oldest son, Sheldon, was about four, we were living in St. Croix at the time, and Hortense had to be gone from the house for a considerable length of time and left me at home to take care of Sheldon and his two year old brother, Haniffe. She didn't leave a prepared dish so the assignment to cook for the boys fell to me. I can't recall with any degree of certainty the exact dish I decided to prepare but I am confident that it must have been something the boys were used to, and I was too insecure about my cooking to try something new. I wasn't that naïve to believe that my cooking would be on par with that of my wife's but I was hoping that the boys would partake and be satisfied until more palatable *food* would be available when Hortense returned home. At the same time, I was completely unprepared for Sheldon's smart remark that he directed at my cooking. "That's not how Mommy does it," he protested. To this day I refuse to cook for anyone else, but myself.

Now back to my friend. I had no doubt that Floyd would have

been treated to a breakfast that would have been satisfying, as well as nutritious. Since Hortense is Jamaican, I expected something festive and cultural: fried plantain, *ackee* and salt fish, or even *johnny cakes* and *callaloo*. I didn't know what she had planned, but I was certain that something good would be coming out of the kitchen when she eventually called us to eat. That morning, Floyd and I were sitting in the kitchen talking. Hortense was not up as yet since it was still quite early and still some time before she would start making noise in the kitchen with the pots and pans; something my mother used to do, that served as an alarm clock.

Floyd didn't say that he was hungry, or that he was ready to eat, but he made a request of me that almost made me laugh out loudly. Instead, I smiled inside, muffled the excitement, and complied without comment. "I need some hot tea to drink. I have *air*," he requested. My initial thought was to correct my good friend by responding with something like this. "In America we don't say I have *air* in my stomach. We say "I have gas." But I remained silent, carefully digesting the request because I had not heard *air* used in that context for years. Even if I had attempted to correct my friend, we would have had a good reason to have something else to laugh about. Floyd enjoys a hearty laugh and I am sure that one would have been in order, had I mentioned it. We joked about it some time later.

Floyd's request allowed me to reminisce, if only briefly, on the amusing life I lived as a boy growing up in Roebuck, and how simple and uncomplicated it used to be. His request also showed me how much I had changed; how much of my own cultural roots I had readjusted since migrating to America, especially in light of the fact that I now had few opportunities to practice the old way of speaking and behaving. And I miss that. Since coming to the US I have learned to substitute air for gas. I now say that I have gas in my stomach, not air in my stomach. I can't help but make the connection with the gas I put in my car. In Roebuck, we never said we had gas in our belly. We had air. Not gas. Gas was something we put in cars. Not that we had many cars in Roebuck. The gas/air thing is only one example of the change that migration has wrought. There may be countless others. Only God knows how many more are lurking in my subconscious.

On a more serious note, my friend's comment about the hot tea and air made a deeper impression on me than it appeared on the surface. It had a way of reminding me that I had lost, or had at least broken the connection from the indigenous mores and folklores of my Roebuck culture. Floyd's question also made me sense that I was living in a state of some kind of cultural deprivation, and led me to understand that I could not afford to misplace my cultural identity, or allow it to become submerged, or secondary to a culture that now appeared dominant, and that I had to work at keeping even simple cultural features like hot tea and air from disappearing from my thinking and from my vocabulary. For this reason, I cherish the occasions when my sisters and I get together here in Ringgold, Georgia, or in Brooklyn, New York.

Reunions and celebrations with my sisters, Elaine, Yvonne, Cheryl, Heather, and their families, and with Aunt Gloria, her husband Clyde and son, David, and with Cousin Jenny and her family, are occasions to rekindle the old way of doing and saying things. For sure, we don't speak American at times like these. I also look forward to joking around with Floyd and Hal on the telephone on a regular basis and also with Jasmine, Laura and Kathy from time to time. It is one sure way to keep the culture fresh while having fun. Last Thanksgiving we all got together at my home, where we had a wild time. My wife, who is Jamaican, and Floyd's wife Shirley, who is American, had somewhat of a difficult time understanding and interpreting as we went full blast into our Barbadian (Bajan) lingo.

On the other hand, the hot tea and air affair also served as a prompt that reminded me of the hard adjustments I had to make very quickly as a new immigrant if I wanted to be understood, or to fit in, especially in graduate school and in the workplace. Modifications in speaking, as well as in writing and spelling, took on an urgent nature. In most cases it was fun to oblige and learn. All of a sudden a bike or car had a flat tire instead of having a flat *tyre*; *labour* became *labor*; *programme* became *program*; *colour* was now *color*, and the letter *zed* took on a new name — zee. A *full stop* became a *period*, whereas, the new name for the *black lead* was pencil, and the *rubber* at the other end of the pencil was now an *eraser*.

A funny thing happened one morning, while I was on bus duty at Loftis Middle School, where I was an assistant principal. I was discussing writing the book with one of my teachers who was on duty with me at the time. Ms. Benson was quick to remind me that a rubber is a condom in America, and jokingly asked if school children took their rubbers to school in Barbados. She even took the matter a step further when she added that it would have been hilarious to her to hear a teacher say "Now class, take out your rubbers..." In Roebuck, the word condom was an unknown. Such a word was not in our vocabulary. But we used rubber all the time when making brakes from scraps of car tires for our home-made scooters, or when burning rubber tyres on Guy Faulks Night on November 5. But condom? Never. That was not a Roebuck word. Later, a new addition to our vocabulary emerged. I don't know where the word *frenchie* originated, but it was our word for the condom. Interestingly enough, as time passed, it evolved to *rain coat*, and even to *protection*.

My adjustments and quest for cultural competence took on other faces as well, even in teaching and learning. Some years ago, I listened with a high degree of interest and excitement as my wife, who was teaching English in St. Croix, U.S Virgin Islands at the time argue with one of her students, Monique, concerning the pronunciation of *mange*. Naturally, my wife who is of Jamaican extraction and British orientation, argued in favor of the long *a* format as proven in the dictionary, while Monique refused to accept her position and maintained that the short *a* pronunciation was the correct form. I am not sure how teacher and student settled their cultural confrontation, but my position is that it depends on where one is from. In other words, it is a cultural thing, and when in Rome, you do as the Romans do. If my memory serves me correctly, I think those two also had some disagreement concerning the word *vase,* but I checked with my wife and she conceded that both the long and short vowel sounds are acceptable in that case, but not with *mange.*

As my progress towards full cultural integration continued, other little things occupied my new learning. As if adjusting to driving on the right was not an ordeal in itself, I now had to learn to water the plants, as my secretary Judy was quick to remind me, as opposed to *wetting* them. And there were some cultural prepositional differences that I had to respect as I now sit *in* the floor and not on the floor. Of course there are countless mini lessons of this nature that I had to learn and respect. And I was happy to do so.

Interestingly enough, some things on the political front were common to both cultures, especially when national election campaigns were in full swing. Some comments from opposing candidates, issued in the heat of competition, though humorous and comical at times, crossed the line in others. I am including the following story only because it highlights the *WC,* a common Roebuck term that I have not heard used in the US. Not that we, or anybody else in Roebuck, had a WC but they had them at Indian Ground School where we went to school.

This public political exchange that was mentioned above; to which the people of Roebuck (and all of Barbados) were privy is said to have occurred between Burton Hinds, the Barbados Labour Party candidate and Asquith Phillips, his rival from the Democratic Labour Party. Apparently, Burton Hinds, publisher of *The Truth* tabloid, had referred to Asquith as Assy (as in ass) at one of his campaign appearances. Asquith, knowing all too well that the ass was another name for the buttocks, had a comeback that stung Burton; a retort that might have made him rethink his initial attack in the first place, especially with a name like W.C. Burton Hinds. Asquith had the last word. Being keenly aware that *W.C.* was an acronym for a *Water Closet,* or toilet, he gently reminded WC Burton Hinds of the relationship between the ass and the *W.C.*

Admittedly, my mind never fails to take me back to the *WC* occasion referenced above each time such political attacks are hurled back and forth when the national political campaign season kicks into high gear in the US. To me, it is not laughable when a President is called a dummy, or a Nazi, on television, or in casual political discourse; or when The Reverend Jesse Jackson thought it was an effective political strategy to yank the testicles of Barak Obama because of a difference in opinion. Or when Mark Levin, on his radio program on July 21, 2008, suggested that former Vice President, Al Gore, drink from the same water he pissed in. The people of Roebuck never went that far in their critique of our politicians and even though these few aspects of the political culture challenge my personal, cultural and moral point of view, there are many others that I accept without question, and am more than happy to adopt.

Even though it was a time of immense change when I first came to live in America, it was also exhilarating to be embracing something new — a new culture. Like many, I was open-minded enough to be less resistant to change. My thinking was, and still is, that I had voluntarily chosen America to be my new home, and that I would not just tolerate it, but would wholeheartedly embrace its way of life in every way, except in those instances where my personal and moral values would be compromised. The latter has not been my experience and in spite of minor adjustments I assimilated well. Almost automatically; the process powered by my willingness to adapt to, and adopt something new and diverse.

To demonstrate that I have absolutely and completely adopted the new culture, I eat colored (coloured) greens and their cousin, turnip greens, and have even tried fried okra. And though after all these years I am still not brave enough to try *grits,* the thought still lingers in my appetite of the future. The more I think about it, I am convinced that my aversion to grits is strictly psychological. In Roebuck, grits are tiny bits of gravel that collect on the side of the road. *Those grits* was exactly how my friend Susie described her serving of grits one day after we had breakfast. "Those grits and those scrambled eggs were so good," she remarked. Why *those grits* and *those eggs* I wondered? How did she know that there was more than one scrambled egg on her plate? I would soon learn that what she said was not an exception, but the rule here in the South. Just like they say *in the floor* as opposed to *on the floor,* like we say in Roebuck

My adjustment to the most popular of US sports was probably the steepest one I had to make when I first moved to America. After my graduate school experience was over and I had a lot more time to pay extended attention to sports I was determined to learn as much as I could, mainly from watching sports events on television. I began my quest by enrolling my sons in Little League ball in nearby Collegedale when we moved to Chattanooga, Tennessee from Riverside, California in 1987. I attended a lot of the games, and did my share of modest screaming and high-fiving, even though I did not understand the rules or the basics of the game. It was easy to relate to a homerun because it was similar to a *six* in my beloved cricket.

It was at my sons' baseball games that I learned a new term. More often than not, a fly ball would make its way to the bleachers where the parents and other supporters were sitting. As a matter of warning to take evasive, or protective action, my American friends would yell "Heads up." I got used to it after a while but initially asked myself, "What does heads up have to do with this?" In Roebuck, an out of control cricket ball would not have evoked a heads up response. "*Look out,*" was the Roebuck thing to say. This brings me to a story I heard a long time ago. An American in Barbados was in a house one day when someone yelled "Look out." Apparently, a rather heavy object was falling from the sky and on hearing the warning he looked out the window. As the story goes, he lost his head that day. As a disclaimer, I can't vouch for the veracity of this story but I am positive that is what was told to me.

I still forget to drop the bat when I get a hit in baseball. The first time I played the game I carried my bat with me, even when I took extra bases, much to the delight of the opponents and onlookers. In cricket, we never dropped the bat when we hit a run. In learning the fundamentals of baseball one question always crossed my mind. I wanted to know why the batter always *ran* to first base even though he drew a *walk*. And I had to learn that even though the batter hit the ball with the bat, it still may not be a hit. And that a strike happens even if the batter did not strike the ball. And sometimes when the batter strikes the ball with the bat, it still may not be a strike. In Roebuck, when I was coming up, a hit was a hit, and a strike was a hit. They meant the same thing. If you hit somebody that meant that you struck somebody. I had several personal experiences with a hit as a young boy growing up in Roebuck. I remember a girl name Gwen hit me one day. I can still remember the hit. It was also a real strike. Gwen and I had a good laugh remembering this incident when I was visiting Roebuck recently.

In the end, I had to learn an additional use and meaning of hit; one that had nothing to do with baseball, or fighting, but with something more exciting and with a romantic attachment as in *hitting on*. This learning experience happened a long time ago and even though I cannot recall the person relating the story, the specifics of the conversation are as vivid today as they were back then. In short, someone was hitting on his girl friend. It was pretty simple to arrive at the meaning of *hitting on* from the context in which it was used but I wondered in silence why the expression was even being applied, especially when no violence or threat of physical harm was intended.

In Roebuck we never said that someone was hitting on somebody, or that they were being hit on themselves. And for that matter, we never said that somebody was *moving in* on another person's girl friend or boyfriend. If somebody had some degree of success in hitting on, or moving in on another person's girl friend or boyfriend, the term for that was *horning*. It was not unusual to hear "Man, he is horning you." In a moment of confession, I am admitting that I was horned at one time or another but I also did my share as well. No more details are available at this time but I continue to wonder about the appropriateness of the term *horning* since there were no visible signs of horns growing anywhere.

It was also painful to learn that a baseball team could bat for nine innings and may score only one run or no runs at all. And that a player, or manager, could get close to a referee's face, close enough to kiss him while screaming and kicking dirt all over him. The first time I witnessed this, I didn't know what to make of it, but as my education in baseball broadened, I grew to admire the confrontation, and even looked forward to the face-to-face match up every now and then. "And why do they call it the bull pen?" I would ask myself. I never kept bulls in Roebuck; only sheep. So I did not have a bull pen but I had seen bull pens and knew exactly what they were like. I am still trying to locate the similarities between a Roebuck bull pen and a baseball bullpen.

When I attended college in Jamaica back in the seventies, there was a rule in the student handbook that read "No spitting on campus." My roommates and I used to joke that if we wanted to spit, we would have to take a taxi to town to do it. What does this have to do with baseball? The first time I saw baseball players spit everywhere, the rule came right back to me, even though so many years had passed. "Why do they have to spit so much?" I would ask; and throw trash around as if there are no receptacles in the dugout for that purpose? I have never had the opportunity to visit a cricket *pavilion* in Barbados, but I find it hard to picture the cricketers spitting and littering as they do in a baseball dugout. Even though the spitting was initially hard to stomach, I have now come to accept it as another aspect of the culture of the game and now feel that the game would not be the same without it.

If it appears as if I am picking on baseball, I am. I am still looking for an explanation as to why the championship series is dubbed The World Series when only teams from America participate in the series? Unless the Canadian teams are classified as foreign. The World Series would be an appropriate name if teams from Cuba and the other baseball powerhouses participated. My only conclusion is that the Series is so called because the individual teams in both major league divisions are made up of so many players from countries outside the US. Incidentally, as I edit this chapter I am inserting that I am watching the third game of the 2013 World Series between the Boston Red Sox and the St. Louis Cardinals on television. Even though I am now culturally educated as far as baseball is concerned, I still maintain my prejudice, that even though cricket and baseball have minimal similarities, cricket is more exciting and more appealing. Americans, I am sure, will be willing to mount a challenge to my position.

As far as sports are concerned, I have had to make the biggest cultural learning curve when it came to appreciating, or even understanding football. The obvious question from a Roebuck point of view is "Why is it that the game is football when the ball only comes into contact with the foot on very few occasions during the game?" But thanks to my sons I have learned to appreciate the game and now understand what the men in tights are trying to accomplish while they knock and throw their opponents *down* to the ground. I initially thought that a first down happened when one man was down, as in first man down, and that a second down occurred when a second player went down, and so on. But my confusion only deepened when I realized that numerous men were going down simultaneously. "And how come there is not a fifth or sixth down?" I used to ask myself early in my education and understanding of the basics of the game.

In all seriousness, I have grown in my maturity and knowledge as far as the game of football is concerned. It has taken some time for me to get over my refusal to consider it a sport I would want to understand, but I have finally come around. I am slowly achieving the status of Sunday couch potato, especially when the Tennessee Titans, and to a lesser extent, The Atlanta Falcons, are playing. I continue to be amazed by the technical skill of the players and also by the play-calling of the coaches. I am enthralled by the throwing game. There is nothing more amazing in all of sports than to witness the accuracy of a quarterback *hitting* (that word again) a running back, or some other position, with a throw from miles down the field, and the receiver going up in the midst of opposing traffic in the vicinity to make the catch. I want to let everyone know that it took a lot out of me to make that confession, especially from someone who believes in the supremacy of cricket. The second half of my confession is that it is my conviction that one day soccer will take a share of center stage in American sports. Soccer is real football. How about that for acculturation?

Floyd's mention of hot tea and air is the motivation for a mini cultural lesson on Roebuck. It may be a bit farfetched as far as teaching a lesson and a moral is concerned but its veracity is beyond question. Growing up poor in Roebuck, my mother, as well as other mothers, firmly believed that a volume of air mysteriously collected in the belly during the night and had to be expelled first thing in the morning if we were to feel good during the day. Ms. Morris believed that. So did Ms. Watson and Rita, and Joycelyn. I am not certain how the air got there because its source was never explained or identified, but tradition had it that it was there and it was better if it didn't stay. The hot tea would bring it up. We didn't question my mother's authority on the matter. We never asked where the air came from. She knew what she was talking about. And we believed her and carried out her request promptly. She was the leader and she knew what was best for her children. Probably, her mother before her made her drink hot tea first thing in the morning. It was clear from Floyd's request that the habit of drinking something hot to break the air was still alive and well.

"You have to break the air," my mother would proclaim. As if air was something breakable, or something to be shattered into tiny pieces. And so, all the children in Roebuck had to drink something hot every morning. Just like millions of Americans must have their cup of coffee, we had our *tot* of something hot. Americans may have their morning coffee because of habit, or as a means of providing the energy to start the day. It has nothing to do with air. For us in Roebuck, drinking a *tot* of hot tea first thing in the morning had one purpose and one purpose only — to break the air. It was all about the air.

My mother probably was on to something more substantive than merely drinking hot tea; something much deeper and more profound; something less scientific but something highly educational. Somehow, with only a primary school education, she knew firsthand how to put the scientific principle that *hot air rises and cool air falls* to the test. I remember how we would stand on the step, or somewhere in the yard, in the early morning Roebuck air, with a tot in each hand, pouring hot tea from one tot to the other, watching the steam rise into the air and witnessing a foamy froth settle on the contents of the receiving tot, as the tea cooled to a friendly temperature that allowed us to drink comfortably. It would have been quite unusual for Roebuck if we did not give a fancy name to the process of cooling our tea. We said that we were *brewing* our tea.

Floyd reminded me on day that brewing may not have been as simple a process as was described and one had to work up to a level of perfection of the skill in order to prevent mishaps. With years of experience and practice, the most skillful among us in the brewing process had the ability to raise the pouring tot as high as possible, raising it higher while simultaneously pouring the hot tea into the receiving tot without missing it. A mistake in the technical process meant that scalding hot tea landed on the toes of the unfortunate person, resulting in a painful accident as experienced by my friend Floyd. This early morning cultural ritual was repeated from house to house in Roebuck. I know for a fact that Deany and her family did the same thing, and that the Scantlebury family did it as well. Small children before setting out for school, and parents getting ready for a long day in the fields on Sedgepond Plantation, brewed hot cocoa tea, Milo tea, or Ovaltine tea. Sometimes we had Horlicks, or even green tea.

Incidentally, I just got up from writing to practice the brewing process. I was excited to discover that I was still able to maintain my accuracy, even after so many years of inactivity. But something was missing. It was not the same as it used to be back in Roebuck. Although the process worked smoothly, the raw materials, the ingredients and the conditions for the reenactment had to be drastically modified. I used two cups since Roebuck tots were not available. And I used cold water, for good reason. And furthermore, I did my simulated brewing performance over the kitchen sink instead of on the front step for fear of my neighbors thinking I was going crazy.

In leaner times we settled for the less upscale but the always reliable *hot water tea*. Sometimes hot water tea was all we could afford. This didn't happen very often but we put it to good use when we had to. Hot water tea wasn't difficult to prepare, and the ingredients were always available and plentiful. We would put some water to boil and then add sugar. The hot water tea was ready to be had by all. It broke the air, and that was what mattered. Every hot drink was tea for us in those days. But our tea did not come in fancy little

tea bags that had to be immersed in hot water to extract the somewhat weak flavor of mint, or chamomile, or red zinger, or even
golden seal. Not so in Roebuck. We did not need tea bags. Our tea
came in tins and cans of Ovaltine, Horlicks, Milo and cocoa. So we
had Ovaltine tea and Horlicks tea, Milo tea and cocoa tea. If we
had coffee, which was rare, it was coffee tea. If we were used to
drinking beer early in the morning, it probably would have been
beer tea. As long as it was something hot that we had first thing in
the morning, it was called tea.

Sometimes we had to drink hot *bush tea* in the morning, especially if we felt a cold, or something coming on, or if my mother
felt it was time for the bitter treatment. That was something she did
from time to time in order to keep our *constitution* up. I don't know
where she learned that word but she used it properly. She never said
that we were going to have herbal tea. We had bush tea. She would
select a combination of bush, vines and tree leaves, boil them, and
make us drink the healthy brew. Ginger tea was more palatable and
lime leaf tea went down a lot easier than the multi bush combination my mother preferred. The bush tea she brewed was real herbal
tea; tea that was as potent as it was bitter. She believed that the
bitterer it was, the better it was for us. And with all that hot tea in
the mornings, the phrase *full of hot air* was a reality for us as it rose
and was expelled in a semi-violent eruption that manifested itself
in the form of a belch or burp. People in Roebuck never said burp.
It was always a belch. I am sure you know full well the fate of the
air that did not rise. It turned into a gas. How interesting!

While I am on the subject, the water and sugar combination was
used with great versatility in Roebuck, and was very handy in leaner
times when hunger and meager finances challenged our creativity
and our survival. A mixture of cold water and sugar produced *sweet
water*, which we had with our meals at times. Note that it was *sweet
water* and not sweet water tea, because the mixture was cold and
not hot, and not very nutritious, now that I reflect on those days

and times. The simple addition of natural lime juice which we got from a lime tree that grew in the backyard suddenly turned the brew into home-made lemonade.

I can still remember us as small children having a difficult time trying to dissolve the extra sugar that settled at the bottom of the *tot* when we used water that was too cold for the amount of sugar we deposited. With spoon in hand we would stir and stir until the residue disappeared. My mother always reminded us to put in the ice after the sugar was dissolved, if we were making ice-cold sweet water. She never used the word dissolve or saturate but somehow she was smart enough to know that the warmer the water, the easier it was for the excess sugar to dissolve. Even with her limited experience with advanced education, she was still able to teach us the basics of living, and how to solve simple, as well as challenging occurrences, that confronted us.

Before leaving the subject, I have to explain the tot that was mentioned earlier. From the context I am sure that its meaning is easy to determine that it is some kind of utensil. Growing up in Roebuck, I didn't think much of it, or if it had a real meaning beyond what I knew it to be. Later, I learned that it had a secondary meaning as well — a small child, as in tiny tot. I am only now, as I write, being made aware of the dictionary's definition of a tot as a British soldier's drinking mug. I had often wondered after I was grown, why we used *tot* the way we did when I was growing up in Roebuck. Now I see the connection. And it is absolutely clear. With Barbados having been under British colonization until 1966, when we became an independent nation, it is easy to come to the conclusion on the derivation of the *tot*. Before I knew better, I held the opinion that *tot* was one of those words that had its origin in Roebuck. Now I have to acknowledge that Roebuck, even though it is known for its uniqueness in so many ways, cannot be lauded for the creation of the tot. But even though the word tot itself didn't have its origins in Roebuck, we were industrious enough to manufacture the actual tot, an example of how creative and resourceful small boys in Roebuck had become in order to solve a problem, or to satisfy a need.

The saying that necessity is the mother of invention was lived out in numerous practical ways in Roebuck when I was growing up there, with the manufacturing of the tot only one of them. We didn't have the luxury of having fine china, tea cups and mugs, so the creation and manufacture of the tot by the young boys was further proof that the poverty that existed among us provided another opportunity to make choices. That's exactly what poverty does. It presents two divergent roads; one leading to despair and hopeless; the other to optimism and resilience. We decided back then to choose the latter. Of course, we didn't articulate the situation in so many words, but our actions spoke in favor of doing something to resolve an issue. Even today I appear to have little patience for people who throw up their arms in disgust before learning the satisfaction of pursuing alternatives and new ways to a desired destiny.

I have never had the good fortune of seeing a British soldier's drinking mug, but my imagination tells me that it was nothing like the tots we assembled in Roebuck from raw materials that were readily available and free for recycling. A British soldier's drinking mug conjures up mental pictures of something exotic; with a degree of expense and class attached to it. Its connotation evokes images of a utensil for personal use that is fashioned from porcelain, or from glass, or some other breakable, or delicate material. The tots we made as boys bore none of these distinctive features

We crafted our own tots for one primary purpose — to drink from. So a high degree of care and personal dedication was spent on their production. We didn't have enough glasses, mugs and tea cups available for common or normal use. Most of the ones we had in our house were kept in reserve for important visitors to our home; visitors who never happen to show up very often, or not at all. Or they were there to put on show and on display as proof that we had a few of the finer things.

The tot-making industry bolstered our usefulness, and had a way of making us feel that we, at least if only in a very small way, were doing what we could to contribute to the economic stability of the home. Tot-making was strictly a boy's activity, and we felt, however unconsciously, that the money we were saving the family as men in training, by practicing this craft, could be used for other necessary items. I hoped this was my mother's way of thinking, as well as the thinking of the other mothers in Roebuck. Besides, tots were inexpensive. Still, they were very sturdy, long lasting, and very difficult to *mash up*.

Girls didn't make tots. My sisters and other girls made dolls by sewing pieces of cloth together and stuffing the head, arms and legs with some of the same material. I now think that they may have also used grass to *stuff* their toys. Already, they were preparing for motherhood and family. Boys were already training to be bread winners and providers. I remember the instant surge of accomplishment when I made my first tot. It was not easy, because I was never good with my hands. But it was a similar feeling to the one I had experienced when I made a grater, crude as it was, in *handwork* class at Indian Ground School, or when I restored book covers in bookbinding class, while the girls were learning to cook in *Domestic Science* class.

We fashioned our tots out of cans — used tin cans. Condensed milk cans. Milo cans. Ovaltine cans. Diversification was practiced in the tot-making business in Roebuck. We had to have a variety of models, sizes, and brand names. This home business put in motion a recycling program that was good for our environment, since the same cans and tins of food we bought from the shop to make hot tea were the very same ones that produced the bulk of the raw material for manufacturing our tots.

After a Milo can or an Ovaltine can was empty, it became

available for the transformation to occur. Truthfully, the can itself did not require much of a change, so the tot was delivered partially assembled. The technical challenge was the making and the subsequent attaching of the handle to the body. That aspect of the production required genius as well as exactness and precision to avoid leaking from around the areas where the actual connection was done. Nobody could do this job as accurately as my cousin, Charleston. He was the master when it came to making tots, as he was at mostly anything that required technical skill. He could do everything.

The handle itself was cut from a piece of tin using a very sharp knife and a hammer; striking the knife with the hammer so that the sharp blade would make incisions in the pliable metal as the craftsmen determined length and width. The rough edges were then turned narrowly inward and then beaten with the hammer to the desired degree of smoothness required. It had to feel comfortable to the touch, or it would be put through the refining process again and again until satisfaction and approval were reached. It had to pass inspection. Tots had to be perfect in every way. Shoddy work was not encouraged, and would be laughed at. The completed work of art brought a sense of pride, usefulness and satisfaction as it took its place in our kitchen, but it commanded a more lofty position when it was in use, holding our hot water tea, our sweet water, or lemonade.

I now realize that way back then my mother, in her own simplistic but profound way, may have used the hot tea and air scenario as a teaching tool to demonstrate lifelong lessons in order to teach and guide her five children to a productive and rewarding future. It was her way of saying that there was something deep down inside each of us waiting to get out, that when set free would transform each of us into a brighter and better individual. This belief in her children's ultimate goodness was evident in the way she treated us, and in the expectations she aimed to extract from deep within us. From early on, she seemed to have perceived a germ of potential buried deep inside our beings. And even if it was not there, she appeared to have willed it, and prayed for it to appear from some where. She wanted it to be there, even if we were too young and too immature to understand. She was thinking of our future and was able to see us, not only as we were, but what she wanted us to become. She talked about our schooling often and demanded that we attend school every day, and on time.

This was important to her, even if it wasn't to us initially. Nothing got in between us and our schooling. Schooling was the hot tea and she saw to it that nothing prevented us from drinking it daily. Not chores, and there were many; not sickness; (thank God we were always a healthy family); and not even poverty. It was because we were poor that we had to go to school, she seemed to think. Schooling was a means to end poverty. Poverty shouldn't prevent schooling. It should encourage it. This seemed to be her way of thinking; her philosophy on poverty and education. She would have stated her position to anyone; only in simpler terms.

Demanding that school attendance was a priority and a privilege not to be taken lightly, was her way of getting something hot inside of us to bring to the surface what was there — that little germ of potential she hoped was deep inside the five of us. And we loved school. We went every day. We drank our hot tea in the morning to break the air, and away we went. One day, my sister Yvonne, and I came home for lunch and it rained so hard and long that it threatened to keep us from going back to school that afternoon. I remember us just sitting there, crying our little hearts out hoping that the rain would stop so that we could get back to class. That's the level of commitment to schooling my mother engendered. It was the hot tea that she served up daily in order to bring up the air of ignorance and hopelessness.

My mother knew firsthand how difficult it was to do *3rd class* labor in the corn *grounds*, in the potato and yam fields, and in the cane *pieces* on Sedgepond Plantation, year-round in the hot Roe-buck sun, and she never wanted her way of making a living to be our experience. "I need something better for you," she would say. But as I got older, I was sensitive enough to perceive a dichotomy and a struggle with which she must have wrestled. "Am I asking too much of these children?" She must have internalized this question to the point of frustration. I may have been misguided in my con-clusion, but I felt very strongly that she must have pondered this situation very deeply, and very often. Of course, she never voiced her dilemma, or discussed it openly, but I can't ignore the possibil-ity that frustrating thoughts concerning what she viewed to be her inability to be an inspiration to her children must have crossed her mind. "How can a plantation worker inspire someone to rise higher than her own personal station in life?" she may have pondered. "What right does a parent with only a primary school education have to expect her children to achieve at a much higher level than she had?" Despite the conflicts with which she may have battled, she never wavered. She would never tire of reminding us that there was something better. "You have to turn out better than I did" was her motto. Education was the key — the hot tea. And she made us drink it.

My mother's questions were answered with the passing of time. Her children went on to complete high school and college, and are making their contribution to society in their chosen fields of inter-est. Completing high school successfully was a great achievement in Barbados, and it was considered cool to land a job in the bank or in the civil service after graduation. Roebuck was not known for producing an abundance of graduates to fill these positions, but few of us were the exception, rather than the rule. Shirley Ramsey became a teacher. Rixford Marshall was a police officer. My cousin, Dorcas, worked in the post office and worked her way up to the position of Deputy Postmaster General. My sister Elaine started out teaching before settling for nursing, later earning a BA when she moved to New York. She continues to work in that field even today. My other sisters Yvonne, Cheryl, and Heather completed their college education in New York, and now work in hotel management, physical therapy, and nursing, respectively. Like my sister Elaine, I initially went into nursing, training at Jenkins, the mental institution in the city, but after a month or so, I quickly learned that nursing was not my calling. I landed a teaching job in 1968 at All Saints Boys School and have not looked back, allowing my desire to climb higher, to take me to Jamaica, the Virgin Islands, Michigan, California, Tennessee and Georgia; working my way up to assistant principal, principal, science supervisor, and adjunct professor, while finding the time to earn a doctorate in education.

Can anything good come out of Roebuck? It sure can. My mother answered that question with a resounding yes. She saw to it that Roebuck earned some dignity and respect. And as her life slipped away in a New York hospital so many years ago, I sensed that she was happy and at peace; that she felt rewarded; that the educational hot tea she made us drink had done its job and that she had lived to see her children achieve a measure independence and success. Something she always wanted.

CHAPTER THREE

Muddah Dearest

But nowhere in Muddah's teaching was she more exemplary than in her teaching of hello and good morning.

Muddah is a term of endearment that is indigenous to Roebuck. To be more specific, it is indigenous to our home and to our family. Nobody else in Roebuck used this word. It was as if we had bought the rights to it and had it copyrighted for our use alone. It is such a unique term that I am not certain of its spelling, or even if it has one. I never saw it written anywhere. You wouldn't find it in a dictionary, or read about it in history. Yet, it has a meaning; a deep and personal meaning to my sisters and me. I am not sure who started the tradition, but it obviously must have been my sister Elaine, since she is the oldest of the five of us. We may never know how she arrived at the term, but she has to be credited for her contribution to the culture of our home and family. When I came along, the name was so firmly entrenched that I had no option but to continue the culture, passing it on to my sisters Yvonne, Cheryl and Heather that came after me.

Looking back, I realize how we used it with so much passion and respect, and with such a sense of caring and reverence. Even now as I write, I am repeating the word several times in silence as a way of reliving and recapturing its beauty and its significance. Obviously, the culturally corresponding American name is Mother. Muddah is to Roebuck what Mommy, or Mom, is to the US. We never said

Mom, or Mommy, in Roebuck. That was too unlike Roebuck. We went for more simple and ordinary names, nothing too fancy or creative, yet very respectful. How we came up with Muddah, I will never know but I still continue to treasure it today, just as much as I did the first time I heard it over sixty years ago.

Not that Mommy was tabooed. It was simply not cultural in Roebuck, or Barbados, or probably in the wider Caribbean. To hear Shirley refer to Deany as Mom, or Clovene to Ms. Marshall as Mommy, or Ken to Ms. Headley as either Mom or Mommy would have been so unnatural for Roebuck. Even our own boys, one born on the US mainland and the other two in St. Croix, US Virgin Islands, have never called their mother Mom or Mommy. She is Ma to them — no where close to Muddah.

In fact, there is one particular incident I heard from my wife, Hortense. She tells a story of how the use of Mom could have been potentially quite costly. She had taken the boys to Dunns River Falls in Jamaica one summer and had previously warned them to keep their mouths closed while she took care of purchasing the tickets, fearing that the attendant might overcharge her if she picked up on an accent that was foreign, or more specifically, American. While she was engaging the attendant in her native Jamaican lingo, our oldest son, Sheldon, interrupted the transaction with "But mom…" As luck would have it, his intervention did not have an elevated effect on the price of the tickets.

When I first moved to America I quickly discovered that there was not much variety in the pet names for mother. It has always been Mom or Mommy. And since taking on this project I have been even more deliberate at paying attention to the pet names that children use to address their mothers. I have even conducted my own unscientific study using some of my students as subjects to determine the most popular pet name for mother. Even though my sampling was quite small, the data led to a solid conclusion that Mom and Mommy are the names most often used. The truth is that the American culture allows for a greater variety in pet names for grandparents. Our friends' children, Kenric and Dana, are quite creative in this regard. They refer to their grandparents as G Mommy and G Daddy, while Bill and Susie's grandchildren refer to them as Papa and Nanny. And our grandson, Max, calls Hortense Oma. Moosie is his maternal grandmother and I am Papa.

No such variety existed in Roebuck culture. My paternal grandmother was simply Grandmother. It was not uncommon to hear us greet her with "Good morning Grandmother." And my maternal grandmother was Ma Ma (mah mah) to us; only because we grew up hearing her own children, Gloria, Wilfred, Perceval, nicknamed Son, and James, nicknamed Brown Boy, call her Ma Ma. In the end, comparing the results of my informal research mentioned above with those from Roebuck, it is safe to conclude that there was a significant difference in how the two cultures use different words to identify mother. American children mostly say Mom or Mommy, whereas children in Roebuck mostly said Ma (mah). This was true of Hugh, Nazie, Dorcas and Sherrod, the children in one Scantlebury family, as well as in the Cumberbatch-Morris family where Keith, Charleston, Golda, Jenny, Henson and Claudette addressed their mother, Sylvie, as Ma. But there were variations on the theme. Andrew and Glendeen and the other children in the other Scantlebury family referred to their mother as Mammy. Muddah was ours.

My sisters and I basked in the uniqueness of Muddah. It was always Muddah this and Muddah that. Muddah, I need this and Muddah, I need that. Interestingly enough, she too appeared to have relished the uniqueness of her name, seeming to treasure it with enormous pride, since she was the only one in Roebuck with that special designation. She was not a Ma, or Mammy, or a *Ma Ma*, for that matter. She was a *muddah*. And we reciprocated with pleasure and delight until the day she died. I recall very vividly the very last time I called her Muddah to her face. The occasion was way back in December of 1988 as her life ebbed away in a New

York hospital. My family and I had driven up from Chattanooga to join my sisters to be with her. "Muddah, I am here," I whispered in between the songs we sang to comfort her. She appeared to have understood. I can't imagine calling her anything else. She was, and always will be *Muddah* to us. Not Mother, but *Muddah*. My father affectionately called her Ms. Mayers. At other times he settled for Iola. Everybody in Roebuck called her Iola or Ms. Mayers but to my sisters and me, she was *Muddah*.

I have already written a little about my mother, but now that I am introducing her as Muddah, our cultural name for her, I want to say a little more about her. And since muddah is unique to Roebuck and virtually non-existent in the US, it is one of those names around which I chose to build a personal story. I have already mentioned how she felt about education; how she believed it was the key for a better life for my sisters and me, even though she could not articulate her position in a way that she would have liked. But everything Muddah did, told us that there was no doubt about how she felt about the direction she had in mind for each of us.

Muddah was adamant about homework. It was as if she wanted to establish a sacred interlude in between the other activities of the household. No one dared to tread on the seriousness of the time that was dedicated and set apart for something special. It was as if she herself was looking forward to this special time to unwind from a hard and sweaty day in the fields on the plantation. She would announce "Elaine is studying," and that would be the signal that complete silence was required, and acquired. The radio went silent. I went silent. We all went silent. Muddah demanded it, and she got it, as our *back house* was suddenly transformed into a sacred study hall.

Muddah appeared to have made homework time important for more than one reason. Ultimately, she determined that Elaine should use the time to get her homework done so she could get good *marks* on her report card. However, there appeared to have been another reason; a personal and selfish reason where Muddah was concerned. Even though it was beyond her academic ability to provide even the simplest bit of assistance with the nouns and the verbs, and the participles and the gerunds, Muddah appeared to understand her role in the educational and academic preparation of her children. If she was asked to articulate that role, she would have said that it was her duty to provide large amounts of moral support in an environment that encouraged learning. She would have used much simpler words, but her intent would have been the same. She absolutely knew that there was something in it for her; that there was a light at the end of the tunnel. She would be at the center of her children's success, and making sure that homework was done, was the most obvious place to begin.

Muddah's almost sacred, or religious reaction to homework time was somewhat ironic in itself. My sister, Elaine, was a student at the Alexandra School, a public secondary school for girls. Many nights she would come home with homework in Scripture or *Religious Knowledge*, as it was called in those days. No wonder Muddah considered homework time a religious exercise. Even though she exacted silence from all, Elaine would sometimes study out loud with monotonous repetitions and chants as she studied the missionary journeys of Paul. It was as if she had read some kind of research on learning that concluded that repetition was a major factor in memorizing and in the retention of content. But Elaine's learning style did not fall on deaf ears. It was because of her learning strategy that I was able to pick up specific facts about the major stops made by Paul, Barnabas, and John Mark on those missionary journeys in Bible times. I can still remember her talking about Antioch in Syria, and Antioch in Pisidia, and how the disciples were first called Christians at Antioch. When it was my turn to study for school leaving exams, had I included Scripture in my list of subjects to study, I would have had a head start, just from listening to Elaine as she studied in repetitive mode under Muddah's supervision.

Muddah kept up a similar homework routine when I started high school. The same restrictions on silence that were strictly enforced for Elaine's benefit were now put in place for me as well. "Sylvester is doing his homework," I heard her announce more than once, and her demands kicked in automatically until I was done. Similarly, as was the case with Elaine, Muddah was oblivious to the fact that she was engaging in parental involvement. Since becoming a teacher myself, and reading and studying the literature on parental involvement and its impact on learning, I now realize that Muddah was very far ahead of her time as far as parental involvement is concerned. She was supporting the theory that says that parental involvement in education means much more than visiting the classroom on a regular basis or accumulating a hundred hours in volunteer work for the school. She never visited a school, never took part in a parent-teacher conference, or showed up for an open house event. Yet, her answer to the parent involvement issue was to make sure that she created a home environment in which her children could study without interruption, and that they were equipped with the tools and materials they needed for school. To Muddah, that was the ultimate parental involvement.

My muddah put her money where her mouth was, as the saying goes. She did not only talk when it came to our schooling. She also acted, if only in so far as her abilities would permit. I want to relate a personal story to support Muddah's passion for education for us, and to prove my point that she did not only talk, but acted as well.

One Saturday night I sat down at the small dinette table around 8:00 to study for my Biology exam on the following Monday. I knew my content pretty well; Biology being my favorite subject in high school. I had an excellent teacher in Mr. Holder. Pooh Holder, they called him. He made the subject interesting and covered the material thoroughly. Mr. Holder was exceptionally skillful at breaking down difficult and complex content into simple and understandable chunks of learning; so simple that he unconsciously provided the occasional cause for giggling that got me into trouble in his class more than once. In one particular class period we were about to begin the chapter on the skeletal system. Mr. Holder began by saying "The skeleton is a bony structure. It is made of bones." Instantly, my eyes locked with David Murray's and we simultaneously broke into laughter. We both suffered the consequences.

On one other occasion, when we were studying a chapter about the various types of root systems, Mr. Holder asked David to read a section of the chapter to the class. He was reading quite impressively until he came to the word *adventitious,* which he pronounced *ad-ven-ti-tee-us.* I was sitting beside David at the time and exploded in laughter. Mr. Holder, who never smiled, did not appreciate my outburst. Still, he was a phenomenal teacher, and was a strong influence in my decision to study Biology in college and teach it to high school students after graduation.

Even though I knew my Biology well, I decided on one last intense final review before the big test. Two things were momentous about that particular Saturday night. Nobody studied on a Saturday night. It was a night to relax. It was a party night, so to speak, although there were never any parties in Roebuck. Still, Saturday night was a fun night. It was a night for *liming.* Secondly, Muddah sat down at the table with me; something she had never done prior to that night. She had always demanded silence, and had gone about her business quietly, until that particular Saturday night. I can't recall ever inviting her company. Maybe she had read my vibes and had perceived the seriousness of the occasion. She took her seat with me at the table, encouraging my study, if only for a brief time.

Even though her spirit was absolutely willing, her flesh was just as weak, because she fell asleep, snoring like a freight train, as only she could, waking up at intervals, but never leaving her post. Muddah slept through studies on the digestive and endocrine systems, protein and amino acids and the personally challenging nervous system. She woke up just before 2:00 AM; about the time when I decided that I had had enough of that green Biology textbook. While this was only one of the many times it was proven that Muddah was special, my only regret is that I never told her how much I appreciated her support and company that night, and how much that particular act of kindness rated very highly on the list of all the good things she had done for me. However, I do recall telling the story to others over the years.

Muddah's all-nighter was all the more appreciated, especially when the nature of the exams I was about to take was taken into consideration. I was in the *fifth form* by then and had arrived at the point in my schooling when it was time to write multiple school leaving exams, Biology being only one of them. In 1968, Barbados, though an independent country, was still a member of the British Commonwealth, and our exams were set in England, either by the Universities of Oxford and Cambridge or by London University. These exams, the General Certificate Exams (GCE), were taken by students from all across the British Commonwealth, from Australia to Canada, Africa, and the islands of the Caribbean, They encouraged a competitive spirit among schools and countries. They required extremely detailed answers of the essay type, as opposed to multiple choice, or completion, or short answer responses. Muddah's presence that night not only kept me company, but also boosted my confidence, and gave me the opportunity to formulate detailed answers in my mind in preparation for my exam the following Monday afternoon.

To show how confident I was concerning my Biology exam, and how Muddah's support had sustained me, I showed up at Kensington Oval on the morning of the exam to participate in the private schools sports meet that was also slated for that day. We didn't call it track and field in Roebuck in those days. It was a *sports* day. However, this boy from Roebuck had two major goals for that day. Both were important in different ways and I would attack each one in the order in which it came. First, I had to win the 880 yards to maintain my standing as a promising athlete. I had to put Roebuck on the athletic map since no one from Roebuck had ever achieved such prominence. It would also make Muddah proud.

I was an athlete in high school, my favorite was the 880, even though I also had some success in the mile which I ran with my friend, Cleveland Yarde. We also ran many road races, or cross country as they call it in the US. Cleveland was a good runner who was expected to win each time. I didn't mind coming in second. It is interesting to note that in Roebuck and in all of Barbados, that the term athlete covered only a specific group of sportsmen and women. Unlike in America, only those who did track and field events were considered athletes. Basketball players were basketball players. Not athletes. Cricketers were just that — cricketers. Not athletes. Even Sir Garfield Sobers, the world's greatest cricketer, was not an athlete. He was just a cricketer. Those who played football (soccer) and *net ball* were not athletes. They were just football players and net ball players. Even the greatest jockey of the day, Challenor Jones, was not considered an athlete. By the way, which one is the athlete, the jockey or the horse?

Incidentally, I won the 880 quite easily, changed into civilian clothing, and caught a bus to Springer Memorial School on the other side of town to work on my second goal of the day, while simultaneously rejoicing with my victory in the 880 and focusing on the exam ahead, buoyed by the preparation that Muddah and I had made.

It was a University of London exam, the questions and directions recorded on pink paper. I remember the occasion that well. I also remember having a very difficult time with the exam; not that I didn't know the answers to the questions. I had prepared adequately; maybe too adequately. The instructions required me to answer question one and any other four. I found myself in a quandary. I knew all the questions equally well, and spent a good amount of time trying to decide on which other four to write. But

Muddah and I had prepared well and I went to work with confidence. When I left the exam room I was confident that I had done well, and was not at all surprised, when after a long wait, the favorable results were returned.

By now you must have concluded that Muddah was a single parent because up to this point I have not mentioned anything very significant about my father. Not quite. My father, like many others from Roebuck, had migrated to England in search of a better life for his family. Times were hard in Roebuck and this was a common practice to seek better working opportunities across the seas. Hattan, my father's brother, had done the same, as well as Leopold and Coursey. People in Roebuck never used the term single parent. There was not a corresponding name for it when I was growing up. I was only made aware of the term when I came to America and witnessed the attention, excuses and blame that were leveled at this class of people, accusing them of the cause of society's ills. I must state that single mothers in Roebuck were not singled out as such. They were not shunned, or blamed. Rita was a single mother; also Aury and Ernesta Cox. Besides them, there were several others that raised their children as single women. I have to be fair in this regard when it comes to my own family, for Muddah was an actual single mother at one time. She had my sister Elaine and me before she was married to my father. That's why our *surname* is Carrington and not Mayers. Muddah was a Carrington before she got married to Fred Mayers. We inherited her last name, as was the culture in Roebuck.

Still, the term single mother was never used in Roebuck culture, even though a rather large stigma was leveled at women who got in the *family way* outside of marriage. In Roebuck, single mothers did what it took to take care of their children. Muddah was such a parent. She was tough, dispelling the notion from some I meet in this country, that "You were spoiled" because I was the only boy among four sisters. "Spoiled by whom?" I usually respond. Not by Muddah. If any spoiling was done to me, it was done by Ma Ma, my maternal grandmother.

Muddah did not show favoritism towards any of us, and appeared to have relished her time as a single mother just to show her toughness at parenting after my father left for England. She was the perfect single mother, working full-time in the fields on the plantation and sometimes in the plantation house, from early in the morning until she *knocked off* in the late afternoon, and still finding time to distribute chores as well as discipline and punishment that were not always corporal in nature. One day she made me wear my sister's blue Alexandra School P.E shorts to keep me out of the street. She used whatever strategy she had at her disposal to get a lesson across. Her actions back then might be classified today as some aspect of child abuse; a decision that might have had a lasting negative effect on me psychologically. But Muddah was not concerned with anything psychological. She didn't use that term. All she wanted was that I keep out of the street. The road, we used to call it. And it worked.

Muddah worked in the fields without complaint, even when the sun was hot and the *driver* was constantly watching. I knew her well enough to know that she would have worked just as hard and just as meticulous whether or not she was being constantly supervised. She was that kind of woman — the kind that always gave her best, no matter the nature of the job.

Quite coincidentally, I am reading a book on the slave trade and came across the word *driver,* and as I write, I am finding it rather easy to compare the conditions under which Muddah and the others labored on Sedgepond Plantation with the conditions that existed during slavery. There, as it had been in days of slavery, was the driver with a white *cork hat* and a *stick*; his symbols of leadership and authority, watching over workers as they labored in the heat of the sun. And the obvious conclusion comes to mind; that right there in the fields of Sedgepond Plantation, while being driven by a driver and even though she might not have been able to reverse her personal situation, the desire that her children would one day be in a position of leadership, respect, and even authority, must have kept her toiling. And so, she pushed education, practically forcing it down our throats, so that we would not be *driven* as she had endured.

Muddah's rewards would come later as the fruits of her labor were manifested in two nurses, a business administrator/supervisor; a physical therapist and a school principal. These sibling accomplishments may appear insignificant to the casual reader but they become more noteworthy when viewed by Roebuck's standards and expectations at the time.

Muddah did not use her singleness as an excuse to shirk her responsibilities as a parent. Neither did she use it as an apology or a reason to set low standards and expectations for us. She ruled with an iron hand, literally. Never did I ever hear her proclaim "I don't know what else to do with this boy," like a weeping parent recently told me in my office about her sixth grade son. She would have never allowed a ten, or eleven year old boy to reach such a level of *civil disobedience* that would drive her to make such an unthinkable admission of defeat. Muddah would never confess to a teacher, or to anyone else, for that matter, that she was failing at fulfilling the most important responsibility entrusted to her. There was no question that my Muddah absolutely knew what to do. And she did it often. She did it thoroughly, and she did it hard, with lots of justice and a lot less mercy.

Muddah was a deeply religious woman and a reader of the King James Version of the Bible. She prayed regularly, kneeling beside her bed and like Hannah of biblical fame, whispered her prayers to God. In Muddah's case though, her whispers were clearly heard but remained undeciphered. As I watched her pray, I concluded back then, and still do today, that her children, especially me, were the object of her communication with her God. As I write this, it is impossible to stop the tears that have begun to form as I relive those tender moments that Muddah invested on our behalf. Yet, it was obvious that she suffered from selective memory when fully engaged in her role as a dispenser of discipline and punishment. Although she read her bible often it was if she had never heard of the verse found in Micah 6, verse 8, particularly the part that talks about mercy. *He hath shown thee O man...but to do justly, and to love mercy...* She was very concerned about not *sparing the rod and spoiling the child* as found in Proverbs 13:24; a charge which she took literally and seriously.

One particular incident comes readily to mind; one that involved my sister, Elaine, and me. To put it simply, Elaine and I got into a knock- down- drag -out sibling fight, the reason for which I can't recall at this time, but we broke down a door in the process. Muddah came home and delivered the goods. To both of us; delivering the message that fighting was not tolerated. And secondly, that it was *dear* to replace a door, especially when money was tight, and neither Elaine nor I was in a position to contribute to the door's replacement.

Muddah lived by a simple and practical motto as far as discipline and punishment were concerned. "*Hard ears, you won't hear; own way you will feel.*" In Roebuck, if I had hard ears, it meant that I had decided not obey her, and if I decided not to obey and have my own way, I would certainly feel; feel something unpleasant and really painful in parts that hurt when I tried to sit. Sometimes Muddah would tell me I was *disgusting.* "That disgusting boy," she would say. But she didn't really mean it the way it sounds. What she actually meant to say was that I was very obstinate. Some time ago I was watching the Rachel Maddow show on television, and had to chuckle to myself when a guest on the show referred to Rush Limbaugh's comments concerning Sandra Fluke, the Georgetown University law student, as disgusting. I suddenly remembered how I, along with other children in Roebuck, was sometimes branded as disgusting when we were growing up. Rush viciously attacked

Ms. Fluke on his radio show, calling her a slut and a prostitute, thereby earning the well-deserved adjective — disgusting.

But certainly Muddah didn't mean that I was revolting, repulsive, or even sickening. She didn't mean that I was a ghastly, filthy, sordid boy. To her, I was not nauseating, or repelling. She didn't even know those words existed. Neither she nor any other mother in Roebuck knew or used those terms. Ms. Watson didn't. Ms. Morris didn't. And Aunt Rita didn't either. But they knew disgusting, and used it often to let us know that we were hard ears. "You so hard ears ...," they would tell us. Never repulsive or revolting. Just hard ears. Not only was I *hard ears* but I was sometimes *gipsy.* "Yuh too *gipsy*," Muddah would tell me from time to time. Other children in Roebuck heard that from their parents as well. But all they meant was that we were *malicious.* But being malicious in Roebuck did not mean that a person was hateful, or mean, wicked or mischievous. It simply meant that we were minding someone else's business.

Being *hard ears* in Roebuck carried some very painful consequences. I experienced this personally because I suffered those consequences first-hand and on a regular basis. But as often as this happened to me so long ago, there is one *hard ears* group event that I will never forget. It was Good Friday and as was the custom in those days, there was all-day prayer meeting at the Church. Of course, my parents had to be there. They would never miss that prayerful event. That morning, a bunch of us took out our sheep to graze down in Sedgepond following a strict warning from our parents not to spend the whole day down there.

Once the sheep were taken care of, we started fishing for *crayfish* in the river; using our feet to s*tamp* in the water to dislodge the fish from their hiding places and then scooping them up in our bare hands and tossing them into a waiting bucket of water for the journey home. We caught a lot of *prongs* and other fish that day and were having so much fun that we had not realized that the time to be back home was upon us. To appease the wrath of our parents, each of us assembled a small bundle of wood to burn in our out-door *fireplace*, rounded up our sheep and set out to climb Sedge-pond Hill on the way home. By the way, I mentioned our fireplace in a casual conversation with a friend one day and she was surprised to the point of asking why there was a need for a fireplace in tropi-cal Roebuck. I took full advantage of the teachable moment to explain the difference between the Roebuck version of a fireplace and a Chattanooga model.

As if by design, our parents did not show up to intercept us all at once; choosing to prolong the agony one kid at a time. Michael got his beating first and Livingstone got his next. In each case the bundle of wood failed to do its job and went flying during each attack. Ms. Morris finally met Charleston and without a single word lunged for his head. In my ignorance, I asked myself "Why is she kissing him?" After a series of screams and yells I discovered that she was not kissing him at all. She was biting his ear. He was *hard ears*. I didn't see when the bucket of fish was sent flying into the bushes but the next morning, it was not difficult to notice a bunch of orange-colored crayfish, our previous day's catch, resting com-fortably on the ground among the shrubbery.

I intentionally brought up the incident while we were visiting with Charleston in Roebuck recently, just to hear his take on it since we had never spoken about it since it happened, and I wanted to hear his account so as to provide validation to what I had already written. He welcomed the opportunity and went into full story-telling mode, which he does so well, as he detailed every aspect of what happened that day and pointing to his ear, where he said he still had Ms. Morris's teeth mark to prove it.

As my luck would have it on the day in question, I was the last to meet my date with destiny; my father meeting me at the top of *the line* between Rita and Aury's house. He didn't bite my ear but he showed me no mercy, apparently taking pleasure in publicly showing, the reputation that he had built for himself as a strict

disciplinarian. When he finally released me, he made it plain that I
still had to fulfill my final chore for the day — grab a milk bottle,
climb Penny Hill and get the cow's milk from my grandmother in
Indian Ground. Some time much later I wondered how our parents
could have been so unforgiving, especially after spending an entire
day in prayer.

Come to think of it, Muddah was a leader in her own right, just
as I am a leader today. I lead a school but Muddah led an organizational structure known as the family. She was not versed in leadership theory or management research but would be the first to admit
that she was a sacrificial leader, doing whatever it took to provide
for our needs, oftentimes sacrificing hers in order to satisfy ours.
Her leadership style was not based on a grandiose reward system,
or on an intricate points program, but it was always clear that her
definition of leadership was her ability to get her children to do
those things which they would not normally do. In other words,
"Do it because I say so." And so, I washed the *wares*, took out the
sheep, fed the pigs and cleaned their nasty pens; not because I
wanted to but because Muddah said so. I abhorred feeding those
hogs, and of all the chores that were mine, I hated none more than
cleaning the pig pens. Heavens forbid if a *boar* or *sow* decided to get
out and run around for a while. I had to catch it and get it back
into the pen. I can still hear Muddah saying "The pig get away, go
and *ketch* it." There was no argument or allowance for compromise.
Her leadership style was from the top down. I did it because she
said so.

There were several other chores I did not like; some which coincidentally involved *picking* something. Even now I am unable to
understand the aversion I had towards picking but under Muddah's
leadership, my dislike for it was not a factor to be discussed. *Picking
rice* was one of them. Picking rice involved picking out the bad rice
grains from the good rice grains before washing and cooking a pot
of rice and peas, or black eye peas and rice, or even split peas and

rice. We would spread out the rice to be cooked on the table and use our index finger to snag the rice grains that were black and remove them from the good ones. It was a slow and boring challenge that had to be met.

There were other aspects of picking that fell under Muddah's leadership and supervision. Because she demanded it, I had to *pick* peas from the pea tree to cook rice and peas. Following the picking and shelling of the peas, there was still more picking to be done. As with the rice, I had to pick out the bad peas from the good ones. And as if all that picking wasn't enough, I was still expected to pick up wood to keep our *fire place* in working order so we could cook our food. Not because I wanted to but because Muddah said so.

I also had to pick *meat* for our sheep to eat. Most times it was pond grass or rabbit meat. To this day I cannot understand why they called it meat in Roebuck. There were just two special kinds of grass that we called meat that our flock of sheep obviously cherished and demanded. Rabbit meat was more of a vine than a grass and it is beyond my imagination why it was called rabbit meat since I had never seen a rabbit eat rabbit meat. I had to go out and find it, especially on those days when I did not take the sheep out to graze for the day. Picking rabbit meat was not among my favorite things to do either, but I could master it fairly easily if I was successful at finding the main root, pulling up the entire plant and going home with a bundle of rabbit meat for my sheep to enjoy. Not because I wanted to, but because Muddah said so.

Muddah's greatest leadership asset however, was her ability to lead by example. She was not only a do as I say leader but was just as effective at leadership by example. She got right in there with us to take the lead in so many chores, just to make sure that her organizational structure, the home and family, not only survived but prospered and flourished. She appeared to have been a firm believer in the proverb: *All work and no play makes Jack a dull boy.* But she was just as ardent in the inverse: *All play and no work makes Jack an equally dull boy.* I never heard her mention the proverb but by her focus on work I was certain that it captured her personal philosophy on work and play. I knew without a doubt that she gladly substituted Jack with Sylvester in each version of the proverb. Nobody can convince me otherwise. After all these many years I still believe it today with the same intensity that I did when I was a kid. She had this annoying stipulation that I do some kind of work on a *bank holiday* or on some Saturday mornings as a prerequisite for playtime, or taking a trip the city, when I was a little older, to *lime* with my friends.

Every year during *crop time* we would help our neighbors *cut* their sugar cane. If Brother Mayers needed help harvesting his canes one Saturday, or on a bank holiday, the neighborhood pitched in to help. When it was Brother Scant's turn, we all did the same. And when it was time for ours to be cut, they returned the favor. Muddah never just sent me to help. She was right there with me. It was her way of getting me involved in community service projects, even though she did not use those fancy words. I did not have my own *cane row* to cut. The cutting was left to the older and more experienced men. My job was *heading canes*, a multi step process that began with picking up behind the *cane cutters* and making small bundles that were heavy enough for me to carry on my head.

In time I became quite adept at tying two *cane tops* together to make a *band* to tie my bundles of cane together. This aspect of the job was made a lot easier because the cane *arrows* were gone from the cane by the time crop time rolled around. The arrows had tiny feather-like parts that blew in the wind that would have been annoying to one's eyes and nose. With the bundle made and ready, someone would give me a *lift*, hoisting it to my head to take to the *cane heap* until the *lorry* came to load them up. I repeated the process over and over again, and even though it was hard work, I never got paid, or expected it, because I was only helping. But I did look forward to the corned beef, *biscuits* and *sweet drink* that were served by the owner of the *cane piece*. Muddah used these experiences to unconsciously teach me her craft. Even though she had loftier expectations for me, it was her way of teaching me to acquire a useful skill; one that I could use to help others when crop time rolled around each year.

More often than not, these work sessions were personal; work that was done for our own home. We had a *piece of ground* in Cabbage Tree that we rented from the Sedgepond Plantation. There we had a *cane piece*, and we also planted yams, potatoes, cassava and pigeon peas. Ever so often, Muddah decided that the ground needed some manure to build up the chalky soil. And so, she and I would carry baskets of *down* on our heads making several trips down Sedgepond Hill to the *ground* in Cabbage Tree. It is still beyond me why we called it *the ground* in Roebuck but it was not uncommon for Muddah to talk about going down to *the ground*.

A much smaller piece of land next to the house, where we planted a little *time*, some tomatoes, lettuce and cabbage, and where *kimber* vines and *punkin* vines ran all over the place, was the garden. But somehow, *the ground* was the much larger piece of land a ways from the house, going down Sedgepond Hill where the *cane piece* was, and where yams, potatoes, cassava and pigeon peas grew in abundance. My friend Hal, supported the distinction between *the ground* and the garden recently when he and I were talking about the time his mother was found dead in their *ground*. He explained that a garden was a smaller piece of land where vegetables grew, while *the ground* was a much larger plot on which larger foodstuff like potatoes, bananas, and sugar cane grew; like *the ground* Muddah had down in Sedgepond.

At certain times during the year, Muddah would charge me with the chore of taking *down* to our *ground* in Sedgepond. We never said the word chore in Roebuck. We had jobs. Not chores. And they were jobs that were not rewarded with an allowance, although we never used the word allowance in Roebuck. If we got any money from our parents it was just that — money; not an allowance. It seemed that Muddah would choose the most inappropriate time to demand that I haul *down* to *the ground* all the way to Sedgepond. As I mentioned above, her choice of day was always a Saturday, or on a Bank Holiday. Never on a Sunday. It was only much later that I learned that I was carrying *dung* and not *down*. Talk about a shock! The dung was manufactured at our house under a spreading *peng weng* tree. That is what we heard it called in Roebuck but I also learned that it had an official botanical name — the *pandanah*. Being the unofficial botanist that I am, I did my research and was able to discover that there is actually a pandanna tree that closely resembles our Roebuck version. That's where we kept our flock of sheep — under the spreading peng weng tree that provided almost perfect protection from the rain and sun. That was their pen; their home. Over time, the unused rabbit meat that the sheep did not eat, combined with sheep *do-do* in a chemical change to form layers of sediment which we called *down*, or manure, if we wanted to be sophisticated. When Muddah estimated that the time was right, the *dung* had to be moved to *the ground* in baskets made especially for that purpose. It goes without saying that this manure did not have a pleasant smell, especially in such close proximity to my nose as it was being transported in a basket on my head. Sometimes Muddah would purchase real fertilizer, as in potash and sulfate-of-ammonia, which did not smell that pleasant either.

I hated those *dung* trips to the ground. And there were several of them in one day, up and down Sedgepond Hill. What made matters worse was the reality that there was never a tangible reward awaiting me. I didn't mind working in the cane field. At least there was a meal of corned beef, biscuits and sweet drink as a reward for a day's work.

Now, I am grateful that Muddah put me through the paces of work, so to speak. Today, I have a healthy appreciation for work of any kind, as long as it is honorable. That's why I had no problems at all working on the chicken farms at Loma Linda University when I was studying for my doctorate. I had years of experience in Roebuck that prepared me for the job. The *dung* experience I endured in Roebuck was adequate preparation for the farms of Loma Linda, and the stench of the potash and the sulfate of ammonia was adequate preparation for the less stronger stuff I experienced while cleaning student apartments in Lansing when I was a student at Michigan State University. It is true that I had more prestigious work experience while working as a graduate assistant in the School of Education at Loma Linda University but the lessons learned in Roebuck, whether taking care of sheep, or working in *the ground*, or carrying buckets of water on my head from the *pipe*, or trying my hand at cooking, or washing and *pressing* my clothes, and even *sprouting*, have taught me a healthy respect and a positive attitude towards work of any kind.

I purposely mentioned *sprouting* above because *sprouting* in Roebuck had a vastly different meaning from sprouting in America. I was laughing inside when Bob Payne from Wildwood, a lifestyle center operated by Seventh-day Adventists in Wildwood Georgia, was educating me on the health benefits of sprouting. As he was demonstrating the process I could not help but remember how we did our own *sprouting* as boys growing up in Roebuck. Needless to say, I was so impressed with Bob's lecture that after his presentation I left Wildwood with a white plastic sprouter, along with several samples of seeds to try my hand at sprouting. Now, Hortense and I sprout several kinds of seeds to add to our meals from time to time.

But *sprouting* in Roebuck was not that simple, and even now as I write about it, I am reminded of a biblical connection, no matter how far fetch the connection may seem. In the story of Boaz and Ruth, Boaz, in an act of kindness, instructed his reapers to leave some of the wheat behind so that Ruth could follow behind and gather enough to feed herself and Naomi, her mother-in-law. The only difference is that in Roebuck, the plantation owners did not instruct the workers to leave potatoes, or yams, behind when they were *digging* them. However, they inadvertently did, not being able to harvest one hundred percent of the crop. Given time, the unharvested potatoes would begin to sprout, pushing up little green leaves above the surface of the ground. That was our signal that it was time to go behind the reapers and dig up the sprouting potatoes to provide additional food for our families. In Roebuck, the entire process was known as *sprouting*.

As a result of the work Muddah mandated while I was growing up in Roebuck, specific impressions, personal lessons, and lasting values pertaining to the dignity of good honest labor were acquired. Consequently, my personal opinion is that children, wherever possible, need to get their hands dirty by digging in the soil; planting something while gaining an appreciation for cultivating the land and producing food. I found it to be an exhilarating and magical experience to disturb the habitat of the earthworms and the other *bugs* that lived there. By the way, we never said bugs in Roebuck, as is the case in America, where every little creature is a bug. The lessons I accumulated because of Muddah's insistence and her respect for the value of work will stay with me for a long time; even today as Hortense and I annually battle to produce a *kitchen* garden from the almost barren soil in our backyard in Ringgold.

There was another side to Muddah. She loved a hearty laugh and a good joke. Although she worked hard, she found time to share her sense of humor. I remember her telling us a joke that still brings a chuckle each time I think about it. She told us a story of a man who wanted to hang himself, but after several attempts he decided not to go through with it. When asked why he gave up on the idea, the man replied that the rope choked him each time he tightened it around his neck. I remember cracking up with laughter when she delivered the punch line. Combined with her humorous disposition was her attitude of contentment. She was the epitome of satisfaction, a character trait that was amazing, especially in light of how little she possessed materially. Each time I read, or hear First Timothy chapter 6, verse 6, I always remember Muddah. *But godliness with contentment is great gain.* That's what the good book says, and it sums up her attitude perfectly. It is not that she did not have goals and dreams of something better for herself and for her children. God forbid.

What amazed me about Muddah was the height and depth of her thinking in spite of her station in life. She had lofty and noble ideals for herself and for us, and she taught by precept and example; lessons in life and living that reminded us that we were to be happy with what we had; learning to do without when we had to. And the best lesson of all was that we had to wait until we could afford something better and never resort to dishonesty in any form to secure anything. Yet, she was a woman with enormous pride. After I grew into a young man, I often pondered how she was able to maintain pride in herself and in who she was, when her station in life was not one to inspire the enormous sense of pride she possessed. Though poor in material acquisitions she was an example in lessons that taught that poverty and pride could coexist. Pride was not a scarce commodity where she was concerned. She had it in abundance. But she was not alone in this regard. The poor people I knew when I was growing up in Roebuck were a proud bunch. Not the stuck up kind of pride, but the kind that motivated them to be better people, and to make life enjoyable for themselves and their children. They had an attitude that forbade them from harboring a feeling of self-pity; an attitude that seemed to dispel the notion of poverty and need. They acted as if they had everything and were in want of nothing. They never thought of themselves as poor people, and because of this mindset, they did not behave, or think in the same pitiful way as most poor people do.

You may find this next statement incredible but I am going to say it anyway because it is true, and because it reveals the true attitude and character of Muddah. I never heard the words poor or poverty, mentioned in our home. They were never talked about; never brought up. It was not important. Our situation was never a topic for discussion. We lived like every other family in Roebuck, probably not knowing, or understanding what poverty was. We knew we were not wealthy, but we refused to think of ourselves as poor. Muddah didn't call regular family meetings to discuss how poor we were, and how unfortunate we were to be in such a predicament that had us *scrunting* from time to time. On the other hand, I did see and hear a lot about pride, faith, satisfaction, and respect. Not in so many words, but they were conveyed via positive attitudes, encouragement and laughter. And we had lots of laughter. We still do when my sisters and I get together ever so often.

Even though I watched Muddah's tenacity very closely when I was growing up and was always a constant witness to her pride, contentment and stubborn will and endurance, I never questioned the source of such lofty qualities, as I was too caught up in the morals and lessons she taught by precept and example. She wanted the five of us to realize that these enduring qualities were the attributes that poor people should accumulate in excess. I am not certain as to the source of this idea, but to me it now appears plausible that her wish is still achievable. After all, each of these qualities costs nothing to own; like grace, forgiveness, respect and faith. They are all free; free to poor people as well as to the wealthy. These are precious intangibles that no amount of money can procure, and the amazing fact is that there is a level playing field on which rich and poor alike can secure these eternal values. Muddah had them all in abundance. They made her rich. They were her wealth.

Even though she was not fortunate enough to own a great quantity of material possessions, or to model the latest trends in fashion, Muddah was astute enough to understand that a neat and clean appearance was more desirable than the quantity of material possessions. Her biblical motto at that time seemed to have been lifted directly from St. Luke 12:15: *Take heed…for a man's life consisteth not in the abundance of things he posseseth.*

That being said, Muddah was far from pathetic when dressed in her Sunday go-to-meeting clothes. She was beautiful in appearance as well as in spirit. And in later years when she could afford a more upscale wardrobe, she was a sight to behold. I marveled with appreciation and pride one Sunday in New York as she was dressed for church. She was well put together. The hat, the gloves, the scarf, the whole works, as they say. That was Muddah at her finest.

As kids we had similar experiences as far as clothing was concerned; experiences which made for some humorous times as well as for teaching life lessons that would last for a long time. Even today I still remember that I never had more than one good pair of shoes at any one time. That one pair was for church, of course. This was one of the first lessons in contentment. Make do with what you have. I did not see the need for more shoes. Even if I did, Muddah could not afford to buy them because they would have been too *dear*, as she had said to us so often. That's how people in Roebuck talked when something they wanted was expensive. "It is too dear," they would say. So I felt comfortable walking barefooted to school and even to Speighstown with my grandmother on Saturday mornings because it was a way of life in Roebuck. Not just for me. If I were the only one without shoes, there would have been cause for worry. Muddah would have never allowed that to happen. She made sure that we kept up with the Roebuck Joneses, so to speak. We did not have Joneses in Roebuck, so we kept up with the Marshalls, or the Ramseys, or any other family in Roebuck. Muddah didn't want us to stand out in a way that would make us peculiar. She made sure that we did not appear better or worse off than others in Roebuck.

Muddah did her best to make sure that we compared favorably with the others in Roebuck. It is true that the situation has changed drastically over the years. I just took inventory of my closet and my tally sheet revealed that I now have four pairs of black shoes, three brown pairs and four pairs of tennis shoes. Actually three pairs. My son, Sheldon, is yet to return the pair he borrowed, or took. My sister, Elaine, also has her stories to tell. It seemed as if she had one pair of black school shoes that lasted her all through her high school years. I remember us taking them to Speighstown at the end of every school term to the shoemaker, Mr. Watson. He would half sole them and Elaine would be back in business until the next visit. The heels were always leaning to one side and Mr. Watson would perform the same miracle again and again. I think Elaine alone kept him in business. I remember her at nights before she went to bed, with her flat, round tin of black nugget shoe polish and a piece of cloth that was once white. She would work on those shoes until they eventually produced what little shine they had left. She did this either before, or after she had washed the white blouse she had worn to school that day to make it ready for the following morning.

It was another lesson in contentment and understanding that was modeled so beautifully by Muddah, especially in light of the fact that my sister might have kept company with classmates and teachers that had much more. It is these experiences that we encountered outside of Roebuck that emphasized our material differences.

As children growing up in Roebuck, it was very seldom that we bought new clothes. We didn't go shopping for clothes on a regular basis as is the case here in America. The fact that there were no expansive shopping malls, mega stores, or super department stores of the caliber that is common to every city in the US was not a contributing factor. While it is true that Bridgetown, the capital city, was home to Harrisons, Foggarty, and N.E Wilson, we were only fortunate to go shopping for new clothes at least twice a year. I can't recall the occasion specifically but on one of those irregular shopping sprees, my sister Elaine had the good fortune to get a new pair of socks (I think shoes as well). Of course she had to try them on, as we used to say back then. Everyone sat watching with absolute excitement. But Elaine had a problem putting on the socks. She was puzzled as to which sock belonged to which foot. She had a dilemma. Was there a right foot sock and a left foot sock? Needless to say, we had one of the numerous family laughs with Elaine at the center of the fun. That's a true story. Today Elaine works as a nurse in New York City and like most women I know, she has more shoes, and probably socks, than she has use for.

We had to take good care of our limited *wardrobe*. In Roebuck, a wardrobe was a container that housed clothes. I remember my parents having one made from a light and colorful plastic material, which they kept in their bedroom. They hung their Sunday clothes in the wardrobe. Other clothes were kept in the *trunk* or in the *bureau*. I remember how I would *skin out* or *emp out* the entire bureau looking for socks or some other item of clothing. My cousin, Dorcas, unconsciously reminded me of *emp out* while she was visiting with us in Ringgold recently. We did not talk about having clothes closets in Roebuck, like the walk-in closets I have grown used to in today's American homes. We did have *closets* in Roebuck but they were not for storing clothes. When we spoke of the closet in Roebuck, its meaning was vastly different; a closet being another name for the toilet that had running water; a *water closet*.

We had school clothes which we had to take off when we got home from Indian Ground School, and put on our home clothes. School clothes were for school and home clothes were for home. In many cases, home clothes were a bit shabby, especially where boys were concerned. I remember wearing short pants with large holes in the behind and since we did not wear underwear at that age, it meant that our *pooch* was exposed for all to see. We didn't say butt in Roebuck. It was our pooch, or our bottom, or behind, or even our *botsie*. Not that we ever mind if our butts were showing. It was a part of the Roebuck culture. All the boys in Roebuck grew up that way. Sometimes our parents would try to cover our nakedness by repairing our pants with *patches* made from other mismatched pieces of cloth, but even the patches became useless if the holes were too large, or if they had to be repaired over and over again. Still, my mother with her *timble,* needle and *cotton* in hand, did her best to make sure my patches were in good working order.

Boys wore a *vest* much of the time. The Roebuck weather was always warm so it was fashionable to go without a shirt much of the time. A vest was enough. We went barefooted most of the time, except in rare cases when some of us were fortunate to have a pair of *pumps.* In Roebuck, pumps were a kind of tennis shoe, usually white, and did not have heels as the dictionary definition says. Sometimes flip-flops were worn by a few people but in Roebuck we called them *slippers*; not flip-flops.

Muddah was much more than the image I described previously. She was a master at the Trickle- down Theory. She had been quite adept at it long before it became trendy as an economic strategy in the US. Her standards on respect and politeness towards others trickled down to us as she practiced her top down brand of leadership and authority. We were expected to behave in a certain way because of who she was, and in accordance with the standard that everybody in the Roebuck community knew that she had set for herself and for us. We were trained to say yes please, and no please, and thanks.

The interesting thing about this training is that it appeared to have happened semi-scientifically, as if by a process quite similar to osmosis. Reverse osmosis to be exact; with our parents extracting pure and moral molecules of good manners and politeness from us via membranes of parental modeling and positive examples. So the osmotic process constitutes the perfect analogy that describes our training in good manners. There were no sit down sessions that were especially designed for the teaching of good manners. Formal lessons were not needed. Do as I do was the method of instruction.

But nowhere in Muddah's teaching, (and in my father's as well) was she more exemplary than in her teaching of hello and good morning. Even though these two forms of greeting others are just as common to US culture as well, somehow I am now able to prove that they made a greater impact, and were taken more seriously by parents and children in Roebuck when I was growing up. Here is where my parents truly showed off their strength as good examples and excellent role models. Now that I am a parent myself, I hope that my three sons will find a role model in me in the same way that I found one in my parents, in this specific area, as well as in other aspects of life. They were almost fanatical about this. So we knew from early that this was important to them, and something which we had to acquire. This was not an inborn characteristic like walking, or crying. Rather it was a trait to be taught, and to be learned. And they were the teachers.

They greeted everyone, and they did it with such vigor and pleasure as if their lives literally depended on it, and they found it necessary many times, to punctuate their greeting with a short conversation. A mere hello, or good morning, was not enough. A brief extension of the greeting usually followed.

So my sisters and I grew up like little robots with an automatic graciousness and a respectful disposition directed towards the adult people of Roebuck. That verbal respect and recognition of our elders was manifested like this on a regular basis. "Good morning Mr. Martin. Good night Ms. Sobers. Hello Mr. Marshall." At the time of writing, I am reminded that sometimes we addressed some people differently. I dared not address Mrs. Sobers as Rita, or Ms. Watson as Lillian. After all, they were older and married. Any approach to them had to be on a higher level than it was for others. Not that the degree of respect was less in any way. But the approach had to be different because of their station in life. Seniority had its privileges. Added to that was the fact that Mrs. Sobers was a woman of distinction in Roebuck. She was the pastor's wife.

At the same time, it was quite acceptable to address Aury and

Osbourne by their first names. Even though they were grownups, they were not married. We learned this distinction from our parents as they too followed the same rule. In either situation I was always very careful to say my greetings loud enough to be heard. Not only because they expected it of me but also because mumbling a greeting might have rendered it inaudible and that circumstance would have had serious consequences. My parents would have been sure to know that I had not spoken to Ms. Griffith, or Mr. Lowe, at one time or another. "Sylvester did not speak to me," they would have complained. And the outcome would not have been a pleasant one.

By the way, this state of affairs was not exclusive to Roebuck. Recently my friend, Hal, told me while we were comparing childhood stories that his mother used to ask him if the dog had stolen his tongue if she knew he had not spoken to one of his neighbors in Benny Hall where he grew up not too far from Roebuck. And a family friend, Joyce, reminded me just recently when she came from New York with my sisters and Aunt Gloria to visit, that if she did not speak to the older people in her neighborhood, they would ask her if she thought they had slept in the same bed the night before.

Incidentally, the old saying that old habits die hard is very true in my experience. It is amazing that I have maintained the practice of speaking to people to this day. Of course the habit is relatively easy to perpetuate in the South where it is common for complete strangers to greet others with a friendly hello, or with a wave of the hand and a genuine smile. Obviously, I find it very natural to return the gesture with candor and familiarity. "Do you know that person?" one of my sons asked one day after one of these polite exchanges with a mere passerby. But it gets worse, or better, depending on how you look at the situation. Let me explain.

The first time I visited New York, you guessed it, I was saying hi to strangers I passed on the street. Not to those in busy Manhattan of course, but to the men and women on the Brooklyn street where my sisters live. I have since learned to modify that childhood tendency after I was instructed that I was drawing attention to myself as a visitor, in the same way my wife, Hortense, still attracts attention to herself by clutching her purse tightly under her armpit in the subway.

Be that as it may, I found it terribly difficult and unnatural to stare in the face of humanity, especially early in the morning, and pass by on the other side without a hearty good morning. I had to learn how not to make eye contact with strangers, completely ignoring them as I went on my way. That being the case, I still remain grateful to Muddah for instilling in me that one aspect of good manners that is as enduring as time itself. I am also thankful for the opportunity to live in the South where I have the freedom to practice this skill without shame, or fear.

One morning, I was returning from a walk around our neighborhood with my dog, Ella. Not too far from my house, I happened upon a gentleman I had not met before. As per my early Roebuck training in good manners, I greeted him with a hearty good morning and just like Muddah used to do, I continued by engaging him in dialog. I was delighted when he briefly interrupted his work in his yard to return the favor with a spirited "Good morning" of his own. Almost immediately, I could tell that he was either a life-long Southerner, born and bred in these parts, or that he had lived here for a very long time. Hugh Wiseman's salutation was so natural, so sincere and very Southern. I find that northerners who migrate to the South still find it a bit challenging and uncomfortable when faced with this brand of Southern politeness. Some may still brand the South as racist, and may even poke fun at the southern drawl but they can't deny that hospitality is still alive and well down here. Ever so often I would be working in my yard, or taking my usual walk around the neighborhood, and passersby, whether on foot or in their cars, would hail me with a good natured wave of the hand, or with a strong verbal greeting.

I soon discovered that I would not be the one to always initiate a greeting and the ensuing conversation. And I was also beginning to realize that once hello and good morning were out of the way, that the conversations that followed began to turn into opportunities to share personal stories and information that are usually reserved for close friends and comrades. Such was the case with Mr. Wiseman. For a man his age, he walks pretty briskly and purposefully. But recently, he stopped to say hello. I managed to see him moving in my direction and correctly concluded that he would stop to say hello. He said that he would not be able to talk too long because he wanted get his walking done before it began to rain, but he would see me next time.

The next time came later in the same week, at which time he graciously introduced me to his wife, Helen, when we met going in opposite directions on our walk around the neighborhood. The next day he interrupted his walk to commend me on the condition of my lawn and to pet Ella at the same time. Our conversation suddenly turned to health and the benefits of regular exercise and a good diet. He appeared eager and happy to disclose that he was 82, and that his father had died at an early age, hence his daily walk. He also voiced his belief that a good diet and regular exercise were great lifestyle choices that tend to override one's predisposition to certain health issues. I was totally astounded when he got down on the ground on his hands and knees in my driveway to demonstrate his modified version of the pushup; and if that display wasn't enough, he seamlessly followed it up with a stretching routine that he did every morning.

He showed me the modified adaptation because by his own admission, he had lost a lot of muscle mass, and in addition to being 82, he was unable to do the regular push up. I could not allow my new friend to perform the private exhibition for me without a word of appreciation. I congratulated him and thanked him for the inspiration and told him that my expectation was that I could be as fit as he when I reached his age. As he walked away, I could not help but to be thankful to my parents for the training they had provided and for the culture they passed on so effectively; effective enough to remain with me all this time.

I continued meeting new neighbors as I walked around the neighborhood and my signature good morning and hello allowed me to add more strangers to those I met earlier on. I now have names to go along with the faces I meet from time to time on my *tour de Meadows* and we now find it a pleasure to converse when we encounter each other on the tour. We are well past the hand-waving stage. We have moved on to a more advanced level on the spectrum of what it means to be neighborly; from a mere hello, or good morning, to in depth conversations and dialogs. It quickly became apparent that I had to devise a method, or a strategy, to aid me in remembering all the new names I was learning. I didn't want to continue greeting my new found friends with hi and hello. Roebuck was small and I knew everybody. My present neighborhood is much larger and I wanted to be more personal with my new hello friends. Just as I had been in Roebuck I wanted to be less generic and general. I am told that in the business world the art of remembering the names of people, clients and associates is a huge plus. Furthermore, I wanted to be certain that I had the correct names in my head so I could practice them with boldness until they became second nature.

Somewhere along the way I have discovered that I have the distinct weakness of forgetting the names of people I meet. This has resulted in an embarrassing situation more than once. Such is the case with Harley. My wife and I had met him one morning several weeks before, when I greeted him with a warm hello. Muddah would have been proud of me. I was sure I would remember his name when we meet again in the future. This particular morning he was talking with Karen, whom we had also met on more than one occasion. She has a bubbly personality and had greeted us warmly when we first moved to the neighborhood. I knew we had exchanged names and as we approached with Ella, I struggled desperately to pull up both names from my memory bank. After an awkward moment we were reintroduced, subsequent to calling Harley the wrong name.

After that rather uncomfortable meeting I began to put a mechanism to work; one that I had heard about some time ago; a strategy that I hoped would help me remember the names of those I would be meeting on a regular basis. I began to connect each new name and person to another person I already knew, or to some event, or experience, in my past. The Harley Davidson motor cycle was my clue for Harley. Mr. Wiseman was the wise man of biblical fame; the wisest man that ever lived, and Ralph Rogers would become RR, or Rolls Royce. I did not need this memory device in Roebuck because Roebuck was so small in comparison to the Meadows, that everybody knew everybody.

I continued to encounter Ralph often, almost every day, walking his two dogs. I would be sure to extend my greetings with a friendly "hello Ralph" as was my custom and training. Ella would try to pounce on his little dogs, and they were as brave as they were small, as they returned the greeting. There was always a noisy tug of war when we met and the pooches never allowed us to get acquainted, until one morning later when I walked without Ella. We exchanged dog names and went on our way since his dogs had become impatient.

Some time had passed since I had last seen Ralph. One evening, I was walking earlier than usual, since I was on fall break from school. We met, going in opposite directions, and from the greeting he gave me, one would think that we were old friends. "I have not seen you in a while," he started. "Where have you been?" Ben and Rocky were impatient as usual and were having a tiff with Ella, but he managed to share that he had had four strokes since I last saw him, and proceeded to give details of his hospitalization and his brush with death. "Like you have lost some weight," he shouted, as Ben and Rocky pulled him down the sidewalk. "Yes," I shot back, but did not have the time to share my experience with diabetes. Once again, I was delighted that the education in social behavior my parents had taught us in Roebuck was paying dividends. I learned to connect with so many people who would have otherwise remained complete strangers.

And so my practice of meeting both unfamiliar as well as customary neighbors progressed, and my constant habit of engaging them in conversation continued; our growing familiarity with one another being the impetus that got us to know more and more about each other. This time it was Harley again. One morning I greeted him as Ella and I were getting ready to cruise down the slope near his house. He was sitting on his front porch high atop a hilly lot at the edge of the forest. No wonder he is visited by wild turkeys and deer. We chatted briefly before I moved on. Several mornings later, he called out to Hortense and me as we were increasing our speed on the downward slope. Among other things, he informed us that a black *burr* (southern for bear) had been spotted in the neighborhood. A few days later, early on a Saturday morning, he was riding his bicycle not far from his house and going in the opposite direction. He came to a halt, poking a little light-hearted fun in my direction by asking if I was getting ready for the Olympics.

My intentions that morning were to get three laps in before getting back home to get ready for church. But Harley wanted to talk, letting me know that he was 62. I complimented him on how well he looked for his age, but declined to release mine. He pointed to his stomach, which was only slightly protruding, telling me that he was trying to get rid of the flab and informing me that he had been very active in volleyball and baseball when he was young. I countered that I also played volleyball and had been involved in track and field for many years as a youngster, so it was not difficult for me to jog around the neighborhood.

This time, I intentionally interjected that I still jogged a little because regular exercise was helpful in controlling my diabetes. He added that his wife Janice was also diabetic. "Type two," he stipulated. I prolonged the conversation by sharing with him that diet and exercise were helping me control my sugar level, and encouraged him to persuade his wife to begin a walking program. He promised that he would. I made several attempts to walk away but Harley detained me each time, intending to educate me on the benefits of healthful living. He shared that one of his relatives juiced so many carrots that his skin began turning yellow. Not to be outdone I countered that I made a shake with cabbage, collard greens, spinach, and celery to have with my oatmeal every morning.

When Harley finally released me I could only complete two of the three laps I had planned. I was not upset, or angry. Rather, I was energized, pleased and amazed that an initial and simple hello, or a good morning, had blossomed into a relationship in which complete strangers felt comfortable and willing to share even personal information with each other. I would have it no other way but to continue to explore the basic tenets of human politeness. Thanks to Muddah for planting the seeds of politeness and respect.

As time went on I continued to rack up instances of more encounters on my trips with Ella around our neighborhood. One lap around was a little more than a mile and the miles continued to add up. So too were the opportunities to run into new, as well as familiar people; some of whom exchanged just a hello and good morning, or good evening, while extended conversations with others cemented a growing relationship. Such is the one contained in the following story; another one in support of my training, and the reason I am delighted that I continue to apply it, even today.

Early on the morning of July 4 I was hurrying to complete my two laps without Ella. My intention was to finish my workout session early because our grandson, Max, was coming over to spend part of the day with us. I also wanted to watch tennis from Wimbledon. The Williams' sisters were playing their semi final matches that day as well. Being an avid tennis player/fan myself, I wanted to have my workout behind me so I would be available to watch their matches on television. I was jogging, huffing and puffing up the incline portion of the journey when I literally ran into Mr. Wiseman, I hated to stop since I was on a mission that morning, but I recognized that a simple "Good morning Mr. Wiseman" was not going to be sufficient for him. He had already come to a halt and was ready for conversation.

"Hugh," he corrected me. I still find it difficult and unnatural to address older people by their first name; a byproduct of the cultural lessons I was taught in Roebuck. He introduced the conversation by wishing me a happy July 4 and continued to lecture me on how great this country is. I nodded my agreement. He explained in detail about his military service in England during World War II and punctuated it with reiterations of how different the world would have been today had Hitler been allowed to have his way. He became personal when he revealed that his son who was now divorced was dating a girl from England and wondered how the British felt towards Americans, especially on July 4.

Hugh returned to his earlier declaration on the greatness of America, and even recounted a story about an immigrant whom he knew that had come to America penniless, and had worked hard to amass a small fortune. Mr. Wiseman also referenced my personal success before we shook hands and wished each other a happy July 4. I asked him about his wife and why she was not walking with him that morning. His response prompted laughter from both of us. "I don't force her to do anything" he said. "That is the reason we have been married for 53 years." We parted, and as I continued jogging I was in no way upset because I was thrown off my personal schedule for the day. In contrast, I was elated and very thankful for the exchange, and wondered what it would have been like had I not offered that first hello and good morning some time ago.

I continued to encounter Mr. Wiseman regularly after that, as I walked with Ella, and we would always stop to talk, sometimes briefly, and at other times more extensive conversations took place. Our talks were usually dominated by the health issues he was experiencing. On one occasion as Hortense and I were walking with Ella, we spotted him walking ahead of us. We caught up with him as he stopped to engage another walker. Just as he was about to end his time with the younger man I had not met before, I greeted the stranger with my signature hello as he left to continue his walk. Mr. Wiseman greeted Hortense and me, giving me a hug and a hello. He was excited to share that his recent surgery had been successful, and that he was feeling so much better. After a ten-minute conversation he left to continue his journey, requesting our prayers on his behalf as he walked away with a warning from Hortense not to overdo it.

Over time, Mr. Wiseman and I have grown pretty close. He appears quite comfortable volunteering confidential and personal information, especially about his own health and that of his wife, Helen. It is amazing how I, armed with a hello and a dog, was able to establish a relationship with complete strangers. Each time I think about it, I can't help but thank my parents for the lessons they taught and the expectations they exacted during those formative years in Roebuck.

Admittedly, I have a sense of guilt as I write this. One Saturday afternoon, Hortense and I set out for a quick walk around the neighborhood; this time without Ella. We had just finished a big late lunch and decided that a quick walk would assist in its digestion; plus it was getting close to sunset and I wanted to be back at the house to watch the Georgia/Tennessee football game. Out of the corner of my eye I glimpsed Hugh still a ways back, and I told my wife to quicken her steps so he would not catch up with us. If he did, I knew we would be in for a lengthy conversation. But the old man was moving at a pretty good clip; catching up with us before we knew it. The talk was on until we found our way back to his driveway, where we stopped to tack on an additional ten minutes or so. Suddenly the football game didn't seem all that important as he led out in a lecture on his days as a young minister; how he opted to pay into social security, and how, since his retirement, has withdrawn more than what he had put in, and that he had told his sons that he was now drawing from theirs. He released us after volunteering details on Helen's surgery and his on-going efforts to make the entrance to the subdivision more appealing with additional lighting. I was happy that I had sacrificed the time to listen to my friend. I would later disappoint him, however unintentionally. I was sitting on the step engaging in a conference call on my cell, with Ella waiting patiently to go on our walk. He stopped and waited, beckoning to tell me something. I could see the disappointment on his face when he had to leave without getting my attention.

As Ella and I continued our walks on a regular basis, meeting familiar faces, as well as new ones, my relationship with her appeared to have been growing with each trip. She was my faithful companion, and with her at my side, we not only got to know the neighborhood a lot better, we also got to know our neighbors. Admittedly, I have to confess that Ella was not my dog in the beginning, even though I have been referring to her as such all this time. Actually, she was a birthday gift to my son, Tristan, from one of his friends. When he moved out, he promised to come back to get her. Although he never did, he would come by to see her from time to time, creating the perfect conditions for Ella and me to bond into an inseparable unit; so much so that one day, some time ago, my friend, Floyd, commented that I had truly achieved the American dream. He was being sarcastic, obviously referring to my relationship with my dog, Ella. He poked fun at me, letting me know that as a boy from Roebuck, I had really come a long way by walking a dog, and even having her in the house at times.

Floyd's observation brought back some painful memories of the harsh treatment dogs received from us as young boys growing up in Roebuck. We thought it cute to pelt them with rocks, and mistreat them in other ways. I remember my family having three dogs. At one time there was Rover. Then there were Fluff and Born Gulley at different periods of time. I don't know what breed they were. In Roebuck, all dogs were dogs. No one cared too much, and knew even less concerning their brand or breed. In the US it is a completely different story. In fact, I heard a news story on the television recently that clearly proves how important dogs are to American families. A reporter was asking a survivor of the recent Colorado floods to relate how she was able to escape the fast-rising water. "I packed the dogs and the kids and left." You will note who is mentioned first in the escape plan — the dogs.

Fluff, as her name suggests, had long white fluffy hair, the likes of which were never seen in Roebuck. Still, she was not a house dog, and was never elevated beyond the level of all other dogs in Roebuck. She was never referred to as a pet, never saw a vet, and enjoyed the same food that we ate: rice and peas, dumplings, banana, and chicken and fish bone. She never tasted Alpo, Gravy Train or Beneful in her life. I never took her walking around Roebuck, nor was she allowed in the house to seek shelter from the sweltering Roebuck sun, or even when it was rainy and stormy outside.

Rover and Born Gulley, on the other hand, were ordinary looking dogs without distinguishable features. Unlike Fluff, there was nothing about them that earned them special attention, except for Born Gulley's name. Yvonne reminded me of the circumstances around which the pooch was so named. Her story is that my father found the puppy in Rock Hall Gulley one day while he was returning home from work as a truck driver for Rock Hall Plantation. From that day on, the dog's name was Born Gulley. Yvonne also confirmed that my father later returned Born Gulley to the gulley after he found out that the dog had been stealing and *sucking* our fowls' eggs.

Since coming to the US I have come to learn of the exalted position dogs occupy in the family structure and in the culture of this place, and I have grown to love Ella very much. Not only is she my walking companion. She makes it easier for me to engage people I meet, giving me the opportunity to practice Muddah's training in greeting others. I have met so many people from having Ella with me on my neighborhood walks, and at times I have wondered if they were more interested in meeting her than they did me, as they reached down to pet her, asking what kind of dog she was.

I show my ignorance about dogs. I know Ella is a chow mix, but I do not know a boxer from a mutt, or a Labrador from a golden retriever, or beagle from a dachshund. At least I do know what a pit bull is. I had a close encounter with one in California several years ago. But whatever the breed or class, dogs hold a prominent position in the American culture. I am reminded of this quite often when I watch HGTV; constantly surprised that right up there with the number of bathrooms buyers want in a house, is the amount of available yard space for their dogs.

Later that day, after Floyd so accurately discovered my new cultural shift, and armed with my new American dream status, I went out with Ella and continued my habit of hailing those whose paths I happened to cross. First, it was the opportunity to put a face to a name, meeting and speaking to Harley's wife, Janice, for the first time, as she sat on her front porch. Without stopping, I did the same to Karen who was tending her garden a few houses down. Close to my house I happened upon Suzanne and her husband Paul, whom I had not seen in a while. This time I stopped long enough to be introduced to her son Billy and his wife, Kristy, who were visiting over the weekend. Suzanne, like me was a new grandparent, so we exchanged progress reports about her Harrison and my Max before I ran off. I took Max by to visit for a few minutes later in the day.

The next morning, with Ella in tow, I said hello to George and his dog, King. It was rather easy to put my device for remembering names to work. King George would be my way to remember their names. My only concern was to be sure to remember which one was King and which one was George. George was a much older man, and I could see that he enjoyed his walk with King. They walked slowly and deliberately. King, appearing to sense that his master was old, seemed quite content to tolerate the man's feeble pace. They lived at a house close to our subdivision but it was not considered a part of the Meadows. Before I met them, I had observed them walking regularly, either early in the morning, or in the late afternoon. My guess was that they walked in our neighborhood so as to avoid walking on the very busy street that ran by his house.

I often admired the close bond between George and King and the strong relationship they shared as they walked back and forth on their regular walks. Months later, on a Saturday morning, Hortense and I were packing the car in the driveway as we were getting ready to leave for church. George was walking back towards his house without King. It was strange to see one without the other; George without King. They were always together, with King frolicking back and forth, playfully waiting on the old man to catch up.

"Where is King?" I greeted him.

"He left me," he announced. Thinking that King had run on ahead or something like that, I said something to the effect that I hope he would be back soon.

"He passed away a few days ago," George interrupted.

"I am sorry," I told him. "Hopefully you can find another dog soon,"

"I miss him a lot," he replied. "I don't know if I will ever get another one. It is hard on you when they leave you."

At that moment, I felt genuine sorrow for the old man. Listening to George talk about King made me feel like he was talking about the loss of a loved one — a human being. Also at that moment, the thoughts in my mind took me all the way back to Roebuck, and I could not help but remember the lowly place dogs occupied in the family structure. *"De dog ded,"* (the dog died) would have been the natural Roebuck response. Nothing else. Nothing remotely humane and mournful like George spoke of King. "He passed away," was reserved for the homo sapiens of the species. Not for dogs.

A few weeks passed and I was somewhat surprised to see George walking with another little dog, almost similar to King. I did not ask what kind or breed the dog was; I never did, for two main reasons. I do not think I would remember, and secondly, I try to preserve my ignorance about dogs and their breed. But I did ask the dog's name. "He is Jett," George told me, spelling out Jett letter by letter. "Jett for short," he reminded me. "Jett Black is his name," he explained. "I am babysitting him for my son."

George and Jett have since joined the list of those I meet on a regular basis, even though we have not yet grown in our relationship to the level at which we exchange personal information, as is the case with Hugh Wiseman. We hail each other each time we encounter one another, usually when I am driving to or from my house. He, however, has formed a friendship with Hortense, and has invited her to visit his garden to get all the greens she needs. And she has graciously accepted.

I met another couple some time later under the strangest of circumstances. I didn't mind it one bit, just as long as the event presented the opportunity to say hello and good morning to someone I had seen in the past, but only from a distance. This particular morning I had just walked out of my driveway and onto the street where Charlotte, with pooper scooper in hand, was trying to yank Starlight by her leash with the other hand to keep her from peeing on my lawn. In Roebuck, dogs didn't have leashes, and seldom went for a walk with their owners. They were left to run wild, even viciously attacking at random. Our dogs did not know the pleasure of taking a leisurely stroll. Neither did we think to, or know how to supply that brand of care and attention. It was not cultural in Roebuck at the time to do that. Dogs were second class, or third class, or no class citizens.

I was without Ella that particular morning and Charlotte and I did a short introduction and chatted briefly about the weather until Starlight was ready to continue her walk. We did not meet very often after that but remained cordial whenever I glimpsed them from time to time when Ella and I did our regular walk. I did not establish the kind of relationship with them like the one that I had built with Mr. Wiseman, or with Ralph, for that matter. Still, I was pleased that my hello and good morning plan got me into a pleasant and first name relationship with my immediate neighbors. It was cultural in Roebuck to know the names of everyone in the neighborhood; something I found disturbingly lacking when I first came to America.

So I got to know Bill and Diane Bice, a retired couple living next door. They are expert campers who spend a lot of time by the lake, dropping in occasionally to check on the house. He lets me know when he is leaving on a camping trip and I usually respond with "We'll be here," my way of letting him know that we will keep an eye on the house. We had the latest version of that conversation a few weeks ago when he was leaving to take his grandkids to Disney Land. Bill and I stop to chat briefly each time we see each other. I have grown to trust him in the short time I've known him; so much so that I also let him know each time Hortense and I leave for an extended trip, asking him to keep an eye on the house for us. When I told him that we would be going to Barbados for a week, I let him know that my son, Tristan, would be dropping by to collect the mail and to check on Ella. He joked that he was glad that I had informed him about Tristan, averting an attack on him, should he encounter a stranger on my property.

"I have something for you," Bill announced one day. "I had it for you for a long time," he said, as he asked me to wait, while scurrying through his garage, disappearing briefly into his house. When he reappeared, he handed me a small pocketknife with the Coca Cola emblem and *Merry Christmas* embolden on the front panel. I thanked him for the knife, telling him that I will always treasure it. It meant a lot to me. Bill had worked for many years for Coca Cola and I was delighted that he had decided to share the memories of those years with me. Suddenly, I once again realized the power of good morning and hello and the good manners Muddah had taught me in Roebuck.

One Easter weekend, while I was mowing my lawn, I had the sudden urge to mow Bill's as well. It was not meant to repay him for the knife he had given me, but just a simple gesture of friendship and the opportunity to build a stronger neighborly bond. I wanted it to be a total surprise for him when he returned from camping, so I hurried as fast as I could, not wanting him to catch me in the act. Being neighborly means much more than saying hello to each other. It goes much further than that. It has an additional component that encourages little random acts of kindness that seek nothing in return.

I didn't mow Bill's lawn to make him feel obligated to do the same for me. I did it merely to help him out so that when he returned from camping, he would have one less chore to worry about. Neither did I do it expecting a monetary reward. Money was not even a part of the equation when the thought to mow his lawn entered my mind. And much later when he volunteered to use his truck to take my discarded carpet to the dump, he did so, refusing my offer to replenish the gas. Even though I knew beforehand that my offer would be rejected, I still went ahead and made it out of simple courtesy. Prior to that, I had already learned a lesson in one aspect of the cultural difference between Roebuck and America; a lesson that I always kept in the back of my mind since coming to this country.

I was driving to work one morning, when I was a principal in another town. I stopped to help a woman change a flat tire (tyre in Roebuck). When the job was done, I was shocked by her response. "How much do I owe you," she asked. "Nothing," I replied. She was surprised that I refused monetary compensation. I was quite taken aback at her offer as she continued to insist and expect me to accept her offer. Several times prior to that event, and even afterwards, people have offered me money for random acts of kindness on my part, and have appeared amazed that their offer was refused. In Roebuck, we did not expect to receive a reward for being kind, for helping to *move* a house; or for helping a neighbor cut his canes. Regular acts of kindness were displayed everywhere and money was hardly offered, or expected.

Michael and Karen and their adopted twin boys live directly across the street from me, and Ed and Joyce Watson, both retired teachers, make up my most immediate neighbors. Eddie and Francis live two houses down the street, just after Bill and Diane. Hortense enjoys a level of comfort with Francis, so much so that she has called her to check on our house when she thought she had left the oven on after she had left for work. By the way, there is an interesting story on how I came to meet Joyce. I had met Ed, her husband, in the gym years before they moved into my neighborhood; also he was always outside working at keeping his lawn perfectly manicured. Meeting Joyce, on the other hand, presented an interesting moment. There was a tinge of embarrassment when I showed up on the first day at Loftis Middle School to begin my duties as assistant principal. "Don't you know me?" Joyce asked as I introduced myself. "I am Ed's wife," she continued. "We live across the street from you." A similar situation would have never happened in Roebuck. Everybody knew everybody.

On my regular walks around my neighborhood, I encounter a very low percentage of racial diversity; Caucasians being the overwhelming majority of the people I meet. There is one African American family I see pretty often but our only contact continues to be a friendly wave of the hand as they drive by when I am sitting on the step or working in my yard. However, we share a slight connection; their son, William, having taught for me when I was principal in another city. I see two black guys jogging on a regular basis but they carry on a regular conversation as they run, so the opportunity to formally meet them never presented itself, even though one of them called out to me to join them on one occasion when I was at the mailbox.

But the situation changed quite unexpectedly late one evening when I ran into one of them walking his dog. We introduced ourselves and Jesse told me that his running buddy, James, had been working out of town. I learned that Jesse was originally from North Carolina and that he had retired to the area after serving in the military. We talked for a while about the racial mix of the neighborhood but unanimously agreed that the subdivision was still a great place to live. By the way, in Roebuck, we never said a person was Caucasian or African American. We referred to Dorin Gill and Mr. Edwards, white plantation owners, as white, but never as Caucasian. African American and Caucasian would have been like a foreign language if they were introduced to Roebuck when I was growing up.

Even though the racial mix of my neighborhood is what it is, I have more than once come into contact with an Oriental family. They are not walkers like I am, but I would see them in the yard, or preparing to get into the car to drive off to work. Most times however, they would pass me while driving back home, or leaving the subdivision. Each time I made it a point of duty either to voice a hello or to wave my hand to communicate a greeting, and they would respond just as politely. Needless to say, I have been longing for the opportunity to engage them in conversation; to know their names, and even to learn a little about their culture. But as of the time of writing, I have not yet been afforded that opportunity. Yet, I plan to ease into the next phase gradually, and with care, being mindful not to intrude on the family's privacy in any way. Muddah would have been proud of me; proud of my willingness to be inclusive, and proud of my attempts to reach out to people of all classes, colors, races and cultures. Even though Roebuck was lacking in cultural and racial diversity, Muddah's training program taught us not to exclude anyone.

I continue to witness the positive vibes I get from this family, and their apparent willingness to adapt to a culture that is different from theirs. Their behavior, in many ways, is at odds with that of many immigrant groups and individuals that call this country home. That some cultural groups refuse to become integrated into the American culture is very evident. They continue to cling tightly to the practices and cultural behaviors that migrated with them from the old homeland, without the slightest attempt at acculturation and integration. They celebrate their own festivals, eat their own foods, and speak their own language, while they gleefully enjoy the services and blessings this country has to offer. Not that it's wrong to honor or preserve one's culture.

On the other hand, there are others who call this country home and work hard to contribute to its greatness and its prosperity. The fact that I am a naturalized American does not prevent me from celebrating July 4 as vigorously as any other American. I look forward to enjoying the fireworks, participating in the parades and parties, eating a hot dog to celebrate the occasion, and even devouring some watermelon, corn and potato salad. But above all, I like to sing the patriotic songs like *God Bless America, the Star Spangled Banner, This Land is My Land, This is My Country*, and *The Battle Hymn of the Republic*. I was driving to the library on the Sunday of the July 4 weekend while these patriotic songs were being played on the radio and I felt compelled to wait in the car to sing along until the program was over. I have also adopted the Thanksgiving holiday and celebrate it with the same intensity and passion, while adding some of my cultural dishes-- rice and peas, curry, sweet bread, *sorrel* and *mauby* to the American menu.

I relayed those true stories to emphasize one important point — that my parents set a standard that was high, and they expected us to meet their expectations and to measure up. They believed that good manners and a polite and gracious attitude towards others, especially older people, was one of the first lessons their children had to learn. Their expectations were modeled every day as they practiced the behaviors they expected of us. They were truly our first teachers, and they regarded their responsibility as a spiritual and moral obligation, not to be delegated to another. To them, the practicing of good manners was as important as schooling and church attendance.

In the midst of all of this training; this preparation for life and for relationship building, my father and mother had one central theme that seemed to guide their teaching and their informal lessons. Respect for adults was expected. Disrespect and unmannerly behavior and attitudes towards those who were elders in Roebuck were not tolerated. "You have no manners," they would scold, if we dared to be impolite or disrespectful. We learned that lesson quickly, and painfully at times. Good morning, good night, and hello flowed from our lips as if we were programmed to react whenever an older person showed up on our radar. Not that they sat us down formally every night before bed time and lectured us in the ways of good manners, or by way of bedtime stories. That was certainly not the case. They taught as all good teachers do. They simply led the way, and we followed. There was an old saying in Roebuck that said that "the breadfruit don't fall too far from the tree." How true.

I grew up thinking that this was the normal way for children to behave. This was all I knew and thought it to be the status quo. It was in Roebuck. In my naïve way of thinking, children everywhere were trained by their parents to be polite and well bred; and that they would mature into well mannered and refined adults. That was the end result Muddah, and my father had in mind for the five of us. Today, it still bothers me to no end when young children stare in the faces of adults, especially early in the morning, and merely pass by on the other side. In my youth I could not have gotten away with this behavior without reprimand. Neither could Jenny, or Glendeen, or the other kids that grew up with me in Roebuck.

At one elementary school where I worked as a school administrator, I witnessed this conduct on a daily basis. Students disembarked from the school bus and stared down adults standing there and went on their merry way without a greeting, or recognition. It is sad to declare, but some adults exhibit a similar attitude towards each other. This is foreign to my belief system, my morals, my ethics, and to the culture I knew in Roebuck. I have never seen my parents decline to greet another adult in Roebuck whether morning, noon, or night. And to be perfectly honest, the greeting usually turned out to be more than just a greeting. As always it turned into something deeper and more meaningful. More often than not it was the impetus for a short conversation with Rita, or with Joycelyn, or Lynette.

At the particular school mentioned above, I made it my business to be intentional about greeting as many students as was possible with a hearty good morning when they got off the bus. Initially, the response was rather half hearted. Happily, progress, although slow, grew measurably. I was encouraged and motivated to continue this practice for as long as I was around. I regarded it as an element of good leadership, a component that was perfected by my parents and the other parents in Roebuck many years ago. Before I left that position, the sounds of "Good morning Dr. C." could be heard more and more. If this is what it means to be *in loco parentis,* I was more than happy to do it for my students; just as Muddah did for me so long ago.

I have since moved on to another school. Presently, I work with older students in middle school and interestingly enough, their conduct perfectly complements that of their younger counterparts. I am usually stationed at the location where students who ride cars to school are dropped off in the morning. From my earliest experiences with these students I was totally surprised at the almost perfect approximation of the behavior of the two groups.

Quite recently, in order to support my position with hard data, I decided to conduct my own unscientific study, and although the findings from my rather small sample cannot make reliable conclusions regarding the 'good morning' attitudes of all middle school children in the US, they appear to support the hypothesis that children of this age are not culturally required to say good morning to adults as was the mandatory culture in Roebuck when I was a boy of their age. Of the 123 students that rode to school in cars on this particular day, only eleven, or 13.53 % greeted me with good morning, even though some of their parents were fairly consistent in greeting me with a wave of the hand, or with a toot of the horn. What is more perplexing is the way the same students hail me and positively interact with me during the day. My conclusion was mixed; either the students did not put into practice the culture they were taught, or they were not the recipients of direct parental instruction in this aspect of child training.

Some time later, I was reading the online version of the Sunday edition of the *Barbados Advocate* and was delighted to learn that certain cultural fundamentals were still being taught in Barbados, and hopefully in Roebuck. In addressing the graduates at Christ Church Girls' School, The Honorable Stephen Lashley, Minister of Culture, Sports and Youth, reminded the students to remember the fundamentals they were taught at school: tidiness, good manners, and how to show respect by saying good morning and good afternoon. I noticed that the Minister did not mention *please for a pass* in his list of good manners and wondered if the children of Barbados and Roebuck still say "Please for a pass" when they want to get by someone who is in their way. It so happened that a seventh grade boy pushed by me one morning while I was on duty, almost knocking me over as I stood in the doorway of the gym. "And he did not even say please for a pass," I said to myself.

I have to thank Muddah and my father for teaching us by their example, the awesome power of hello and good morning. I have tried to do the same for my sons, not in a formal way, but primarily by my example. Just like our parents taught us. I had begun to wonder if I was getting through to them, at least in a small way, until one of my neighbors who recently moved away told me one day that my boys were very polite. I was elated.

Muddah had her economic strength as well. As I relive our financial status for the purpose of writing this chapter, I have to wonder how she was able to take care of our needs, especially keeping our *board* house in repair. She would go down to Spieghstown and *truss* boards and *pine* from Plantations Limited to fix up the house to keep it from leaking when it rained. We never said trust or credit in Roebuck. It was always *truss*. Only later did I realize that the correct word was trust. Little by little, Muddah would pay the bills when they were due and still was able to take care of my school fees and the needs of the five of us. I am smiling to myself as I write, remembering how Muddah pulled it off. I have already mentioned how hard she worked on the plantation, but she had to supplement her pay in order to make ends meet.

To do this, Muddah took part in a regular *meeting*. Even though she was a deeply religious woman, I am not talking about Monday night church meeting, or Tuesday night, or even Wednesday night prayer meeting. It was a meeting of the minds; women of Roebuck getting together to pool their money to solve their financial woes. I am not really sure why they called it a meeting, because they hardly met, and there were no notes taken, books kept, or financial reports given. There was not even a president, or secretary; the only officer being the person collecting and keeping the money. But they pooled their money, each person contributing a basic amount per week. This was called a *hand.* Each person had the option to *throw* one, or more hands, if she wanted to collect a larger payout when her *turn* came. Knowing my Muddah as I do, I am sure she must have thrown more than one hand. The meeting system was more remarkable in many ways. It took a rather large leap of faith in the person designated to collect and keep the money, and to pay it out each week to the investor that was predetermined to receive her turn. The accounting had to be perfect as no banks were involved. Being aware of her financial obligations, I am sure that Muddah must have looked forward to receiving the returns on her investment when it was her turn. With a large stash of cash in hand, she was able to continue running the business of the household, patiently waiting until it was time again to begin throwing another hand.

Muddah was a tough woman in excellent health when we were growing up; her physical strength and endurance probably resulting from her labor in the fields. She never had reasons to visit Dr. Gilmore, or he her, and never had to spend a day in the *horsepital.* She was usually tired after her daily toil on the plantation but hardly complained of sickness or unusual pain. She was never so sick to be described as being *poorly.* One particular night was different, however. She was in her bedroom, with just a partition separating hers from the one where I slept. I was quite small then, but I was very aware as to what was about to happen in the next room. Muddah was being attended by Mrs. Worrell; Ida Worrell, the local midwife. My maternal grandmother, Dorris Worrell, was also present. I knew she must have been in unbearable pain when I heard her scream "Lord have mercy." She must have been really *sick.* In Roebuck they usually described a woman as being sick when she was experiencing her menstrual period or when she was house-bound for a while after giving birth.

A little brother was born that night, but did not live past infancy. Later, two more brothers would suffer a similar fate, dying much younger than the first. The emotional pain she endured must have been much more unbearable over the years. We said good bye to those babies without fanfare, or visible signs of mourning. No medical intervention or *post mortem* to determine the cause of death, as is done in America. And no funerals, or memorial services, private or public, for either of them — David, Floyd, and one without a name. In Roebuck we weren't too keen on giving babies their names until after they were born. I can remember my father making a *box* for one of them. I can't remember which, but I clearly remember him putting it on his bicycle and pedaling off to All Saints Church to burry our little brother. Just like that. But Muddah remained strong and resilient until she became *poorly,* before she was finally overcome by cancer in 1988 in a New York City hospital.

I can't think of Muddah without a what-if question interrupting my thinking. I have had many what-if questions over the years. What if I had not left Roebuck, what would my life be like now? What if I had not joined the Seventh-day Adventist Church? What if I had married another woman instead of Hortense? Every time I think of the what-if question concerning Muddah, I end up with the same answer each time. And it makes me happy because it tells me that Muddah was as unchanging as the answer to my what-if question. What if my three brothers had lived, would Muddah have done her best to support eight of us, giving all of us the same opportunities that she worked so hard to provide for the five of us? Each time I come up with a resounding yes. That was the heart of Muddah. It is impossible to see her work harder than she did but I am confident that she would have done whatever it took to provide all of us with an equal opportunity to be successful.

PS: We had to put our Ella to sleep only recently. One afternoon, minutes before I got home from work, she was hit by a car while crossing the street. Her injuries were too severe to save her. I miss her every morning when I come downstairs and she is not there to greet me. I miss her excitement when I get home after work, as she was usually there to welcome me home. I feel her loss each time I take a walk around the neighborhood.

CHAPTER FOUR

Our Two Houses

She knew that her limited experience with schooling made it impossible... She made up for it by providing the space, the dedicated time, and by securing an environment that supported learning and invited success.

The title of this chapter is quite misleading to say the least. It appears as if we owned two houses in Roebuck as the title suggests. The reality is that nobody in Roebuck owned two homes. The Roebuck people could hardly afford one house, not to mention two. No one had a first home in addition to rental property. They were all satisfied with the one house and I am quite certain that apart from not owning two homes, nobody in Roebuck knew anybody that had a primary residence in Roebuck, plus a beach house in Christ Church or a mountain retreat in Hillaby.

The Roebuck people did not think like that. They were not business people or people of means and luxury. Muddah and the other residents in Roebuck lived the culture of the district. They were plantation workers at heart and by profession; sugar cane, potato and yam farmers, who owned sheep, cows and goats. They were not interested in the real estate business. It was not a priority to them. They were at peace taking care of the one simple house they had; keeping it fixed up so it wouldn't leak when it rained.

But come to think of it, we didn't have just two houses. We actually had three; the outhouse being one of them, and two others. But in Roebuck, we never talked about having an outhouse, or going to the outhouse. The outhouse was a name I learned much later. We went to the toilet. The toilet was iconic. It was a common fixture in Roebuck culture. All houses had them in one fashion or another, and in locations that varied from house to house. We did not even speak of going to the restroom, or to the bathroom. The latter creates an impression of something more sophisticated, with a sink, toilet paper, hand towels, a commode and running water; none of which was available in our Roebuck toilet.

In addition to the outhouse, there was a *back house*. I am tempted to use *back house* in a sentence so as to provide a contextual clue as to its meaning but I'll refrain because its meaning appears to be so ridiculously obvious. At least it is to me. Yet, its simplicity and relevance may be as foreign as other aspects of Roebuck culture. Simply defined, the *back house* was the back part of a house. Naturally, from the explanation provided, there was a *front house* as well — the front part of the house. The *back house* and the *front house* were not separate structures. They were connected at the time of construction, or in some cases when finances or other circumstances dictated that only one section could be built, a *back house,* or the *shed roof,* was added later to form one house. A Roebuck *back house* is comparable to the den or family room in today's American homes. We never said den in Roebuck; only *back house*. Den might have conjured up the notion of place where lions lived, and the only wild animals known to Roebuck were those pesky monkeys.

We spent a lot of time in our *back house*. Other families in Roebuck did the same. It was the meeting place, the family room, so to speak. There was not a formal dining room so we ate at a little blue *dinette se*t, a four-seater that we acquired later on, but prior to that, we made ourselves comfortable wherever we could in a *back house* that was sparsely furnished, or not furnished at all. In fact there was one piece of furniture that was a fixture in our *back house* in the early days that could be considered an antique today. This special piece will be discussed later. But sitting on the floor (in the floor, as Americans say) to eat our meals was not uncommon. It was a way of life in Roebuck and our family was not different in this regard. It was part of the culture that we embraced as normal and natural.

We knew we had arrived at a minute degree of affluence when the dinette set appeared. But the pre dinette days found us occupying the floor at meal times, especially when everyone was at home when it was time to eat and the couple chairs we had were taken by our parents. But we seldom ate together as a family. There was no set time for dinner, or supper. By the way, we didn't speak in those terms. Dinner and supper were not a part of our vocabulary. We ate food, not dinner, or supper.

Incidentally, while writing this section of the book I took a break to go downstairs to my breakfast nook and recreate the memory of floor-sitting. I was the only one at home so I was free to appear silly and childish in complete privacy. My wife, had she been at home, might have understood; but if my children were still living at home they would have looked at me funny and wonder if dad was beginning to lose it at such an early age. But there I was, sitting on the floor with an empty plate beside me trying to resurrect the childhood *back house* behavior from my past. Strangely, I was not sure where to put the plate. I couldn't remember the details and the specifics of how we did it back in Roebuck. First, I tried placing the plate on my lap, then to my right, and then to my left, and even between my legs on the floor. It was awkward, uncomfortable, difficult, and even strange, to say the least. However, the most difficult aspect of the entire reenactment was the task of getting up from the floor. How did we do it back then? Or more appropriately, why did we do it? Because we had to. It was all we knew. We had to be creative and inventive back then.

My friend, Floyd, reminded me later during a telephone conversation that we also had another seating arrangement. He was kind enough to remind me that sometimes we even sat outside on the back house steps to eat our food. I had forgotten this detail and was thankful to him for bringing it back to me. I jokingly said to him that I would one day sit on my step and eat my dinner in order to gauge the reaction from my neighbors. I do sit on my front step and enjoy peanuts from time to time but I am yet to muster the courage to relax there and eat a plate of rice and peas, or a bowl of chicken soup. When I do, I am prepared to be dragged before the home-owners association to be charged with indecent exposure.

Interestingly enough, there was no homeowners association in Roebuck, even though everybody owned their own homes. And there was nothing indecent about sitting on the step and enjoying a meal. Rather, it was decent and welcomed. It was as accepted as it was culturally correct. Before Floyd and I were disconnected, I could hear him begin to share my folly with his wife, Shirley, who is from the U.S, and who I thought would certainly not understand this cultural feature. But he did share with me that he and Shirley sometimes sit on the floor to eat in their Washington home — proof that some elements of acculturation are transferable, and still possible.

Like all other families in Roebuck we ate in our *back house* but we didn't cook there; at least not in the earlier days when cooking was an adventure at our house; an adventure that was both danger-ous and taxing. Early in our poverty we cooked over an outdoor *fireplace,* which we made by placing two *rock stones* wide enough apart for a pot or *coal pot* to sit on. We would get the fire started by pouring a little *kersene oil* on dried twigs before igniting with a match. Larger pieces of wood were added very soon after to get the real fire going. At times it was difficult and even impossible to keep the fire burning long enough until the food was cooked. We would get down on our hands and knees, and with our faces as close as possible to the fireplace, blow some puffs of air on the smoldering wood to get the fire going again, only to get up with fire-red eyes and smelling like a fireman.

Sometimes we would put our creativity to work by making a fan out of cardboard, or even with the aluminum pot cover to rekindle the flame. My guess is that the phrase *fanning the flames* was manifested right there in Roebuck. Later on, when we added on a small kitchen off the *back house*, we installed an indoor fireplace but the process to keep it working efficiently was the same as the one with the outdoor model. As time passed, we moved up to a two-burner stove that stood on four tall legs with a round glass *kersene* container on the side.

The fridge was long in coming to our *back house* because it took almost forever for electricity to arrive in Roebuck. Once it finally came, my mother made certain to put it to good use. The fridge was the only thing we had to plug in. We had no fancy lamps, electric can openers, blenders, or food processors. None of that fancy stuff. I liked having the fridge because it made me feel important. I would open and close the door just to see the light go on and off. The fridge was of the type that had to be defrosted ever so often; after an abundance of ice had built up in the small freezer compartment at the top of the unit. We would put a bowl of hot water in the freezer to speed up the defrosting process. More often than not, we would simply unplug the fridge for a while and wait for the melting action to be completed before plugging it in again.

We had plenty ice and sold ice cubes on occasions but we never had the volume of disposable food to keep in the fridge, and quite often it was very spacious inside. "There was enough room inside to hold a party." That's exactly how Clyde, my Aunt Gloria's husband, described somebody's fridge. His description was also certainly true of ours most of the time. The acquisition of the fridge and a television by my mother was not her way of competing with others. She was simply trying to raise our standard of living, little by little.

Our *back house* was also home to one piece of furniture that was a forerunner to the blue dinette set. Sitting along the *partition* that separated the *back house* from a very small bedroom was a bench-like piece of furniture that was about five to five and a half feet long and about two and a half feet wide. It didn't have a backrest so when we sat on it we had to lean our backs against the partition, with our legs hanging down. I never knew where it came from. It was there for as long as I could remember. My father probably built it since he was very crafty at carpentry. I don't know that for sure. But what I do know is that nobody in Roebuck had this antique piece which we called the *ortaman*. That's what my mother called it and that's what we all called it. That's what we heard and we did not question anyone as to its meaning, its pronunciation, or spelling. I had never seen it written in a book and was therefore unable to question its existence as a word, or its etymology. Phonetically, it was easy to spell but still its place in the Queen's English was questionable. As young children we did not have the foresight to check it out in a dictionary. It was one of those words that my sisters and I accepted without question. *Ortaman*. It was there to sit on, and that is just what we did. We sat on it.

I want to explore this situation a little deeper. In Roebuck, as children we repeated what we heard. That's how we learned the culture of the place. At least we repeated what we thought we heard. I am sure that as you read this, you can recall some words that you heard, or repeated, in childhood, only to discover later that you were completely off base. Such was the case with my sisters and me. We heard and repeated the word *ortaman* as children, only to discover much later that the correct word was ottoman, and that the ortaman was one of those words that had its birth in Roebuck.

I learned later that this state of affairs was not limited to Roebuck, and I have two hilarious examples that support the point I am trying to make. When we moved to Chattanooga in 1987, our youngest son, Tristan, was almost four. We soon began attending a series of evangelistic tent meetings that was sponsored by our church. Before the preacher got up to preach each evening he was always preceded by a rousing song service in which a number of songs and choruses were sung by the congregation under the direction of the song service director. Tristan grew to love one song more than the others; the words go something like this: *Redeemed how I love to proclaim it. Redeemed by the blood of the Lamb…* Some of you may know it since it is a fairly well known song. Some time after the meetings had concluded, we were having our own family devotion one evening. My wife was sitting at the piano playing the songs that were requested by the other four members of the family. When it was Tristan's turn, the four year old suggested that we sing *Redeemed Cow.* The humor was intense and Tristan was as serious as he was persistent. How could he have interpreted *Redeemed how* as *Redeemed cow?*

It is still difficult for me to understand how he arrived at that conclusion. But he did. That's what he heard. And that's what he repeated, being too young and innocent to understand that cows aren't redeemed.

Another unrelated incident happened later on. And once again Tristan took center stage. My wife and I had purchased a collection of LP records with religious songs for children. We both love music and we did our best to expose our three boys to wholesome music. We would put on the music regularly for the boys to listen and sing along, especially at bed time. After a short time they knew the words and the music to the songs and could sing them verbatim. They were catchy tunes and easy for young children to learn. I too would find myself singing along at times to The Bill Gaither Trio and the Sunday School Picnic and Orchestra, and also to the music of the Heritage Singers' album, *Heaven is for Kids.* One album that I liked really well was *Kids of the Kingdom* with Annie Herring. I would even sing the tunes to myself even when we weren't playing them for the boys' enjoyment. My intent is to have them recorded on a CD to play for my grandson, Max, when he comes to spend the weekend with us.

One day, out of the blue, Tristan asked his mother, "Who is Willie?" Hortense was baffled at the question, since there was no conversation between her and her youngest son that would inspire that question from the boy. We had a friend that went by that name but surely Tristan wasn't inquiring about Willie Hammond. Only later did she understand the question and Tristan's reasoning. One of the lines in one of the songs to which he listened went like this: *He will take you right now if you are willing.* Tristan had heard *He will take you right now if you are Willie,* and wanted to know who this Willie was. I still laugh to myself each time I remember the innocence of my youngest, even though he is now a young man. Probably, my mother was saying ottoman all those years but we heard *ortaman.* Can you blame us?

I have one more to share. However, this one does not involve Tristan. But it does tell the story of a little kindergarten chap whom I do not know but who, like Tristan, repeated what he thought he heard. This hilarious story came via e mail some time ago to Hortense and me from my friend, Floyd. I am writing it as I received it so as to preserve its full impact. Some of you may have already come across this one. If you have, please forgive the duplication, but it does support the point I am trying to make. Here we go.

A mom was concerned about her kindergarten son walking to school. He didn't want his mother to walk with him. She wanted to give him the feeling that he had some independence but yet know that he was safe. So she had an idea of how to handle it. She asked a neighbor if she could please follow him to school in the mornings, staying at a distance, so he probably wouldn't notice her. The neighbor said that since she was up early with her toddler anyway, it would be a good way for them to get some exercise as well, so she agreed. The next school day, the neighbor and her little girl set out following behind Timmy as he walked to school with another neighbor's girl he knew. She did this for the whole week.

As the two walked and chatted, kicking stones and twigs, Timmy's little friend noticed that the lady was following them as she seemed to do every day all week. Finally she said to Timmy, "Have you noticed that lady following us to school all week? Do you know her?" Timmy nonchalantly replied, "Yeah, I know who she is." The little girl said, "Well, who is she?" "That's Shirley Goodnest," Timmy replied, "and her daughter Marcy." "Shirley Goodnest? Who the heck is she and why is she following us?" "Well," Timmy explained, "every night my Mom makes me say the 23rd Psalm with my prayers cuz she worries about me so much. And in the Psalm it says, "Shirley Goodnest and Marcy shall follow me all the days of my life, so I guess I just have to get used to it."

On second thought, the *ortaman* had an additional function. My uncle, Garfield, used it for a bed. Uncle Garfield was Ma Ma's brother, who apparently never had a family, or had a home of his own. My mother invited him to sleep at our house after my father migrated to England. My guess is that she felt more secure having a man in the house, especially at night. The *ortaman* became Uncle Garfield's bed for a very long time and a place to lay his head night after night. That must have been a very uncomfortable and punishing substitute for a bed. It was hard and sturdy and smooth to the touch. It appeared to have been finished with a thorough dose of sand papering, but without varnish, or stain, or paint. It had turned dark with age and use. I don't recall Uncle Garfield ever using a pillow of any kind, or even asking for some form of bedding to soften the impact of the hard, wooden ortaman. He slept without question and without complaint. But that was his personality. That's the kind of man he was. He was a very quiet man, who never said much. He was not reclusive, but he kept pretty much to himself most of the time.

Uncle Garfield was as tall as he was lanky, with one distinguishing feature, which we thought to be intriguing. The first finger on his right hand could not bend at the joint like normal fingers do. It remained permanently straight for as long as I knew him. And this was the only finger that had this special feature. All the others were as normal as mine. We never had an explanation from my mother, or from Ma Ma, or from anyone in the family. He did not volunteer to share any information. And we dared not ask. We did not make fun of him either; like we made *mock sport* of little boys and girls in Roebuck when they got a bad haircut, or when a bee sting had swollen shut the eye of the unfortunate one. Kids were as cruel in those days as they are today.

By now you may have come to the conclusion that the *ortaman* and the ottoman look completely different from each other and have completely different functions. Mine was nothing like the ottoman I came to know many years later. I never knew what a real one was like until I came to live in America in the early eighties. None of the houses in Roebuck had those fancy ottomans; the kind you rest your feet on. However, my theory surrounding the history and development of the ortaman will most likely not be disputed. It probably was the forerunner to the modern version that has undergone a series of slow evolutionary changes to reach the climax it is today.

Something else happened in our back house that has a way of humbling me every time I think about it. I mentioned it to my wife, Hortense, and my sisters and I make it a point of conversation when we get together to reminisce. The conversation is usually accompanied by laughter and frivolity, but at the same time it is always a sobering reminder of the road we have traveled to reach where we are today. Ever so often my parents would treat us with something special. Not because we were good, or because someone was celebrating a birthday, or an anniversary of some sort. They simply treated us. And it is one of those fun times, simple and plain though it was, that had a way of bringing our family together. We would always be at our happiest during this time of merriment. We would laugh and giggle without reason as we anticipated what was to come.

Without warning they would bring home a can or two of Exeter corned beef and some *biscuits*. The slaying of the fatted calf was about to begin for us. My mother or father would empty the contents of the corned beef can on a plate and untangle them with a fork before working in a generous amount of chopped onions, a little black pepper and some *lard oil* to moisten as needed. We watched and waited for what seemed an hour for the preparation phase to end, with our mouths watering more and more with each passing moment. The actual feast was not without order and precision as each of us took a biscuit, loaded it with corned beef, covered it with another biscuit and returned to sit on the *ortaman* to eat. We would repeat this ritual, until the plate was empty.

Preceding the feast was a practice that was common in our house. It was the culture in our home to say the *grace* before meals; a prayer my father taught us; the one we used whenever we ate together. We knew it by heart and it quickly became an automatic practice, even when our parents were not around. I still remember it, even though I have not personally used it on a regular basis since leaving home, or passed on this aspect of my culture to my children. It is forever etched in my memory, as is Psalm 23, Psalm 34, Psalm 100, Proverbs 3 and the *times tables* that we learned by constant daily repetition as kids at the Indian Ground School. Our family grace went like this:

> *Dear Jesus, thank You for this food*
> *Bless me and bless it also*
> *In Jesus name*
> *Amen.*

My mother continued the corned beef and biscuits practice long after my father left for England. She must have noticed how happy we were and how we ate and laughed ourselves silly for no apparent reason, except for the pure delight of eating corned beef and bis-cuits. She must have noticed how excited we became whenever she treated us this way, and appeared to have saved the moment for when she thought the time was right. I grew to love corned beef but I have not eaten a lot of it since leaving home, even though my cousin, Charleston, once described it as the most stupid prey he had encountered; his reason being that the corned beef locked itself in a can and left the key on the outside, making it easy for its preda-tors to find it. This one example provides an accurate insight as to the kind of person Charleston was when we were growing up in Roebuck. He loved to *sky lark*. It was like second nature to him.

As I reflect on these back house celebrations, I can't help but conclude that my mother's thinking at that time went far beyond serving up a treat of corned beef and biscuits. Far beyond "eat, drink and be merry." She believed that it was her responsibility to give us something positive to look forward to on a regular basis, to excite and encourage us, no matter how poor we were. She appeared to have had the determination that her poor children were going to have a bright future and that our present condition was not to be looked at as a predictor of what we were to become. She not only served up corned beef and biscuits. She served up much more in the form of educational opportunities, along with the constant reminder that "You have to turn out better than I did." Too many have been brainwashed into believing that poverty is a life sentence in a maximum security prison, without the possibility of parole. My mother, on the other hand, embraced an opposite interpretation, and used it to reinforce hard work, ambition and priorities. Lessons well taught in our back house.

I can't forget the only source of light in our *back house* once dark-ness came every evening. The reliable *kersene* oil lamp protected us from the darkness which arrived early in Roebuck. We could count on it knocking on our door around six, no matter the season of the year, rainy or dry. It was cultural, and quite unlike it is in the US where the sun does not care about setting until close to nine in the summertime. Darkness didn't find me outside the confines of our *back house* too often. I was afraid of it and tried my utmost to be back inside in time, especially if someone in the neighborhood had died and there was a funeral, or one was being planned. I could not sleep at night. I was certain that a *duppie* would get me. In those days the *undertaker* that had the *turn out* would bring the remains of the dead person back to their home to *lie in state* for a couple hours or so before the service at The Pentecost Church at the end of Roebuck. That was scary for every little boy and girl in Roebuck. In Roebuck we didn't talk about the *remains* of a person that had died. We simply called it the body. The only time we used remains was in a completely different situation; when Ms. Redman or Ms. Nicholls at Indian Ground School gave an arithmetic problem in division to the class and asked us to work it to find out what remains after dividing 5 by 4.

Nothing was more terrifying than coming face to face with a hearse, especially at night. I was not the only one in Roebuck that was afraid of the hearse. All the boys and girls in the district felt the same way about it. It was as if being scared of a hearse was part of the culture of Roebuck. In those days hearses played music and songs like *Nearer My God to Thee;* the kind of haunting music that made every little boy and girl scared to death. I clearly remember the day when Lemuel Harris from St. Lucy parked his hearse at the top of Penny Hill, right between Indian Ground and Roebuck, and was playing hymns for a while. I later learned that it was his way of advertising his new coach. That was one day I dared not venture outside. It was a form of self-imposed *back house* arrest. It was like punishment for doing nothing wrong. I could hear the music clearly from the *back house*. It was haunting and downright frightening. The only other time I was forced to stay in the house during daylight hours was, as mentioned before, when my mother made me wear my sister's blue PE shorts. That was her way of keeping me out of the street.

One night, as was my custom, I was carrying cow's milk from Ma Ma's to my house in Roebuck. Ma Ma, my maternal grandmother, lived in Indian Ground. This was my favorite chore for more reasons than one. I got to eat at Ma Ma's house every evening. I ate at my house as well, but Ma Ma always left me a *share*. Her food always tasted better than the one my sisters cooked. I loved her very much and if I was spoiled in any way, Ma Ma was the one to do it. My mother never did. For a long time I was Ma Ma's only grandson until David came along years later and she found a way to make both of us feel special. I also liked to visit Ma Ma's because it gave me the opportunity to get in some good long distance running. I would run all the way to her house and then do the same when returning home. I never checked the distance officially but my estimation says that it was about a mile and a half each way. I loved to run and I still do a little today. Running to and from Ma Ma's house every evening provided good practice when I specialized in the mile and the 880 at The Modern High school.

On this particular evening I was enjoying the run back home as usual, with more than half the distance behind me. I had just crested Penny Hill and was about to slip into cruising mode as I made my decent on the other side of the Hill, allowing my effortless strides to carry me to the bottom before calling on my reserves to propel me through the *pond bottom* and finally into Roebuck proper. The familiar *mist* that usually filled the pond bottom was missing, so I could see fairly well in the dark of the evening. Plus they were no *sleeping policemen* to impede my natural speed. I had repeated the scenario countless times. But my strategy suddenly changed when I came face to face with the unthinkable — a hearse; just sitting there. I was already running so it was not difficult to kick it into high gear. The milk bottle shattered into a million pieces but that was not a good enough reason to stop running, until I reached the safety of my back house.

At dusk my mother usually gave instructions to "light de lamp" and one of us would grab the small box of Safety matches and light the wick of the old *kersene oil* lamp that had its familiar place in the back house. I refer to it as the old lamp because for as long as I can remember we never had to purchase a new one. The lamp was a sturdy, permanent fixture in our back house. However, it was a different story with the lamp shade, or the *chimney,* as we sometimes called it. The chimney was an appropriate name at times because of the black smoke that escaped from the small opening at the top, or because of the thick black soot that collected on the inside of the *Home Sweet Home* lamp shade.

We broke the chimneys too often for Muddah's liking. After all, they were so thin and fragile. No wonder they broke so easily. My mother's reaction to the breaking of her lamp shades was far from calm. Many of the mishaps happened during the process of cleaning the thing. Taking a piece of rag in one hand I would gently maneuver it through the opening in the base of the chimney to remove the soot that had accumulated the night before, only to breathe a sigh of relief at completing the task without committing the unpardonable crime. The job of cleaning the chimney was suited for my older sister, Elaine. She was physically better suited for this delicate work. Not only because she was older. There was another reason. Elaine had these long, skinny fingers that were perfect for the job. And it was too delicate a responsibility to be assigned to my younger sisters, Yvonne, Cheryl and Heather (Neats, as she was better known) until they were much older. One of us invented a clever method to get the job done without the risk of having to force our hand through the small opening at the base of the lamp shade. We made a tool by wrapping the cleaning rag around a narrow piece of wood and used it to clean the chimney — probably the first chimney sweep.

With the chimney cleaned, the wick trimmed, and a generous amount of *kersene oil* carefully poured into the base of the lamp with the aid of a funnel, the lamp was lit by striking a single match from the box of Safety matches and our little back house was instantly transformed into a space with a purpose; a serious purpose that would last for the next two, three, or four hours, or however long it took. It was homework time. My high school sister, Elaine, was about to study and on my mother's orders the place had to be quiet. No radio. No talking or laughing. Only quietness. This was serious time. Consecrated time that was important to my mother as Sunday school and church were to her. This nightly affair confirmed my mother's commitment to education and how seriously she regarded its place in our development and our future. And when my time came, the ritual was just as intense. "Be quiet. Sylvester is doing his homework," she would demand. My mother referred to me as Sylvester only when I was in trouble, or when the situation at hand was a serious one. Homework time was always the latter; a serious time; a Sylvester time. In less important times my name was always Syl. Not Sly. Sly is American.

I recall with excitement when a lone sixty watt bulb suspended from the ceiling of our *back house* replaced the old and faithful *kersene* oil lamp with the *Home Sweet Home* chimney. Electricity had come to Roebuck and my mother saw to it that we were one of the first to have the upgrade. For me, it was like having a new toy. I would turn the switch on and off without reason. Just the pleasure of seeing the light flicker on and off cemented the reality of how far we had come. But homework did not miss a beat. It went on. It had to go on. My mother said so.

Surprisingly, we kept a *monkey* in our back house. Many people in Roebuck did. I have heard stories of people in America having snakes and other exotic pets in their homes but we kept a *monkey* in ours. We cherished it for a long time, getting rid of it just after we brought the fridge. What is the connection between the monkey and the fridge, some may ask? It is a simple one if you lived in Roebuck when I was growing up. The *monkey* was a large kettle-like container made from pottery for the purpose of keeping drinking water cool. We kept the *monkey* on a shelf in the back house and withdrew cool water to drink when needed, filling her up again when the supply was low. Our *monkey* became obsolete only after the fridge appeared; when we could now store bottles of water for cooling.

Our *back house* was home to another piece of furniture — the *larder*. I was surprised to find larder in the thesaurus because all this time I was of the opinion that it was one of those words that was made up in Roebuck. The thesaurus defines the larder as a cupboard, or small room, for storing food. Pantry, the word Americans use, was never mentioned in Roebuck. Our larder was never as well stocked as my pantry in Ringgold which has a variety of canned goods, cereals, flour, sugar, pasta, etc. And it seems that the stash grows noticeably each time Hortense returns home. Most of the food consumed in Roebuck was not of the type to be kept in a larder. Although we ate a lot of rice, much of the food we consumed was *ground* food. Our yams, potatoes, cassava, eddoes, carrots and beets, were harvested from the ground and were classified as *ground provisions*; not the kind of food to store in a larder.

We never used the term *produce* in Roebuck and harvesting the ground provisions was a process known as *digging*. So to get some of these foods ready for cooking, we had to go out and dig them. Still, other provisions like breadfruit, green banana, sour sop, pears, limes and other fruits were picked from trees in or near the back yard, or grew in the *ground*, a plot of land that was rented from Sedgepond Plantation.

When my sister Elaine did her homework in the *back house*, my mother demanded silence from even the radio. The Redifussion, as it was known, was a kind of radio that had only one station and was available in two models; a rectangular table model and a triangular-shaped one that hung from a *wall*. If memory serves me well we had the latter model hanging in our back house. The Redifussion provided only partial programming and *went off* at a certain time during the day and came back on later in the afternoon and went off again at midnight. I hated to be awake when it was going off. The playing of the national anthem at that time of the night was kind of spooky and scary to me as a little kid. However, there was something positive and personally educational about the Redifussion — the 7:00 AM and 7:00 PM news from London. After about four or five beeps of the radio signal, the announcer would always begin with "This is London Calling." I listened to the BBC news as often as I could and as a result I was able to learn quite a bit about numerous international countries, their capital cities, and the names of their leaders, prime ministers and presidents.

My favorite weekend Rediffusion programs came on Sunday afternoon — two comedies, *The Clitheroe Kid* and *My Word*, the latter probably largely responsible for my lingering interest in words. On week nights, two popular radio dramas on the *Rediffusion, Portia Faces Life* and *Dr. Paul,* commanded the attention of many in Roebuck. Sometimes I made myself available to tune in but I was not hooked on them like I was on the 7:00 news. The BBC news on the Rediffusion was my window to the world in those days. Even today, I still enjoy listening to the news on CNN or MSNBC, but sometimes get the feeling that they are not as educational as the BBC news I listened to as a kid in Roebuck.

On the other hand, and in spite of the positive side mentioned above regarding the Rediffusion that hung in our back house, there was something slightly frightening about it that I still remember. Every morning around 7:15 and just after my beloved BBC news, the programming switched to something of a more morbid nature — the obituaries. Not that we ever said that word in Roebuck. My mother always said that she wanted to hear the *deaths.* I can't recall another person who loved funerals more than my mother. I hated to be at home alone when the *deaths* were *coming on.* Earlier on, I thought they were announcing the *deafs,* and wondered if such programming was necessary, even though the announcer always began with "We regret to announce the death of the late" so and so and would go on to provide detailed information concerning the funeral. Similarly, I wondered about the meaning of *the late* but never had the heart to ask. There were some questions I never asked in Roebuck. This was one of them.

A multitude of fond memories was created in that *back house* of ours. And it is not difficult at all to retrieve the scenes that are forever stored on the hard drive of my consciousness. Having said that, the most outstanding back house memory in my personal experience is the one I detailed earlier about one particular Saturday night when Muddah sat up with me as I studied in preparation for writing my Biology exam the following Monday. As previously mentioned, I never looked my mother in the eye that night, or even after the results of the exam were returned, to tell her how much I appreciated her gesture, or gave her a big hug for what she had done. This is one regret that will always stay with me. She deserved to hear that from me and I never said it. But we were never a touchy, huggy, family. We rarely expressed our emotions and feelings in words, or by hugging and embracing. In fact, we never told each other how much we loved one another. Yet, I knew that our love for each other was strong and always present. Love and appreciation were understood; taken for granted, but felt by all. It was demonstrated but never verbalized.

My mother however, would have brushed away my attempts to bestow gratitude with a smile, or with "That's okay." That's the kind of human being she has always been. That's the kind of mother she wanted to be. And she was. She lived vicariously through the successes of her five children. Her reward was Elaine's success in nursing school. Her rewards continued later when I graduated from high school and became a teacher. I could feel her pride. It stuck to me. I knew her eyes were on me that first morning I walked out the back house to begin my teaching career at All Saints Boys School in September, 1968. She continued to accumulate other accomplishments when the younger siblings Yvonne, Cheryl and Neats achieved personal success in business, physical therapy and nursing respectively. None of us became an attorney, a physician, or an engineer but if you knew Roebuck well, you would have to agree that these milestones were huge accomplishments.

My mother found her niche and filled it well. She knew her limitations and was comfortable in the areas in which she was strong. She knew that her limited experience in schooling made it impossible for her to help us with homework when we grappled with the weekly essay assignments for English class, or with the steamy romance themes of Romeo and Juliet, or with memorizing and identifying the chambers of the heart and their role in the circulation of blood. She made up for this by providing the space, dedicating the time and securing an environment that enhanced learning and invited success. And it all happened in our *back house*.

The fact that there was a *back house*, the obvious question is whether there was also a *front house*. And there was. Unlike the *back house*, our *front house* was like the road less traveled, or much like the most holy place described in the sanctuary services of the Bible. If you know or understand anything about the biblical sanctuary and the restrictions that were placed on who was allowed in and how often, you would understand why I have so reverently described our *front house*. Access to the place was guarded by two swinging doors that were always latched to keep out wanderers and casual visitation. Unlike the *back house*, our *front house* was mostly reserved for important people that hardly came a-calling, or it was viewed as the show part of our house. Everyday visitors like Ms. Watson, or Ms. Morris, or Cadogan were not entertained in there, nor did they expect to be greeted in there. It was like the living room, or great room, that is common in American homes today.

Our *front house* housed my mother's best furniture: Morris chairs made from mahogany, with soft cushions, the *cabinet*, and a rather large chair my father had built. A black and white Zenith television set came much later and some of the boys from the neighborhood were allowed to watch it but only from their place on the front step. In Roebuck we never called the cabinet a china cabinet; just a cabinet, probably because there was no real china kept in it. It was a short piece of furniture without the lower storage section that is characteristic of today's modern pieces. It sat on four short legs in one corner of the front house and was home to some drinking glasses as well as a set of knives and forks, none of which we ever used. I don't recall seeing any plates or wine glasses, or fancy china.

The floor in our front house was not carpeted, or covered with area rugs. These luxuries were not included in the culture of Roebuck. Our *front house* floor was made of *board*. We did not say wood, or hard wood, or floors, in those days. I am still amazed while watching HGTV when people make comments such as "I like those floors." It was always the floor in Roebuck. Not those floors, as is so commonly said in the US. And there were *window blinds* that that decorated the *jealousy windows,* which we kept open much of the time so that the wind could blow through the front house, fluttering the blinds as it passed through.

The information I just gave concerning our *front house* was done to create an atmosphere of a neat and tidy space, and to show that care and effort were exerted in keeping it that way. It was a nice-looking space, if only by Roebuck standards. My mother made sure it was always painted and that it was a place to relax, even though it was not used very often. Still, it was still due a makeover at least once a year at Christmas time, even though it was always in mint condition. The Roebuck culture demanded it and the sights and smells of Christmas were very present in our front house. My mother was in charge of the makeover project but my sisters and I provided the free labor. Chairs had to have a new coat of varnish and the floor a fresh coat of polish, even though they didn't need it. But it was Christmastime and the smell of new paint, varnish and wood stain was festive.

What is Christmas without a Christmas tree? Our *front house* had to have a tree — a freshly cut tree. Not an artificial store-bought tree but a real tree. In actuality, we didn't have a Christmas tree. We had a Christmas branch. When the time came to put up the *tree*, we went to the *grass piece* and simply cut off a branch; just a branch, from a tree we called the mile tree, so called because it grew so tall. I once heard that its botanical name was the *cassarina* and right away I concluded that it was one of those names that had been manufactured in Roebuck, even though it sounded semi-official and semi-scientific. However, I did not have reason to conduct a research on our festive friend until now. I was driving to a picnic one Sunday afternoon, while talking on my cell phone to my friend, Hal. At one point in the conversation he mentioned that he was going to Barbados in the near future and I took the opportunity to ask him to take a picture of a mile tree and send it back to me to include in the book. I am uncertain as to which one of us brought up the name *cassarina* but the one thing of which I am certain is that we were both united in our conclusion that *cassarina* was the incorrect spelling. Hal had the presence of mind to put google to work right then and there and was able to come up with casuarina, an Australian pine.

Be that as it may, a branch of The Casuarina tree took its place in a corner of the front house and was promptly decorated, primarily by my sister, Yvonne, who wasted little time adorning it with a collection of silver decorations that were crafted from the packaging she retrieved from boxes of Trumpeter cigarettes. Not that she smoked. She was only interested in the sliver paper inside the cigarette box. The *tree* had no lights; no bells, no ornaments, or gifts wrapped in Christmas gift wrap; just silver paper from cigarette boxes. Hanging close by, on a string, were the few Christmas cards we happened to receive. Christmas gifts and toys were rare in Roebuck in those days, so we didn't expect them. I remember getting a cheap and flimsy *mouth organ* that I ran around blowing into; it did not last very long. Other boys in Roebuck had a similar mouth organ experience. At other times, a comb covered with paper produced a more durable mouth organ.

However, the Christmas festivities were not confined to the front house. We had to have a white Christmas, even in tropical Roebuck where the temperature at Christmastime reached close to 90 degrees. Before the *snow* fell, we used a *chopper*, a hoe, a *cutlass*, a *bill*, a *peck*, or whatever useful tool was available to remove all the grass that grew between the rocks around the front house. This was no easy task, especially when it is understood how rocky and uneven our yard was. Just in case someone may be wondering, a cutlass is another name for a machete. We never said machete in Roebuck. A *bill* is more difficult to describe, but it is much shorter and wider than a cutlass, with a sharp rounded bottom edge and a slender pointed hook at the front that made it easy to dislodge the grass that grew between rocks. However, the bill was primarily used in the harvesting of sugar cane. In Roebuck we called it *cutting canes.*

Obviously, snow didn't fall in Roebuck, so we had to manufacture its counterfeit in the form of *marl.* Armed with a long slender iron we named the *grabble urn,* and a bucket or some other container, we would go to the *marl hole* and dig white marl. But we never referred to it as limestone in Roebuck. It was marl to us. By the way, I am thinking that *grabble urn* was in all actuality a gravel iron. *Grabble urn* is what we heard growing up and that's what we called it. By now you will have understood that the people of Roebuck manufactured names as they saw fit. In any case, we would spread the white marl to cover the ground outside the house, and with most homeowners in Roebuck utilizing the same process, Roebuck was transformed into a white and tropical wonderland, only without reindeer and Santa Claus, who was *Father Christmas* to us. It was only then that the song *Dreaming of a White Christmas* really made any sense to us.

Behind our *back house* was our back yard. The back yard did not receive the same treatment as the front at Christmas, even though it was exposed for all to see. It did not have a *paling* so it was easy to see what was going on back there. In fact, many houses in Roebuck did not have a paling. Some might have had a partial one but the houses in Roebuck were not known to have a fence. We never said fence in Roebuck. It was always a paling. Incidentally, at the time of writing this, I am discussing with Hortense our need to fence our back yard. We would probably still have Ella if our property was fenced.

A Roebuck *paling* was made of galvanize. We did have a small paling around the toilet to give us privacy as we *bade* outside. I remember as children growing up, how we hated taking a bath behind the paling as the smell coming from the attached toilet was very prohibitive, especially if it was wet outside after a shower of rain. "It smells stink," we used to say. We were too *scornful* to go back there under those conditions that almost made us puke. Even now I can hear Yvonne making the puking sound without anything coming up. She was also scornful to walk outside when the ducks would splatter their do-do all over the back yard. She would attempt to throw up at the slightest thing.

I had to laugh as I recalled a related incident at my school. One boy had left the class quite suddenly for the bathroom just after he had returned from lunch. The teacher asked me to check on him, while telling me that he looked just fine when he entered the classroom. As expected, I found him in the bathroom and in obvious discomfort, with his face over the sink. When he was in a position to straighten up I asked him what was wrong. His response triggered the lighter side of me, so much so that I could not contain myself, even though the situation was quite serious. "The student teacher has a sore on her lip and it made me gag when I looked at it," he told me. Back in Roebuck, we would have said he was scornful and that the sore made him throw up. We never said gag in

Roebuck. It was always throw up, or vomit. Not gag.

As I am describing the various rooms in our Roebuck house, I think it is appropriate here to mention our *half bath* and our *full bath*. Our home in Ringgold has three full baths that look nothing like the baths we had back in Roebuck. In Roebuck a half bath and a full bath were something we did. They were verbs instead of nouns. They were not rooms in our house. I had a half bath twice a day; one in the morning, when I got up and was getting ready for school. Sometimes we called it a *wash up*. A basin or a small bucket of water was all that was needed, for all that was required was that I wash my face, my feet and hands, and brush my teeth, sometimes with the lather from Lux soap, or Lifebuoy soap, or Palmolive soap, or even with ashes if Pepsodent toothpaste was not available. The term *washing out your mouth with soap* had real significance for us in Roebuck in those days, even though we did not say bad words at that age. It has just crept back into my consciousness that at times we were quite creative as well as health conscious when it came to brushing our teeth. We used natural and recyclable ingredients found at home in our outdoor fireplace; materials formed as we burned wood into ashes while cooking. Ashes, as a cleaning agent, made our teeth sparkle. Nowadays, the politically correct name is charcoal but to us in Roebuck, it was ashes, and we had it in abundance.

In Roebuck when we said that were washing our hands as we were washing up, we really meant that we were washing our arms. We called the whole arm the hand. And so it was with the foot. Washing our feet meant that we were washing our legs but we called the whole thing the foot. We made sure we did not smell *musty* when we went to school, so we had our half bath in the mornings before leaving home because we had to pass inspection when the teachers at Indian Ground School did a thorough job checking our faces to make sure there was no dried up *dribble* around our mouths from the night before, or *cold* in the corner of our eyes, or *snot* running out of our noses.

They checked our hands and our feet and under our finger nails to make sure they did not find *dirt*. They also checked to see if our hair was combed, making sure it was not *knotty*. In Roebuck we did not say our hair was *nappy*. It was *knotty*; rolled up into little knots on our head like "rat shit on a ledge," as Charleston so perfectly described somebody's hair. Ms. Redman, Ms. Edwards and Ms. Nicholls were like drill sergeants, ready with a ruler in hand to attack any dirty parts they found. It didn't matter if you were in *infants A* or in *class six*. They would line us up in the school yard for inspection every morning before we were served our biscuits and a cup of milk before school started. Many times I breathed a very deep sigh of relief when I knew I should have failed inspection, were it not for the layer of Vaseline that put a shine on those spots that my half bath did not cover.

As per the Roebuck custom I had another half bath before going to bed. My arms and legs would be *rusty* after taking care of the sheep, or playing in the grass with other children. I could not go to bed rusty. I was listening to Jim Leyland, the manager of the Detroit Tigers after his team lost the first game of the World Series to the Giants. He said that his pitcher was rusty. I had to smile to myself as I recalled the meaning of a Roebuck rusty and how rusty our arms and legs used to be after fishing for *crayfish* in the river in Sedgepond. We never said craw fish in Roebuck; only crayfish. After playing in the grass our hands and feet would itch while we were washing up or taking our half bath for the night. But we never said itch in Roebuck. We said that our hands and feet were *biting* us. As if they had teeth.

We took a *full bath* every Sunday morning. Sunday was special and we had to be clean for Sunday school and church. A full bath was the complete works; complete with hot water to boot. It was as if we were washing off all the dirt that had accumulated on us during the week and a full bath was the way to clean us up. Obviously, a full bath required more water than a half bath, so a larger container of cold water from the pipe under the breadfruit tree by The Marshall's house was required. Not a basin, or a bucket this time but quite a large pan. The term pan gives the impression of a much smaller container than a bucket or basin but a Roebuck pan was quite large, resembling a tub in size. We would boil water on the stove and dump it into the pan of cold water, making it comfortable enough for the full bath. Secured behind the paling by the toilet we would get a good lather, making sure that the one pan of water lasted to wash us from head to toe.

The *front house* and the yard were not the only places that got a festive dressing up for Christmas. By the way, in Roebuck we were not afraid to say Christmas for fear of being politically incorrect as is the case in some sectors of the US. Happy Holidays was fine but Merry Christmas was the festive greeting of the culture. After all, it was Christmas.

We got all dressed up on Christmas afternoon to go down to the New Testament Church of God at the end of Roebuck to say our *pieces,* or to sing in the choir for the Christmas program. A piece was a recitation or a poem we had to learn in order to recite it for the program. The Christmas program was the highlight of the season and people came from far and near to listen; crowding the church, or standing on the steps just to get a glimpse of what was going on inside. Small boys and girls, and even some older folk, would go up on the *platform* when their names were announced to say their pieces. Boys would salute and the girls would bow, or curtsy, before they began. Too often, stage fright would take over and some, nervous and *trembling*, would forget their lines, and sometimes the impatient crowd would *clap them down*, ending their chances to say their Christmas pieces.

Christmas was one of the rare times when we got new clothes. Muddah would make sure of that. She too was at her happiest and very festive at this time of the year, and she worked hard to ensure that we had the best in clothing and food. She always bought a ham, the only time we would have ham, and just the smell of the boiling ham was the announcement that Christmas had arrived. We would also have red apples, which we called English Apples. She baked sweet bread and cooked rice and peas and stew, and *pepper pot.* Incidentally, I looked up pepper pot in the thesaurus and learned that it is *a Guyanese or Caribbean stew made with meat, rice, and vegetables and seasoned with cassava syrup.* The ingredients in the Pennsylvania version include tripe and sometimes dumplings. But as far as I can remember my mother's pepper pot was all meat; cow hoof boiled down to a thick and delicious meaty stew.

I usually got a new long sleeve shirt, a tie, and a short pair of pants that sometimes had a *fob.* Long pants came much later. By the way, we never said a pair of pants in Roebuck; just a pants. A pair of shoes and socks completed my list of Christmas clothes. Interestingly enough, I did not go to town with my mother and Aunt Gloria to fit my new shoes, and the *coolie man,* who came around often did not sell shoes, so my mother, like most mothers in Roebuck, designed a method by which she arrived at my correct shoe size. She would get a straight narrow stick, ask me to stand on it and would cut it off exactly where my heel ended. That was my shoe size. And she never bothered to *measure* both feet, just one foot. Nor did she measure the width. That too did not seem to matter. Off to town, she and Aunt Gloria would go to shop for my shoes. Sometimes the method worked perfectly, while at other times the shoes *burned* my feet, as they said in Roebuck.

Charleston weighed in on the shoe size issue when we went to see him recently while visiting Roebuck. And even though he himself had recently had a leg amputated, he was his old self as he entertained Hotense, Cheryl, Heather and me on the back deck of his home one Sunday afternoon after church. He literally cracked us up as he retold the story, adding that after the shoes were purchased and brought home, they were put away until the day they were to be officially worn. I could not contain myself when he added the final details on how he bent up so many spoon handles, using them as a shoe horn to force his feet into the shoes; and reminded us how we used to grease our heels with Vaseline to make it easier to slide our foot into the shoe. Still, the tight shoes made us *scotch*, as we tried to walk comfortably, especially in the blazing Roebuck sun.

Our visit with Charleston reminded me of the gut-wrenching laughter we used to enjoy at his hands when we were growing up in Roebuck. As we were about to say goodbye, I witnessed the serious side of him when he asked for Hortense to come to him and I too became teary eyed as he paid her a most sincere compliment. He told her that he admired how well she fit into the family and how much he appreciated that she was not shy or reserved, and how much he admired how she pitched in to lend a hand in whatever needed to be done. In other words, he was telling her that she was not *poor great*.

Boys in Roebuck did not get underwear for Christmas, or at any other time for that matter. Our culture back then did not demand them for young boys. So we did not wear them like little boys in America do from a very young age. In all honesty, we were in our early teens when we began the practice of wearing underwear. While girls were wearing *puff-legged* panties, or bloomers, boys went without underwear until they were a little older. Only recently, my friend and I were joking around about this very thing; about not wearing underwear under our short pants on the school bus. Of course, he had to bring up getting a *hard on* while talking to girls on the school bus with no underwear to act as a buffer to *hold it down*. I had to remind him that that is not the purpose of underwear. In Roebuck I did hear of older men wearing a *BBD*. It was not until much later that I understood them to be wearing a BVD.

While in this trend of thought I think it appropriate at this stage of the discussion to interject some further contrasting aspects of the two cultures that relate to the theme mentioned above. Boys in Roebuck did not have the word penis as part of their vocabulary. We never used that word. It was always a *dickey* or a *doggie,* as if it was meant to bite someone. A true story is appropriate here. I was driving to school one morning while listening to local talk radio on a station in Chattanooga, Tennessee. The host, Jeff Styles, was talking about a gentleman he had not seen in a while but had run into him the night before at a social function in the city. Styles described the man's appearance, saying that he was all dressed up; even wearing a dickey. Understandably, I could not contain myself, wishing I had someone to share the laughter, or even wishing I could call in to the radio station to let Jeff know how much I appreciated him starting off my day with such a healthy and vigorous laugh. I am positive I would have lost control of the car had Jeff mentioned *pokey* in the same breath.

As if the above incident with Jeff Styles was not sufficient, a similar one was played out almost word for word quite recently. I was again driving to work on the morning of January 5, 2015, and was again tuned in to Jeff's radio show, *The Morning Press.* This morning in particular, he was having a conversation with Bill Lockhart about men's fashion, when Jeff happened to mention something about not liking to wear neck ties. "That's right," Lockhart chimed in, "You are a big dickey guy." Needless to say, I had another invigorating early morning laugh.

More hilarious is the fact that we did not even know of the term *erection* in Roebuck when talking about a dickey. In all fairness, we knew what it was but we did not call it that. That too was a term too scientifically advanced for us at that time. The common parlance was less dignified. Hence, we spoke of being *set.* Set to do what? I don't really know. The more advanced street name *hard on* would be added later.

I hate to continue in this vain but the cultural terms are as interesting as they are vast when considering the present topic. Maybe two illustrations will suffice. I was doing cafeteria duty at school one day, when one of the workers left her cash register to find me. She was obviously pretty upset but managed to complain, pointing in the direction of one boy and telling me that "He is talking about having a *boner* in my line." I had never heard the term before but judging from her attitude, I knew that the boy's remark must have been highly inappropriate and that I had to address the complaint with the student as soon as possible. So, in order not to appear ignorant, I pretended that I completely understood what she was talking about. In retrospect, I should have used my background knowledge to come up with the meaning. I certainly knew what a bone was; something hard and firm, but did not use my schema to arrive at a meaning in that specific context. Pulling the accused aside after he had finished his lunch, I sat down with him to address the complaint.

"What did you say in the lunch line?" I began

"Nothing," he said, with a guilty look all over his face.

"What is a boner? I continued, and waited while he looked at me as if I was from another planet.

"You know," he answered.

"I really don't know," I admitted, and again waited for his explanation. Finally, with a little bit of coaxing from me, and with some degree of embarrassment on his part, he opened up.

"An erection," he told me.

Another story as seen through the eyes of a child, or spoken from the mouth of a child, is as innocent as the one above was willful. Hortense and I had taken our grandson, Max, who was about two at the time, to visit her girlfriend and her family in North Carolina one fall break. One morning we were down stairs having breakfast and Max called from upstairs telling Omah (his name for his grandmother) "I want to pee." Both of us lingered for a while as we continued eating and talking at the table. In the meantime, Max, realizing that nobody was responding to his emergency, shouted down to us with a little more urgency, "Omah, I want to go to the bathroom, my penis is getting long." That got our attention right away as Max got the help he needed. In his own little innocent way, he had invented his own cultural language to interpret the standard way of saying things, so as to get his message across. No mention of boner, or erection, or any of that adult stuff; just that his penis was getting long.

Chapter Five

Sleeping Quarters

Even in simple things and in those tasks that appear insignificant and without priority, there is a pride and a standard to be reached and cherished, even by the poor.

Not very long ago, after my friend, Floyd, moved to a new house in Washington, he mentioned that he had bought a new bed and was about to go shopping for a mattress. In our conversation he voiced our mutual confusion when he said that in Barbados the bed was the actual thing we slept on. We also wondered why Americans talk about making their bed in the mornings when in all actuality, they do not sleep on the bed. We concluded that they sleep on a mattress and should be talking about making the mattress in the mornings and not making the bed. We shared a short laugh at discovering how the two cultures differ so widely in their use of the vocabulary surrounding something so simple. He understood when I mentioned that we used to say bedstead to mean what Americans call the bed; the *bedstid*, we called it in Roebuck. Still, bedstead is not a household word in America. I don't hear Americans talk about their bedstead. But when I was growing up in Roebuck, it was commonly used, even though it was the *bedstid* and not the formal and correct bedstead. In my youth, the *bedstid* was the accepted cultural term; one that was commonly used in our Roebuck community. Now, as I write, it is somewhat comical how we utterly destroyed the Queen's English in Roebuck to arrive at our own unique version

130

of some words as dictated by our culture and dialect. This is a startling phenomenon, especially when viewed in light of the fact that we have a reputation of being one of the most educated countries in the world, with a literacy rate hovering permanently around 99%.

I doubt very much that *bedstid* is currently used in Roebuck as it was when I was growing up. This may be one of those words that has been completely eradicated from the literary culture of Roebuck. The infusion of technology and the availability of financial resources that create an elevated standard of living, have a way of altering the culture of a people. As a result, *bedstid* may have fallen by the wayside, along with so many other words we thought were standard and acceptable; like the word *ortaman* that was detailed previously. But I feel justified in my attempt to resurrect the *bedstid* in order to serve the purpose of this work. The *bedstid* was the frame on which our bed rested. I am going to explain *bed* a little later but for the moment, please understand that the terms box spring and mattress will be mentioned only sparingly, since they were unknown entities when it came to sleeping in Roebuck.

Legend has it that our bedstead was constructed by my father. I was not a witness to the construction but one has to draw that conclusion since he had expertise in carpentry. He built houses all over the place. When I was a little boy I watched him work on the *house top* of a house that was being built quite a distance away and being intrigued by the late arrival of the sound of his hammer to my ears a few seconds after he struck the nails. I actually waited to hear the sound of the hammer come to me. It was fascinating to watch and listen. This incidental teaching strategy, though unconsciously and involuntarily performed by my father, was an early science lesson in the concept that sound travels. I also remember him building a chair. It was quite a large and sturdy one that seated about four. My father did quality work and he was proud of his skill and his workmanship. I witnessed him apply the varnish, a chore we as children would perform every year at a certain time to keep the masterpiece fresh. It made for very comfortable sitting once the cushions were in place. So the obvious conclusion is that my father made our bedstead out of wood. A strong supporting argument in favor of this position is the fact that we never saw bedsteads of this nature or model in Courts, or Plantations Limited, or in the other fine furniture outlets in Barbados. Not that we were regular shoppers.

One feature of our bedstead is that it was one piece. It did not have moveable parts for the purpose of assembling, or disassembling as necessary. Unlike the manufactured and mass produced structures of today that come with attachments and metal parts that slide easily into slots to secure a headboard and legs, our bedstead was a one-piece creation of very fine workmanship. I often wonder where the bedstead and the chair my father made are today. I hope that the lucky owners realize that they are sitting and sleeping on a piece of history.

Our bedstead in Roebuck had space for two or three *larks*. They didn't fly, and they didn't chirp. But they were there. The larks were the narrow pieces of wood that we spaced parallel on the bedstead to prevent the bed from falling through to the floor. My only other reference to *lark* has to do with the bird, and I find it impossible to associate it with such an important mechanism that was a part of our bed in those days in Roebuck. I was beginning to think that I was the only one that called them larks, as it was difficult to get confirmation from others; that was until Hal came for a weekend visit. We were sitting around reminiscing about growing up in Barbados, when I broached the question to test his knowledge. We both burst into a hearty laugh, with Hal asking why they were called larks and making reference to the lark as a bird; even repeating the saying "Happy as a lark." As I write this, I am still convinced that larks are still in use today. To satisfy my curiosity, I got up from the computer and checked under the box spring in one of my bedrooms to be certain. There they were, sitting in their place.

I still didn't know the American name for their larks, but I was sure there had to be one. I promised I would not rest until I found out about this one firsthand. Until then, I would continue to call them larks, just like we did in Roebuck.

Luckily, I did not have to wait very long. One afternoon, after leaving work, I realized that I could not wait any longer to get the scoop on larks, so I pulled into the parking lot of *Rooms To Go* and grabbed a pen and some paper to record my findings on this very simple research. I introduced myself to Steve, the salesman, and surprisingly, found him quite interested in the book and ready to help.

"What do you call those pieces of wood that you put on the bed to prevent the box spring from falling through?" I asked.

"Slats," he answered, without pausing to think.

But Steve went further, walking me over to one of the models on display. He lifted the box spring and showed me the three slats. I thanked him vigorously but he had more knowledge to pass on; giving me an education in slats, and again using 'show and tell' strategy to get his point across. I followed him briskly over to another showroom nearby. As before, he lifted the box spring, this time revealing six to eight slats. "This is a slat row," he instructed, adding that the slat row is popular with people who prefer a lower bed because they can get by without a box spring. I thanked him again, shaking his hand to leave, not wanting to use up more of his time. I should have anticipated his next question but he caught me unprepared.

"Where are you from?" he asked.

"Barbados," I told him.

"I've been to many of those islands down there," he said, mentioning Antigua, Jamaica, St. Maarten and St. Lucia, taking the time to tell me that he thought that St. Lucia is the most beautiful.

"St. Lucia is beautiful but you have not seen Barbados," I countered.

"Do you want to know what we call a slat in my country?"

"What?" he asked.

"A lark."

"A lark?" he repeated, while at the same time trying to contain a laugh that was both loud and honest. "Every culture has its own way of saying the same thing," he said when he was fully composed.

I thanked him for the last time, leaving with much more than I had expected to learn about larks and slats, and best of all, with the aid of his last statement, I now had a larger focus on a title for the book, since I had not up to that point, settled on one. As can be imagined, I was completely ecstatic when I left Steve at *Rooms to Go*. My plan was to go straight home to record our encounter in my manuscript. But my thirst for more knowledge on larks and slats was suddenly unquenched when I realized I was soon to pass by *Ashley's Furniture*. Lydia welcomed me gleefully, expecting to make a sales pitch.

"I am not here to shop," I announced, "but I have a question." I am writing a book about how different cultures say the same thing differently," I explained. Like Steve, she was interested and ready to assist. "How can I help you?" she asked, adding something to the effect that furniture is the same everywhere.

"What do you call those pieces of wood that you put on the bed to prevent the box spring from falling through?" I asked.

"You mean the slats," she replied. "Some people call them center support," she continued.

"We call them *larks* in my country," I added. She too had a spirited laugh, though not as intense as Steve's. I thanked her for her help after she jokingly called out to some of her colleagues, "Do you see any larks flying over there?"

More unique and much more creative than the *lark*, was the bed itself — the thing we slept on. As a boy growing up in Roebuck I spent some time sleeping on the floor. Our house had two *chambers*, one of which belonged to my parents. Since I was the only boy in the family, it was necessary to be creative when it came to sleeping arrangements. We practiced ladies first, in our home. I simply spread *bedding* on the floor and went to sleep, leaving the bed for the females. This was not an isolated practice. It was common in Roebuck. Other little boys slept in the same manner. Sleeping on the floor was a part of the culture. It was part of our growing up; a rite of passage, so to speak. I am not sure how old I was when I graduated from the floor, but one thing I do know, is that I have no problem sleeping on the floor today. At least my floors are carpeted. Now, when our family gets together, sometimes the floor provides additional sleeping space, with air mattresses providing comfort and protection from the hard floor. We are used to it. At least those of us that were born in Roebuck. For those of the family born in America, floor-sleeping is a new way of life. I was amused when our grandson, Max, came to spend the weekend with us as he always did. Max was almost a year old and always insisted on sleeping in our bed when he visited. However, Hortense was not satisfied with his rest one night, for according to her, "He was tossing and turning all night." On the next weekend visit she had a plan in place. She prepared a bed out of a comforter, sheets and pillows, and set it down on the floor in the den. She and Max slept well that night. I didn't join them but watching them sleep brought back fond memories.

We changed beds often. We had to, and for good reason. They wore out like shoes and demanded replacement. And it was easier for us to acquire a new bed than it was to get a new pair of shoes. I didn't get new shoes that often but I got a new bed fairly frequently. It was a common practice in Roebuck. People replaced their beds on a regular basis. Later, I wondered if wealthy people practiced such luxury. But the poor people of Roebuck did; trading in their beds once, twice, three times or more each year. They did not own golf clubs, cars, or television sets that they could replace when they wanted to, but they were fortunate enough to come by a new bed whenever they needed one.

The bed was one item that poverty didn't, or couldn't, deny Roebuck's families. They would not allow it. They played games with poverty and came out victorious every time. They saw poverty as a condition that was perfect for driving its victims in one of two directions. It could take them here, or it could take them there. There was only one alternative. There was no in between. They knew full well that poverty could have sent them stumbling into the bottomless pit of despair and hopelessness, or it could have been a circumstance that could motivate them to find endless creative alternatives to satisfy their needs and make life a little easier for them and their families. And so *Muddah* and the other mothers in Roebuck chose the latter. They did not whine or complain. They were smart enough to know how to make lemonade out of limes. And they knew about making lemonade, literally. The bed story is only one example of how they dealt with their deficiencies like the champions they were.

When it was time for a new bed, my mother went shopping at the grocery store. At the shop, we used to say back then. At Mr. Gill's shop in Indian Ground or at Mr. Scantlebury's shop in Roebuck; shopping for a bed at the same shop where she shopped for sugar, flour, and *lard* oil. And because she shopped at Scantlebury's or Gill's, the bed was always cheaper and without a down payment, or a monthly bill with added finance charges tacked on for late payments — extra burdens that she did not need to incur. She shopped for, or more accurately, she begged for flour sacks but we called them flour bags. I actually remember my mother asking these two shopkeepers at one time or another to save some empty flour bags for her. I don't think she had to pay for them, and even if she did, they couldn't have cost much. Then again, my mother had such a good relationship with them, as she had with others, that they were willing to grant her request with pleasure. In those days, flour was delivered to the shops in large white bags that were made from a rather durable material.

I can remember the delivery men hoisting the forty pound bags on their shoulders and ambling up the steps to the shop to deposit their load. I am positive that they were as consciously aware that they were delivering flour for food as they were unaware that they were also supplying the raw material for bed-making. It is rather interesting to discover that a recycling program that was good for the environment was in place in Roebuck back then, before recycling became the fashionable project it is today in the USA.

One thing we knew for certain was that our new bed was going to be white in color. We also knew that it would be hand-made, and that it would be authentic; that it would be one of a kind; not mass produced; and not sold in stores. The bed-making process was multidimensional and took some time to complete.

First, the flour bags had to be torn apart and washed by hand. There was no other way to wash them. Everything was hand-washed in Roebuck. My mother would put some water in a pan, or a tub, and armed with a bar of blue soap and a *jooking board* she would make herself comfortable on a slightly elevated rock, with the tub between her legs, as she completed the first cycle by fiercely working each soapy flour bag back and forth several times on the *jooking board* before rinsing them in a tub of fresh water.

I am positive that some may have some notion of what a *jooking board* is, but at the same time, others may not. It is what is known as the wash board today. We called it a *jooking board* in Roebuck, not a wash board; *jooking* being one of those words you will not find in a dictionary. It is a cultural term that is specific to Barbados and to Roebuck. Incidentally, *jooking* had an additional meaning in Roebuck. It meant to punch, or stab with a pointed object. It is the latter meaning we used when we *jooked* another student with a *black lead* at Indian Ground school.

After the rinse cycle came the bleaching phase of the process. The bags had to be bleached and cleansed to perfection because they had gone through many hands by the time they were handed to my mother. The bleach rotation was a completely natural phase that was green and harmless to the environment long before going green became fashionable. Clorox bleach, or Spray and Wash had not made their way to Roebuck at that time. My mother used solar energy as her bleaching agent. She didn't have to collect it. It was there for the taking, everyday of the year in Roebuck. That's one of the reasons we could have a new bed at any time. The energy was free and it was effective; two factors that the poor and creative people in Roebuck used to their advantage. Muddah would spread the wet flour bags flat on the grass, in full view of the blazing sun and would *sprinkle* them with water from time to time to prevent them becoming completely scorched in the hot Roebuck sun. I can plainly recall her reminding us to sprinkle the clothes from time to time while they were being sun-bleached.

A second rinse cycle followed when the bleached bags were placed in the tub of fresh water. This was the shortest phase in the washing process and one that was quite mysterious to me as a young boy growing up in Roebuck. In fact, it is still a mystery to me as to why my mother added *blue* to the water and it did not affect the color of the clothes except to make them whiter. Muddah would dunk the bags in the blue water, swishing each one in the water before holding it up as if to admire her work, or as if she was inspecting them for defects before putting them back into the tub for one last swish before preparing them for drying.

Prior to drying, the excess water had to be removed from the bags. They had to be put through the *wringer*. My mother was the wringer. She had a special wringing technique which she accomplished with ease; one that I learned to use when it was time for me to do my personal laundry, and one that I occasionally use today when necessary. She would take each bag, dripping with water, fold it in half, and turning each wrist simultaneously, but in the opposite direction to each other, while at the same time, moving her hands down the length of the material until most of the excess water was expelled. This is the best explanation I can provide to an uncomplicated procedure but I can tell you that it is the same method I use today when I wring a wet kitchen or bath towel.

The drying phase was the final chapter in the laundering of the flour bags; the would-be bed. In this phase my mother combined the forces of solar energy and wind energy. The flour bags were hung out to dry on the clothes line, flapping in the breeze as the heat of the sun speeded up the evaporation process. In the meantime, other raw materials to be included in the manufacture of the bed were being readied; also by a natural process.

Cuss Cuss grass, a tall slender plant, was already cut and spread under the blazing Roebuck sun. I am not sure if there was ever a scientific name for the cuss cuss but that didn't matter. We had the habit of attaching our own name to things in Roebuck. And even though it was cuss cuss grass to us, its proper name is Khus Khus. Apparently, nobody in Roebuck ever consulted with Ratty concerning its botanical name. He, being the resident botanist who worked in agriculture down in Sedgepond, would probably have known. By the way, Ratty was not his real name. Not many knew that his actual name was Cleon. I did not know that until very recently when I was writing this section of the book. To fully understand the extent to which his real name was hardly used, not even his nephew, Floyd, had ever heard the name Cleon, until he called his sister Jenny, in Barbados for verification at my request. We had a big laugh at our discovery, while once again agreeing how deeply entrenched nicknames were in Roebuck, and how, in many cases, they were the preferred names.

It now occurs to me that I should have been more aggressive in researching the botanical designation of khus khus since I was a diligent student of botany; having passed the subject when I took my GCE exams before leaving high school. But my interest in this natural renewable resource only began to expand during the evolution of the book; so much so that I did my own research into the khus khus with some rather amazing findings. I discovered that its botanical name is *vetiveria zizanoides*, a native of India, and known for its oil that is used in medicine. If the people of Roebuck had only the slightest inkling of its medicinal value, we would have been drinking khus khus' grass tea as well. Additionally, the khus khus was used for making hand fans and mats, and for preventing soil erosion. The oil has a sedative effect and aids in the treatment of emotional outbursts, such as anger, anxiety, restlessness and nervousness. No wonder it delivered such a restful sleep. The people of Roebuck had to have had the awareness, no matter how small, of the restful characteristics of the khus khus, and were ingenious enough to put it to a good and appropriate use.

In either case, a rather large patch of khus khus grew near our house, and we were careful to treat it kindly, knowing that it would be needed time after time. My mother didn't plant the khus khus. Nobody did. There were no khus khus seeds to plant; like we planted lettuce, or carrots or beet seeds. It just grew there and we sort of claimed the rights to it, even though others living close by cut from the patch as well. For sure, Deany Ramsay that lived across from us cut from the permanent supply from time to time. It was a kind of a natural community resource but where it came from, nobody knew. It was as if it was just placed there, destined for some important function and the people of Roebuck were creative enough to perceive a specific purpose for it. I also discovered from my research, that the khus khus is the main ingredient in the perfume with the same name. No wonder our sleep was so sweet.

Khus Khus was a sturdy grass, though I could never figure out why it was called a grass, when most all the other grasses I knew, like pond grass and rabbit meat, grew close to the ground. However, khus khus was tall and grew back rapidly after being harvested with a sickle. It provided a hiding place when we played games in the late evenings. I remember us playing in the khus khus when we were small children, running through the tall grass while playing childhood games. This caused our arms and legs to *bite* us when we took a half bath before going to bed.

Drying the grass, as we named the process, was the next stage in bed production. The green khus khus was laid out on a flat surface near the house, a permanent spot chosen especially for the drying process; a spot in full exposure to the sun by day and the moist dew that *fell* at night. In those days, we in Roebuck believed that dew actually fell from the sky in the same way that the rain did. We supported our belief with the fact that the grass was always wet early in the morning, so our conclusion was that the dew must have fallen from the sky during the night. It was my mother's belief that the dew would make us sick and would encourage us to cover our heads because "the *dew is falling,*" as she usually said. On a more humorous note, I used to think that my mother was saying that the *jew* was falling. In fact, that was exactly what she said. Only much later did I learn that neither the dew, nor the *jew* was falling.

I can remember my mother ordering us to go and turn the grass so that the sun could work its drying magic on the green color, which would eventually begin to turn brown, like hay. Drying did not mean that the khus khus was wet. All it meant was that the grass had to turn brown before it could be used to make a bed. And the drying process needed the *hot, hot, hot* Roebuck sun. That's how we used to talk in Roebuck. It was in our culture to repeat some adjectives three times for emphasis, as if no one would believe us if we were not repetitious; as in my head is hurting bad, bad, bad, or I am hungry, hungry, hungry. Only recently, I was talking with Floyd about a woman we both knew from Roebuck and to hear Floyd describe her as being a miserable, miserable, miserable woman was hilarious.

Periodically, we would turn the grass so the sun would dry it and in time we would observe the slow chemical change taking place before our very eyes; one without the addition of chemical formulas, test tubes and experimental laboratories. The heat from the sun was all that was needed, and even though it rained on the khus khus from time to time, we did not pick it up and hide it from the showers when we saw that the rain was *setting up*. We always said that the rain was setting up when rain clouds threatened that a downpour was imminent.

I have often wondered why the people of Roebuck never thought of adding more variety to their grass beds. Why did it always have to be a dried-grass bed? It has surprised me that no one had dared to experiment with a green khus khus grass bed. At least a second model would have provided an option and a choice in beds. It would have encouraged competition and diversity to the bed-making industry. And who knows? A green khus khus grass bed might have proven to be the stronger and more durable of the two models. Probably, the Roebuck upper class and its culturally elite might have opted for one over the other to distinguish themselves as being superior in taste, or in status. "I have a green khus khus grass bed," they might have boasted. But that distinction never happened, thereby preserving the singular model production.

Meanwhile, the flour bag material was stitched together in such a way as to form a container, or a receptacle, to receive the dried khus khus. An opening was left for that very purpose. We never categorized our beds into single beds, queen size beds or king size beds. Those sizes and distinctions were unknown to the residents of Roebuck, so my mother did not set out to make a single, a queen or a king. She simply made a bed without paying attention to measurement, size or brand. And each time the final product was perfect in every way.

Muddah seemed to know exactly when the drying phase was complete. She was the experienced authority that oversaw the bed-making project from inception to completion. We could tell without formal and direct instruction that the cultural art of bed-making was being passed on to our time. Her management of the project told us that she had done this all her life. The great thing about lessons in culture is that many behaviors are caught rather than taught. Bed-making fell into both categories because my mother took time to demonstrate how certain aspects of the project were to be done.

Chronologically, the *stuffing* procedure followed the drying phase. This was my favorite part of the entire experience. I can remember being totally involved in the action of the stuffing phase. It was a joint effort but we were not without direction and supervision. My mother was very particular concerning this aspect of the venture. She was specific. It had to be done right. As I write this account, I now realize that she was teaching us valuable lessons using the bed making process as her teaching aid.

Muddah was actually teaching us that good values and pride in a job well done are not held in reserve for a certain class. Neither are they meant to be monopolized by a privileged stratum or group. Even in simple things, and in those tasks that appear insignificant and without priority, there is a pride and a standard to be reached and cherished, even by the poor. And the bed-making venture, along with so many other teachable moments, was responsible for transmitting not only a culture but also life's values and principles. My sisters and I owe my mother a debt of gratitude, which is going to take a lifetime to settle. The only way we can do this successfully is to pass on these lessons to our children. I hope I can do it half as well as I have been taught.

"Stuff the corners first," my mother would instruct, accompanied by an accurate demonstration. The opening through which the green-to-brown khus khus, now *posturpedic,* or *tempurpedic* material was introduced was always wide enough to accommodate the stuffing material but it was usually difficult to get it into the corners with the perfection and the precision Muddah demanded. Consequently, she always had an answer that was practical and precise. Taking a long stick she would demonstrate how to poke the khus khus into the four corners first, making sure they were stuffed to their capacity until they bulged. The protruding corners signaled the completion of this one aspect of the job. And with the corners inflated, it was then safe to proceed with the not so precise part of stuffing the middle of the bed.

We randomly dumped the dried khus khus into the open space with only one requirement as a guide — making sure that the grass was distributed as evenly as possible. We didn't have to use a spirit level to test our accuracy but instinct and a keen eye told us when our stuffing was satisfactory to my mother's standards. The entire stuffing process took place outside our house in the same area where the drying occurred. Tracking grass in the house would have resulted in creating extra clean up and unnecessary work. The entire process was set up like a factory system to ease and alleviate as much difficulty as possible.

I refer to the next phase as the delivery phase; that of moving the bed to its final resting place inside the house to take its place on the bedstead. I equate this aspect of the process to moving a rocket, or space shuttle, to the launching pad in preparation for launch. Surprisingly, the comparison is not too ridiculous, for in retrospect, the sight of that big, high, white, flour bag bed now reminds me of some form of an extraterrestrial body waiting to fly back to its home in outer space when conditions were perfect. But it never flew. It remained there for the entire warranty period, or for its natural life span; whichever came first.

Moving the bed to the inside was the last phase and all hands were needed. The finished bed was not heavy but was awkward to carry; in the same way as lifting a mattress. If you have ever helped someone move, you know exactly what I mean. Since moving to the U.S I have often helped friends and church members move from one house to another and each time the mattresses were tricky to lift and carry. In Roebuck, once the bed was done, we would grab hold of the corners and lift; keeping it flat until we reached the door to the back house, where we would turn the bed on its side, without allowing it to drag on the ground, and ease it through, being careful not to tear the material as we went through the door and into the bedroom to set it down on the bedstead. The opening through which the khus khus was poked was left open on purpose so that we could *make up* the bed when we got out of bed in the mornings. We didn't *make* the bed when we got up. In Roebuck we *made up* the bed. The first step in *making up the bed* was to put our hand through the opening and stir up the khus khus to help maintain the shape and condition of the bed for as long as possible. Floyd reminded me that for many of us, *making up the bed* in the mornings simply meant taking up the bedding off the floor.

With everything in place it was time for my mother to issue the final word of waning — the manufacturers' limited warranty statement. It was a verbal one. Not a written one attached to the product itself. It was also a personal one, and it was directed towards me. It was concise and issued in plain and simple language in the imperative form. "Don't pee this bed." That's it.

It was a warning that was prompted by my history and reputation. This bed would die a death similar to those that preceded it, and like those that would come later. They all had one common enemy. Me. I would pee my bed almost nightly. And several times a night. Not that I suffered from an incurable bladder ailment, or that I didn't know that I was peeing in the bed. I knew that I was lying there peeing away; conscious of it all the way. And to be honest, I was not the only little boy in Roebuck who was wetting his bed every night. Others did the same. And like me, they would *hang out* their wet clothes and wet *bedding* on the line every morning to dry in the hot Roebuck sun. My mother would warn "Make sure you pee before you go to bed." But that warning, though well meaning, didn't always help the situation.

In my defense, there were several situations that were to be blamed for perpetuating the bed-wetting habit that my peers and I perfected with time. I am hoping that a brief explanation will be enough to garner a measure of understanding and even sympathy. Not only for myself but for all the other little boys who grew up in Roebuck with me during the bed-wetting era. During *crop time* when sugar cane was plentiful, we would *suck* so much cane that by the time we were ready to go to bed our *bellies* were full of cane juice.

We became experts at peeling the cane using our sharp canine teeth and sucking the juice from cane after cane until we were satisfied. Stealing sugar cane from Sedgepond Plantation was easy if Mr. Straker, the watchman, wasn't around. Georgie Straker, we used to call him, was also known to *run* us for *teefing* bananas as well as coconuts, which we picked to get at the coconut water and the soft white *jelly*. In time, we gained expertise in finding and *breaking out* only the best quality *canes* from the particular *cane piece* where they were planted. Brown Skin girl, with its clear skin, soft texture and distinct taste was by far our favorite. Other types of cane were sweet as well but were no match for Brown Skin Girl.

But there were also legal sources that contributed to our bedwetting and our parents played a large role in this aspect. They would bring home a small supply of sugar cane after working in the *cane piece* all day. This supply was supplemented by another exciting and fairly dangerous action on our part. It was fun to run behind A33, the Austin lorry and A115, the Bedford, doing our best to pull out a cane or two as the loaded lorries made their way to one of two sugar factories; Haymans in St. Peter, or Porters, in St. James. Sometimes we got some from an unlikely source. Occasionally, the men riding on the moving lorries loaded with sugar cane, would throw some down for us to chase after as they raced through Roebuck on their way to the cane factory. I now think they had as much fun as we did as they watched us compete for the sugary treats.

Lorries were not the only means of transportation of sugar cane to Porters or Haymans. At times, a Massey Ferguson tractor, pulling one or two loaded trailers would also make their way from Sedge-pond through Roebuck on their way to the factory. With all this cane available, it was not uncommon to find a small stockpile in many homes in Roebuck. And so, we sucked cane until we were full. As a result, it should not have been at all surprising that our young bladders were incapable of processing such a large volume of cane juice in such a short time before bed time. And bed time came early for young boys in Roebuck. The only logical place to find relief from the overflow of cane juice was the bed.

In addition, I was afraid of the dark, and didn't want to get up at night to go outside to pee. We never said urinate in Roebuck. It was always pee. We usually kept a basin, or a *topsy*, also known as a *poe*, under the bed for that very purpose. I would use them sometimes but it was a lot easier to lie in my bed and pee; especially if it was storming outside. I didn't mind the rain because the sound of heavy rain beating down on the galvanized *house top* was like music, ser-enading us as we slept. Thunder and lightning were a different set of circumstances; frightening circumstances. There was no way I was going to get down off the bed to pee under those conditions. I was terribly scared of thunder and lightning. And if my fear of thunder and lightning was bad, my dislike for the darkness was amplified ten fold, especially if someone in the neighborhood had died. Roebuck culture taught that the dead person would come back during the night in the form of a *duppie* to get us.

I remember when Hartley Bishop from Indian Ground drowned in the dam in Sedgepond. He was a young boy like me. I knew him well. We used to take out our sheep together to graze in the morn-ing and go back to bring them in in the evening. And when George Best hung himself in a tree in the grass piece, I was scared to death for a quite some time. Getting up to pee in the middle of the night was out of the question. There was no way I was going to get out of the bed to pee. I did it right there in the bed. My mother's admoni-tion to "Go and pee before you go to bed" did not work for a long time. Like other things, I had to grow out of it.

Before leaving this discussion on pee and urine, there is one true story to tell, and this one truly distinguishes the differences between the Roebuck culture and that of the American way of doing things; or saying things, as is the case in the following case study. I was the new principal of a small church school in Chattanooga at the time this happened. One morning, one of the teachers came to me and informed me that one of her students had had an *accident*. Thinking that he was involved in a vehicular accident or something of that nature, I immediately inquired as to how he was doing.

"He had an accident in the classroom," she said

"What happened," I inquired. "Did he hurt himself?

"He had an accident in his pants," she explained.

"What kind of accident? I asked, thinking that the boy had injured his private area because he had fallen, or was involved in an altercation with another student. "He did number one in his pants," she replied, while at the same time noticing my apparent lack of understanding. "He wet his pants," she concluded, laughing at my complete ignorance of the cultural language surrounding such matters.

Eventually, she got around to teaching me that there was also a number two that had to do with the other stuff. But I had two silent rhetorical questions as we dissolved the conversation. Why was it called an accident in these parts? And why did they have to attach a numerical value to personal bodily functions? In Roebuck we did no such thing. We made it as uncomplicated as possible. An accident happened when two cars smashed up in each other; not when a boy messed in his pants. "He peed in his pants," or "He *do do* in his pants," we used to say; without assigning numbers.

But pee and dried khus khus grass were not supposed to come in contact with each other. They were the bitterest of enemies, and when that combination happened in Roebuck, at least three unpleasant situations were sure to develop very soon. First and foremost, it created a breeding ground for *chinks*, and a visiting *cockaroach* or *santapee* every now and then was not uncommon. Somehow, *muskeeters* did not appreciate those conditions and decided to stay away. By the way, we never said bed bugs in Roebuck. They were chinks. Their population increased noticeably as they appeared to relish the *rank* conditions that encouraged the explosion in their numbers. The hungry little visiting creatures would come around often to feed on my blood, and in time they were not so little anymore. They grew measurably from the nightly nutrition I was providing them. And so they came back for more night after night to withdraw from the blood bank. When I felt them crawling I would trap them between my thumb and fore finger and squeeze them until they popped, spilling blood in the process. The bed bore the marks of the evidence, as the once white flour bags were now dotted with the blood of my victims.

In addition to the chinks, the wet grass would generate a putrid stench, which my mother would describe as *pissy* and *rank*. She would say from time to time that "It smells rank in here." I am certain she said rank. That is what I heard. And she was correct. I had to look it up in the dictionary only recently while working on this manuscript. It means to have a rancid and offensive odor. How did she know how to use that word, especially since it has multiple meanings? I couldn't find *pissy* in the dictionary, but I am sure that you get the idea. But my mother did show signs of intellectual brilliance ever so often. This was one of those times.

As was to be expected, the nightly drenching had a rotting effect on the grass, hence its destruction was imminent, and plans for a new bed would once again be considered, and the manufacturing process would once again be put in motion. Anyone who has, or had a history of bed wetting, knows the discomfort that comes with lying in a wet bed and wearing wet clothes all night long. It seemed as if morning delayed its coming on purpose, just to prolong my misery. I relived this awful experience countless nights while growing up in Roebuck. Nevertheless, the *cocks* crowing at dawn was long anticipated music to my ears. It meant that relief was on the way and that the time to end the sodden wretchedness was almost at hand. It would soon be time to get up and hang the soaked clothes on the clothes line to dry in preparation for a repeat performance the following night. Incidentally, the proverb *misery loves company* is true. And I certainly had lots of company. Without a doubt, many little boys lived the rank experience as well.

CHAPTER SIX

Biscuits, Gravy, Bakes and Crackers

What I do remember very clearly is the truth that racism and other aspects of racial hatred and bigotry had no place to grow, or even thought of in Roebuck.

When I decided to move to the USA, I knew right away that I had to adapt to a way of living that was drastically different from my simple way of living in Roebuck. Although we had lived several years in St. Croix in the US Virgin Islands before the big move to the mainland, and had picked up a little of what to expect as far as cultural shifts were concerned, I was still in for a rude awakening when the actual move finally happened. Leaving behind the eighty degree weather of the tropical Caribbean to land in the frigid fall of a Michigan September was only a very slight foretaste of what was to come; a series of adjustments that began with me having to *draw up under* Hortense at night much more than I was used to.

Understandably, in Roebuck I had no need for a sweater. I never had one. Didn't need one in Roebuck where the average yearly temperature was about seventy-five degrees. And I could get by quite comfortably without long sleeved shirts. I hardly wore a hat, or cap, even though the sun would beat down unmercifully most of the time. In Roebuck, I was used to dressing light; a shirt, pants, and shoes and socks as needed. But to be suddenly forced into layers of clothing that did not even keep me completely warm was a bit much, and downright uncomfortable. Now I had to wear a *vest*.

151

It took me quite a long time to refer to it as an undershirt. In Roebuck it was a vest. We did not speak of a vest as part of a three-piece suit. That was *waist coat*, pronounced *west cut* in Roebuck — the part of the suit that was under the jacket; the suit coat, as it is called here in America. Not that anybody in Roebuck wore three-piece suits any way.

Then there was the thermal underwear. Long Johns, they called them. And they were long. In Roebuck I never heard about long underwear. We were lucky if we had short ones but having to make the shift to lengthy underwear took some time to get used to. Then I had to hide my shirt under a sweater and cover the sweater with a heavy coat, cover my ears with ear muffs, plus wear a hat, thick socks and winter boots that did not always keep me from slipping and sliding in the snow. And a scarf, of all things. Having to wear two pairs of underwear was not only comical at first. It turned out to be one of the biggest adjustments I had to make when the real winter finally rolled around.

At first, the long johns made the case for a personal wardrobe malfunction that provided a good laugh on many occasions until I managed to maneuver the mechanism with ease. I remember the first time I wore them and had the need to rush to the public restroom in a store in Benton Harbor, Michigan. I almost wet myself trying to maneuver the complexity of the double underwear situation. I was an expert in handling one pair but that evening I had to work feverishly at mastering two pairs. Before I left Michigan two years later, I had become an expert in handling the short john-long john mechanism. Why long johns? I used to ask myself. Why not long James, or Peter, for that matter?

I had come a long way from Roebuck to be a graduate student at Andrews University in Berrien Springs, and later at Michigan State University in East Lansing. Yet, I had problems accepting everyday scientific principles as they related to winter and the strange impact it had on nature, and on people. Many a day I became rather depressed when the days were dark and overcast and the sunshine was absent, so much so that I lost my motivation to attend classes. And when the sun finally came out for a day or two, I wondered why it was shining so brightly and still the weather was so cold. One more thing that was terribly troubling that added to my quest for adaptation was the appearance of the trees once the really cold weather showed up. They had no leaves; quite unlike the trees in Roebuck that always had theirs. It was not easy to accept why a natural phenomenon as simple as leafless trees was so psychologically depressing, and even physically draining.

Later, when the summer finally arrived and the sun was at last on full-time duty, I prayed that it would *go down* a little earlier, around 6:00 PM as it did in Roebuck; instead of 9:00 PM, so that I could tell that the day was over and I could fall asleep. In Roebuck we did not speak of the sun setting; only of the sun going down. And we also spoke of the sun *coming up* in the morning, as opposed to the sun rising.

As if the dressing situation was not enough, driving provided major complexities as well. In Roebuck we drove on the *left hand side* of the road. Even in St. Croix, an American territory in the Caribbean, where we lived for four years, driving was done on the left. It took me a while to get used to this aspect of the American way of doing things. And having to drive in layered clothing, coupled with the problem of having to remember to drive on the right, provided its own set of near misses on the road. We had purchased a huge 1973 LTD Ford rather cheaply, and driving back from Benton Harbor to Berrien Springs one day, after coming to a *major stop* I made the turn and proceeded to drive on the left, only to encounter a large truck barreling down on us. Thankfully, I managed to self-correct before a major catastrophe occurred.

As tumultuous as the dressing and driving adaptations might have been, there were numerous other aspects of my adopted culture that were quite interesting and somewhat humorous and very comical to say the least; especially when it came to food and eating. A reminder that this book is primarily about words and how they define a culture is relevant at this juncture. The sections that follow, set the scene for the cultural scenarios that centered on food, its preparation, and the adjustments we had to make. Hortense is extremely good at striking a balance when preparing food that I was accustomed to with the new American dishes I was to adopt. Still, the clash of culinary cultures was inevitable and happened quite frequently. As in the case with biscuits.

In Roebuck we ate a lot of biscuits with corned beef, or sometimes with butter. So I grew up confident that a biscuit is a biscuit, no matter where I went. Even though they came under various name brands and variations, to me a biscuit was a biscuit in England, in America, or even Australia. But once in America, I came to discover in quite an interesting encounter that a biscuit was not a biscuit, and that I had to restructure my thinking, as well as my appetite, as far as the biscuit was concerned. I think it would be helpful at this point in time to draw a distinction between the American biscuit and the Roebuck version, and also to draw attention to the truth that this is one of those cultural realities where a word, such as biscuit, with a similar spelling and exact pronunciation, has a completely different meaning and interpretation. An American biscuit is *a small round piece of bread that rises with baking powder or soda and is then baked in an oven*. I lifted the definition directly from the dictionary so it has to be accurate.

But Nola from Roebuck would have held on to her *belly* and laughed so hard until she cried in disagreement, if she only knew that the Roebuck biscuit was not the only kind of biscuit there is, and that the appearance of another model was vastly different from the flat and dry versions that Roebuck enjoyed back in the day. By the way, we never said stomach or tummy in Roebuck. Always belly.

"Biscuits are made of flour," Nola would agree. "But they are flat and square and dry, and sometimes round, or sweet, as is the case with Shirley Biscuits," she would say. "And we don't put them in the oven," she would continue. "We buy them from the shop." My cousin, Charleston, would concur without question, but would go a little further in his description, and refer to the biscuit as a square meal. Charleston was the comedian in the family. He was the same one who once said that a corned beef was the most stupid food he knows. His reasoning being that the corned beef locked itself in a can and left the key on the outside. I now wonder after all these years, if Charleston should now alter his assessment of the corned beef, especially in light of the fact that Eucklyn Thompson from nearby Indian Ground, who was nicknamed Corned Beef as a boy, presently holds a prominent leadership position as Senior Superintendent of Police on the Barbados Police Force.

I was introduced to biscuits in the South; Chattanooga, Tennessee to be exact. I had spent two years in Southern California while attending Loma Linda University and I can't recall having an encounter with biscuits during the time I was there. I had a good American friend, Susan, and while our families ate together occasionally, she did not introduce me to the American version of the biscuit, probably because it was not a Californian cultural item.

One Sunday, shortly after my family arrived in Chattanooga, I was invited to attend a breakfast meeting in connection with the job I had landed as principal of our church school. On arriving at the meeting venue I heard biscuits and gravy being discussed as items on the menu "Biscuits and gravy?" I mused to myself. Keeping in mind Nola's definition of a Roebuck biscuit I was sure I knew what biscuits were and I was positive that I knew what gravy was. In Roebuck we used to call it gravy sometimes but it was *sauce* most of the time.

We had lots of sauce in Roebuck. We would serve it with rice, coo-coo, or with *stew food*. My mother would get upset with Lane (Elaine), my oldest sister, when the sauce was too watery. She would laugh and say that the food was swimming in the sauce. Somehow

Elaine seldom got it to the right consistency.

Ms. Scantlebury did not sell gravy mix in her shop so Elaine made hers in a frying pan in our kitchen from a combination of *lard oil*, onion, tomatoes, black pepper, water and *salt fish*, or *red herring*. It was always salt fish in Roebuck. Not cod, as is the popular name today. I am sure she added other stuff as well. She made her own *browning* by burning sugar in a frying pan. When flying fish or chicken back was available, she would switch between flying fish gravy and *chicken back* gravy. So we would have fish sauce or chicken gravy with our food, but never biscuits with gravy. Who thought of that idea? What would it taste like? What would it look like? Would it be enough to satisfy my hunger? These were some of the deep questions running through my mind as I waited for breakfast that morning. After all, the biscuits and the gravy to which I was accustomed were two foods that never associated with each other. They never mixed. They were like enemies. If Elaine had ever attempted to serve biscuits with her gravy in Roebuck, it would have been disastrous. I could not imagine a marriage between the two.

When breakfast was finally served I chuckled in silence and with some degree of amusement at the sight of the biscuits and I was unable to resist the urge to comment to the person ahead of me in the buffet line, "Those are not biscuits. Biscuits are flat and thin and square." Surprisingly, the gravy was whitish and thick and lumpy. Not watery and thin as I had expected. But after all those questions and misgivings, I must admit with all honesty that the combination went down surprisingly well. It was tasty and satisfying and a second *share* was in order. Some time after that I learned that my Roebuck biscuit was actually a *cracker* in the United States. As time went on, I had to adjust my thinking concerning the use and new meaning of cracker; that it was not always just a food item, but that it also carried a stigma that was ugly and derogatory. Strangely enough, I had encountered the *C* word in Indian Ground a long,

long time ago, without even having the slightest inkling of the racial implications and the alternate meaning it carried in the United States. But more on this later.

As I mentioned earlier, we ate biscuits regularly in Roebuck. Biscuits were a staple; like rice, yams and eddoes, or cassava. I remember my mother dunking biscuits in her tea at times to make a kind of sop. On Sundays when breakfast consisted largely of a bowl or a *tot* of *oat flakes* we had biscuits to accompany the cereal; at that time not fully understanding its nutritional impact. We probably thought it was a food item reserved for poor folk. Today, I rely on my oatmeal to provide me with the energy I need to begin my day. My mother thought it was special; there was something nutritionally superior about it. She didn't use those big words, choosing only to say that "It is good for you" and reserving it for Sunday breakfast.

Muddah would make a large pot full of oat flakes every Sunday morning to keep our bellies full to last us all day through Sunday school at 10:00 and church that followed an hour or so later. We did not have oat flakes during the week, so when we thought of Sunday, we automatically thought of oat flakes. I remember how Muddah would bring a generous mixture of water and cow's milk to a boil, being careful not to let it boil over, before adding the flakes, stirring it with a long pot spoon until it was thick enough to the desired consistency. She would sometimes sweeten it with sugar but most times she used sweetened condensed milk, always adding a couple leaves of *bay leaf* for added flavor.

We didn't eat our oatmeal. We drank it. My mother did not make it into a thick food as is done in the US. She made it so thin that we could put the tot or the bowl to our *heads* and drink it off. We could use a spoon if we wanted to but we still drank our oatmeal. Hers was more liquid than solid, so we never ate it. And I still prefer it that way today.

I had an interesting encounter with oatmeal when traveling in another city. I decided to order a serving from the breakfast menu in the hotel restaurant where I was a guest. I think it was in San Antonio when I was attending a conference there. When the waitress returned with my order I immediately thought that she had misunderstood my accent and had brought me something else instead. She had to convince me that what she had brought me was indeed oatmeal. It was thick and brownish and very ugly and unappealing. Nasty, as some American children would say; the same way my students describe food served in the cafeteria that is not to their liking. Try as I may, I have not yet reached the place where I can describe food as being nasty. That's an American thing. In Roebuck, nasty was reserved for something dirty; like clothes, or shoes, or someone's house, but never food.

I laughed to myself the first time I heard someone say "Those oats were so good." In Roebuck we never said *those oats* like Americans say *those grits*, or *those greens*. We never pluralized our oat flakes in this way. We reserved the plural form for things like peas, or potatoes, or tomatoes. But never those grits, or those greens, or even those eggs that are prepared in a scrambled form. "Those eggs are good," I heard someone comment about the scrambled eggs served at a breakfast when I first came to this country. I was aware that there had to be several eggs that were scrambled together but I was quite surprised at the '*those eggs*' comment. On second thought, we did say those eggs in Roebuck but only when counting the number of eggs we regularly found in the bushes, left there by one of our *fowls* or ducks in a hidden nest nearby before they were hatched into chickens or ducklings.

In order to cool our oat flakes in the morning we would stand on the step and pour the oatmeal from one tot or cup to another, watching the steam rise until the oat flakes were safe to drink with biscuits, or with *salt bread*, a name that was quite misleading since there was nothing salty about salt bread; a loaf that is fist-size, almost round, and without a definite taste unless smeared with butter, or with a slice of cheese, or eaten with fried flying fish.

In Roebuck, biscuits came in three versions. Eclipse and Sodabix were flat and square in shape, so it should not be at all surprising that Cousin Charleston once joked that they were a square meal. The Eclipse was my favorite. It was much harder than the Sodabix and could easily dislodge a *shaky* tooth if one wasn't careful. In Roebuck we never talked about a tooth being loose. It was shaky. But there was also a round biscuit, the Sunrise. Sunrise biscuits were even harder than the Eclipse, and could prove difficult to chew by small children, and even by some adults, especially in cases where teeth were missing. No wonder my mother would soak them in her tea, or in her oat flakes. Not that she had missing teeth. It was just her way of softening her biscuits.

Eaten by themselves, biscuits were somewhat dry and almost tasteless; except for the Shirley biscuit that was sweet to the taste. Regular biscuits demanded a thorough chewing and a lot of *spit* before swallowing. In Roebuck we did not speak of saliva. Spit was the local term. We got our biscuits from Mr. Scantlebury's shop and would spread butter on them and eat with *sweet water* for lunch when we ran home from Indian Ground School and there was nothing else to be had. Very often they were served as part of a full meal, or as a snack at other times when we were hungry. Besides, fried flying fish with biscuits was a real tasty treat, especially during flying fish season when the fish was cheap and plentiful. But biscuits served with corned beef, was always the best.

In Roebuck, we didn't make biscuits in our kitchen like American make theirs from scratch or purchase them from the store and finish them in the oven at home. But we did make *bakes* from scratch. At face value the word *bakes* may appear to be a verb, especially to those born in the US culture, but used in context, it is quickly recognized as a noun; a thing; a naming word; a food item. And what is more misleading about bakes is the fact that they are not even prepared by the baking process. They are fried. Deep fried. Practically everybody in Roebuck had bakes for breakfast on a regular basis. Sometimes, along with *tea*, they were all we could afford. They were as standard a breakfast item as pancakes or waffles are to the American breakfast menu.

Interestingly enough, bakes were not considered a poor man's delicacy in Roebuck, simply because we did not believe that we were poor. Poverty was never discussed. But whatever the reason, bakes were had by all. As a boy I could smell them in the crisp early morning air as they were being fried all over the neighborhood. I never heard of anybody complaining of not liking bakes. Not that complaining would have helped. We had to eat them or "starve to death," as my mother would jokingly encourage.

I laughingly remember the first time I tried to explain how to make bakes to some American friends. After I had carefully gone through my presentation, one of them blurted out, "You mean pancakes." Obviously, I had not done as splendid a job as I had hoped. But bakes are not pancakes. They may strike a slight resemblance to miniature pancakes but they are not even close to pancakes. They are not pancakes even though the ingredients may be almost similar. One thing is for sure; you won't find bakes mix, like pancake mix or biscuit dough in a can or box in the baking goods aisle of your favorite food store. Neither can you pick it up in the frozen section of the local supermarket. Better yet, bakes would not qualify for inclusion in the products that line your local heath food establishment. They would never pass the health test. Too greasy. Really greasy. You have to mix them in a bowl in your kitchen from scratch. That makes them authentic and truly Bajan (Barbadian).

I never claimed to be good at making bakes. I hardly tried my hand at making them when I was growing up in Roebuck. I usually left that job to those in my Roebuck family who had the expertise. I don't know why but all of a sudden my sister Yvonne, has emerged as the official bakes maker in the family, making them in New York from time to time. Strangely enough, there was no official Roebuck recipe for making bakes. My guess is that the cook in each family added his or her special twist to the standard ingredients. Whatever the variations in production, bakes were Roebuck's main breakfast food; except on Sunday. Even today they remain quite popular. At the time of writing, my friend Floyd, and his wife Shirley, were visiting Barbados. He called me all excited to let me know that he had stopped by his sister, Jenny, and she had made some bakes for them, and that his American wife had thoroughly enjoyed them. I doubt Jenny opened up her favorite cookbook to find a recipe on how to make bakes. She, having studied *Domestic Science,* must have whipped up a batch of the fast food in no time. My mother and sisters didn't consult a cook book either when making bakes, or anything else. Nobody in Roebuck did. And yet, they cooked peas and rice, boiled chicken soup, and made stew food to perfection. Or close to it.

Surprisingly, there are official recipes for making bakes; one that I found while researching the topic in *West Indian Cookery* by Phyllis Clarke, a former lecturer in *Domestic Science* at the Government Training College for Teachers in Trinidad and Tobago. And another one I found in *Sky Juice and Flying Fish,* written by Jessica B. Harris. Much later, my friend, Floyd, sent me one as well. But I didn't try my hand at following any of these recipes, simply because they are not authentic by Roebuck standards. These recipes had one common feature. They all called for measured ingredients. And the people of Roebuck did not measure anything when making their bakes.

I confess that I had come up with a recipe of my own before I found those that are mentioned. At the same time, I must admit that I have not put my method to the test prior to making it available to the world. I am certain that many in Roebuck will want to weigh in, either to compliment me, or to wonder if I have forgotten my Roebuck roots. Before we proceed, it is to be understood that I am basing my methodology on the practice that the people in Roebuck perfected when cooking; meaning that there is no mention whatever in my recipe of measuring the ingredients: no cup of this, or a teaspoon of this, or a tablespoon of that. That's how the people in Roebuck cooked. My guess is that they still do.

Here we go. Make a batter with flour and water in a large bowl. Keep in mind that batter is not a word we ever used in Roebuck. We simply mixed the flour and water together. However, the mixture has got to be fairly thick but still not as thick as when making bread. Add a little salt, black pepper, onion and sugar to taste. Heat a generous amount of *lard oil* in a frying pan until it is hot. Hot, hot, hot, as we used to say in Roebuck. Use a large spoon to dip out individual spoonfuls of the mixture and place in the oil, keeping in mind that the bakes have to be flat and not too thick. Turn each bake over when it appears brown around the edges. Remove and place on a plate to cool. Eat warm or cold. Bakes go well with tea or juice. They may even go well with beer or wine but I have not tried the latter combination so don't hold me to it.

One thing to keep in mind is that there were no low fat, low calorie bakes in Roebuck. What Roebuck bakes lacked in nutritious value, they made up for it in grease content. One way to check the grease and caloric content was to put a couple of them in a paper bag and let sit for a brief time and observe what happened. The physical makeup of the bag underwent a dramatic transformation. It was as if a chemical change happened that produced a completely different product, complete with color change, as well as a new texture.

As if the difference in biscuits has not already ginned up enough cultural disagreement, there is one more thing that I find rather alarming. Although I can't recall with any degree of specificity the first time I heard an American say that she was *eating* soup, I have heard it said so often since the initial time that it has to be included it in the list of cultural differences that exists between the two cultures. In Roebuck, we didn't eat soup. We drank soup. And for the life of me, I can't figure out why Americans say what they say about soup, because there is hardly anything to eat in a bowl of American soup. Granted, there may be a few pieces of noodles, or the occasional piece of chicken or beef in a bowl of American soup but by and large the overwhelming majority is the watery broth to drink. Yet, they say they eat soup. Some time ago I placed an order for potato soup in a restaurant. Needless to say, there was no noticeable potato in the soup when the order arrived. And the bowl was small. Not that I was expecting a huge bowl but by Roebuck standards, but the bowl was tiny, and the soup was nothing like the potato soup I was used to in Roebuck.

In Roebuck, soup was a big affair. It was a conglomeration of everything from chunks of sweet potato, yam, green banana, breadfruit, and dumplings, to wedges of beef, or chicken, all boiled together with split peas acting as the thickening agent. That's the reason we always said we were *boiling* soup instead of cooking soup. Our soup was a real carbohydrate and starch convention. Although there was a lot more to eat in a bowl of soup, people in Roebuck still said that they drank soup. People in Roebuck made real dumplings; not the small weight loss imitation type as is the case with the American chicken and dumplings. The Roebuck version of the dumpling was fist-size, and the baking powder made them rise and float on top of the soup like white cumulus clouds. I was traveling on a plane a while ago and had a private laugh when the clouds reminded me of the dumplings my sister, Elaine, used to make when she *boiled* soup. She never seemed to get the dumplings just right. Even her husband, Kenneth, made fun of her dumplings years later.

In Roebuck, dumplings were also a major item in a dish known by all as *stew food*. Like soup, stew food was a combination of the starches but the difference was striking. In stew food, the *ground provisions* were thoroughly boiled *down* and served without the soupy liquid as is the case with soup. Stew food was served with a lot of salt fish gravy, flying fish gravy, or even with *red herring* sauce.

We never said smoked herring in Roebuck. To us it was always red herring.

Even rice in America is not like rice in Roebuck. Cooked American rice is plain. Just rice. There is nothing in it. In Roebuck however, rice came with several options: pigeon peas and rice, split peas and rice, black eye peas and rice, even green banana, or bread fruit and rice. People in Roebuck were very creative with rice to prevent monotony. A wedge of *salt beef* or a *pig tail* was sometimes added for flavor. As per my mother's instructions, the peas were boiled first before adding the rice. More water was added as needed until the rice was cooked and the pot *dried down,* as my mother would say.

By far, the most popular dish in Roebuck was *cou cou*. There is no food or dish in the US culture that is a counterpart to cou cou; maybe corn meal porridge, but that's not a fair comparison. We never called it corn meal cou cou in Roebuck; just cou cou, even though the Roebuck people also cooked banana cou cou and breadfruit cou cou. Simply put, cou cou is corn meal cooked with okra in a pot of boiling water. But there is nothing simple about cooking cou cou and it is not as simple to prepare as I just described it. It takes an expert to cook it, so much so that my mother did not leave its preparation to anyone else. She was the resident expert. Elaine was not allowed to cook it. She could be trusted to boil the okra until my mother got home. The rest was left to Muddah. I can see her now pouring the unmeasured corn meal into a pot of boiling okra water, sweating as she *stirred* the mixture with a *cou cou stick,* a paddle-shaped tool made especially for stirring cou cou. You had to say stirring the cou cou; not mixing the cou cou. Stirring was the cultural term and had to be used in cou cou preparation. It was not uncommon to hear my mother say that she was stirring cou cou for dinner.

The trick to preparing cou cou was in the stirring of the thing. If the stirring was not expertly done, the end result would be *lumpy* and uneven, and quite awkward to eat. Cou cou was also served with gravy, especially flying fish gravy that was made with either fried or *steam* fish, as we used to describe it in Roebuck. That being said, I was never a fan of cou cou. To this day, I still don't like it. I am probably the only person from Roebuck, or Barbados, for that matter, who does not fancy our national dish. I adore corn meal porridge, but not cou cou.

My wife Hortense, who is Jamaican, was first introduced to cou cou by a friend from Trinidad when she was still in college. She told me afterward that she did not find it tasty and had vowed never to try it ever again. That was until she visited my family in New York and my mother *stirred* cou cou for dinner one day. She was sold, and since then has continued to proclaim that my mother was the best cou cou maker ever. When I was a boy growing up in Roebuck, I thought so much of my grandmother that I would always go to her house in Indian Ground every evening for a second dinner, especially when cou cou was on the menu at my house in Roebuck. One day, when I arrived at Ma Ma's house a big disappointment awaited me. Mama had cooked cou cou as well. But like all good grandmothers that spoiled their only grandson, she hurriedly prepared me something else.

I mentioned the word *cracker* previously and promised to give it further attention at a later point because there is a story I wanted to tell. One day, when I was still a small boy, I had gone to Indian Ground to visit my grandmother, as I so often did. We were standing outside and my aunt, Gloria, was joking around with Coursey Marshall, a young man that lived close by. That was the personality of Aunt Gloria. To this day she is still full of humor and still known for making others laugh. I can't recall the exact exchange that took place between her and Coursey, who was of a *clear* complexion, or what he had said to Gloria that elicited her response but I remember it today just as clearly as if it were yesterday. She jokingly called him a cracker and everyone, including me, as well as Coursey, had a hearty laugh. And that was it. I thought nothing else about it.

By the way, in Roebuck we described people as being either *clear skin* or *dark skin,* hardly using the term black. I had never heard the term cracker in Roebuck. We didn't use it in Roebuck in any context. But I did hear *nigga man* every now and then. It was not uncommon to hear someone say "That nigga man ..." Years later, I learned that a cracker was what we called a biscuit in Roebuck. Much later, as my education expanded, I was surprised to learn that it had racial overtones. I had often wondered where Aunt Gloria learned that word in that context. She had never been to America, and back then television was yet a long way off in coming to our neck of the woods. In short, I do not know the story of her exposure to that word, and I didn't question her about it when she used it to describe Coursey because it meant absolutely nothing to me at the time, and probably not to her.

Knowing now that the meaning of the word is as demeaning and humiliating as the *n* word, do I think that Aunt Gloria meant to be ugly towards that young man? Absolutely not! All these years she has been, and still is, a model of decency to my sisters and me, to her husband, Clyde, her son, David, and to all who know her. And what's more comforting and satisfying is the fact that I have not heard her use that word in a racist context since then. I simply wonder how she came to know such a word and its implications as far as this one aspect of the American culture is concerned. I didn't think that she remembered the incident after so many years had passed but when I asked her about it while preparing this section of the manuscript, she laughingly told me that she hadn't forgotten, and went on to tell me how they jokingly used to call clear skin people crackers.

What I do remember very clearly is the truth that racism and other aspects of racial hatred and bigotry had no place to grow, and were not even thought of in Roebuck. The reality is that all the natives were black but having said that, there were still some facts of life that could have been the impetus for such feelings to germinate. One obvious scenario was that the plantation system was in full swing, where the plantation owners were white and the black people of Roebuck worked in the fields of the plantation cutting canes, planting yams, potatoes, eddoes and cassava. Some Roebuck women like Muddah, even worked as servants and cleaners for the white plantation owners that lived in the plantation house on Sedgepond Plantation just down the hill from Roebuck. As far as I can recall, the only other interaction with white people happened very sparingly, such as when Dr. Gilmour, a white doctor, made house calls. Still, those relationships were always cordial and respectful. The locals went about their business as though the word racism was not known. That was the culture of Roebuck.

When I moved to America, everything suddenly changed and my education and experience with racism began. Not that I know of a time when I was personally targeted in a racist way but suddenly everything was viewed through the black/white prism. Prior to that, my somewhat limited education and exposure to racism came by way of the Rediffusion. As a young boy, I keenly followed the civil rights movement of the sixties, with its marches, dog attacks, water hoses attacks and brutal treatment of black people, without the minutest thought that I would one day live in a state that was once one of the hot beds of the civil rights upheaval. And to spend almost thirty years here, longer than I have spent in my native Roebuck is even more astounding.

While this chapter is not intended to launch into a dissertation on race relations, it is appropriate at this juncture to contrast the racial cultures in the same way that other aspects of culture are discussed elsewhere in the book. Let me begin with a story. I was very early in my principalship of a small church school in Chattanooga, Tennessee in 1987. A church member, a retired teacher, was volunteering in the office when the telephone rang and she promptly answered in a very polite and professional manner. What happened next caught me completely off guard. She handed me the telephone, with the comment that the call was for me and that it was "somebody from the other side." Seeing my confused state, she explained by adding "It is a white person." I took the call but immediately thereafter returned to ask some clarifying questions.

"How did you know it was a white person on the phone? I asked.

"I just know," she answered.

"But how do you know?" I countered.

"You will learn," she promised.

And I did learn. And without even trying. It would have never crossed my mind in Roebuck to listen that closely to be able to distinguish the difference in the voice tone, or quality, of black and white people. Now, when I pick up the telephone, or listen to the television, surprisingly I am an expert on the race of the person speaking on the other end. While I do not consider this particular ability an aspect of racism, it must be said that I was quick to discern that this Christian woman had harbored some unchristian feelings as far as those on "the other side" were concerned.

"Why did you say the person on the telephone was from the other side? I continued

"Because she is," she replied.

"What is the other side? I continued

"She is white," she told me.

Suddenly, I did not want to continue the discussion but allowed her to deliver a speech on how bad white people were and how they should not be trusted. I listened with a heightened sense of disbelief, not only because my volunteer professed Christianity but also because the lady on the line, and from "the other side," was of the same religious affiliation. I had only moved to the South a couple of weeks earlier, and wondered why I had not experienced a similar encounter in racial awareness when we lived in Michigan, or in California, our most recent place of residence.

Indulge me again as I relate a story that I have heard more than once, and it continues to intrigue me each time I hear it. And what is more troubling is the fact that of late, I too have been guilty of a similar line of thinking. Probably you have as well. A news item on the television dealt with an incident in which a gunman had killed several people. "I hope that fool is not black," one person was heard to remark. When another gunman killed twelve and injured close to sixty in a Colorado theater one person was heard to remark "I am glad he is not black." I have heard incidents like these play out over and over again but never had the courage to ask for an explanation or reason for the comment. But they always leave me asking myself a series of questions. Do white people make similar comments like "I hope he is not white?" Are they being racist if they do? Are black people being racist when they make comments of this nature? Or is it their way of *wishing* Blacks out of serious criminal activity?

There is one more thing in the racial cultural difference that has landed me in somewhat of an uncomfortable situation on more than one occasion. It obviously annoys some when I appear not to be as enthusiastic and jubilant as they think I should be, especially in those instances when Blacks and other minorities are appointed to major political positions, or when they make notable achievements in sports, education and business. I admit that it has never been my intention to belittle the remarkable accomplishments of any group. Similarly, I tend to applaud those accomplishments with a sense of pride and admiration but apparently with less vigor and fanfare, according to the interpretation of some. If this scenario is indeed true, then I have one possible explanation for the misunderstanding; and it does have a cultural foundation. I grew up in Roebuck where it was commonplace in Barbados to see blacks in high positions in government, law, education and sports. The Prime Minister, Errol Barrow, was black. The Minister of Education, Erskine Sandiford, was black. The attorney general was black. I hope the point I am trying to make is clear — that from an early age I was used to seeing Blacks in positions of leadership and authority. Apparently, I do not get carried away enough when it happens in this country.

History teaches that our island was once a British colony, where the Queen's representatives occupied the highest and most influential positions in the land. But history took a turn on November 30, 1966, when independence was won from Great Britain. About the same time, the civil rights movement in America was in full swing, and while Blacks in Barbados were filling the political, legal and educational leadership roles in the country, their black counterparts in America were being subjected to Jim Crow laws, being attacked by dogs and water hoses, and engaging in countless marches to win their freedom. So if my behavior is suspect, it is not because I do not respect, or understand the struggles and the vast changes that have taken place in America as far as the racial divide is concerned. That is so far from the truth. The fact is that I have history on my side; a history that had me experience the exalted status of Blacks long before it was possible in America. I was used to it long before it was fashionable in America. It was a part of my culture much earlier, and this may be the reason I appear not to dance in the street, or turn cartwheels when it happens here, even though I do share in the jubilation and excitement when such accomplishments happen.

I mentioned previously that I can't recall ever being racially targeted in this country. At the same time, I tend to be very naïve where such matters are concerned, and would probably have to be confronted face to face and called an ugly name if I am to conclude that I am being targeted. Fortunately, or otherwise, I am not one that is able to conclude that racism is to be blamed if I am not successful in a job interview, or considered for a promotion, or something of that nature. But looking back there have been a couple incidents that happened years ago, which may be far-fetched, and may be even stretching the point a bit. But I still want to relate the following stories that may not even be applicable to the discussion at hand, or to the point I am trying to make. It is not that I am looking for incidents from my past that had a personal racist attack. Rather, I recite these experiences to shore up the cultural differences I experienced; happenings that I would have never encountered in Roebuck.

We were living in St. Croix at the time. There was an empty lot between our house and the neighbor to the right. Many times I would notice bags of garbage that produced an obnoxious odor, discarded among the brush. The stench was impossible to dismiss, especially in eighty degree weather. This particular day, I caught the neighbor dumping a bag of garbage and I proceeded to confront her.

"Why are you dumping your trash there" I asked, probably with a detectable degree of irritation.

"Why don't you go back home, you alien? She retorted.

"I may be an alien, but I am not nasty," I countered.

My comment got her stirred up and we went back and forth with a few exchanges, with me calling her a bad name before it was all over. I am sure it was not the *b* word because I am not known for using that kind of language, no matter how upset I may become. But I did use the *n* word — *nasty*, more than once.

Obviously, this incident was not a racist attack on me because she was as black as I am. But what it did was to highlight two aspects of culture that were striking. First, how did my adversary know that I was an alien? After all, I had never spoken to her before. My accent obviously gave away my secret. Secondly, and most importantly, her use of the word alien hit a raw nerve and I reacted just as offensively. In Roebuck, and in Barbados for that matter, we never used the word alien to describe people that were not native to the island. We called them *foreigners*, a term that is less horrific. I put the alien comment on the same level as the *n* word or the *cracker* word, for that matter.

Here is one more story. I was working on an Ed.S degree at Michigan State University. This was way back in the early eighties. One evening in the winter the professor in charge of my Futuristics class asked us to think about one thing that we thought would radically change in the future, and come back to class the following week to share with the group. I thought really hard during the ensuing week but was unable to settle on an idea until one suddenly popped into my head the very evening I was riding the bus to class.

Back in class I thought I was on to something really big, and was anxious to share my idea when it was my turn to speak. Even though my deep Barbados accent made it difficult for many of my white classmates to understand me much of the time, this time I spoke clearly and with passion on the idea that in the future, we would be able to see the person with whom we are speaking on the other end of the telephone line To make a long story short, Professor R (I'll yield to my better judgment and not mention her full name) shot down my idea rather coldly. Although I can't recall her exact words, her reaction was that my concept was a dumb one and had no chance in the world of ever happening, even though in my way of thinking, my futuristic notion was much better than the majority of those submitted by my classmates. Of course, I scored a victory of sorts much later with the invention of Skype and Face Time, two technological features that have completely revolution-ized communication of late. Was this an act of racism leveled in the direction of a black student? I didn't think so then, and I still feel the same today, even though I felt defeated and deflated at the time. Even though some in my class might have been quick to say that the race card was played in this case, I was less excited to point fingers, which was probably due to the fact that the culture in Roe-buck — the culture in which I was born and raised, did not support this kind of thinking.

CHAPTER SEVEN

The Line

"You, Fred son, you will never amount to anything good."

I remember learning a long time ago that a line is a geometric figure that has length but no thickness. I think I learned this piece of geometric information while I was still in elementary school at Indian Ground School. Primary school, as we used to call it in Roebuck. But in Roebuck, some words, as you may have come to discover, took on a different meaning to match the culture of the place. So was the case with the *line*. I lived down the line in Roebuck. If I went away from my house, I was going up the *line*. Going down the *line* meant that I was walking towards home. When I was attending high school, I would wait on the step of my house and watch for the postman coming down the *line*, especially when I was expecting my report card to come in the mail.

Since coming to America, down the *line* has taken on a whole new meaning for me. Now, in addition to the Roebuck meaning, I have to get used to it as it is used in baseball lingo I regularly hear on the radio, or watch on television when a batter hits a ball down the line, whether down the first base line or third base line. I often chuckle inside when listening to Atlanta Braves baseball on the radio and hear Chip Carey or Don Sutton comment on Chipper Jones or Jason Heyward hitting a ball down the line. More often than not, it brings back fond memories of my own *down-the-line* days in Roebuck.

Obviously, the line in Roebuck was some kind of road or street that led to somewhere. But since I began writing the book I spent a lot of time trying to unravel the mystery surrounding the reasoning why the *street* where I lived was called the line. And what is more intriguing, everyone I consulted had their own idea as to why the *line* was so named. So as far as the origin of its name is concerned, much is left to conjecture and speculation.

The idea that the houses were built almost in a straight line crossed my mind but I soon dismissed that line of thinking. Whatever the case, we grew up calling it the line, walking and running, and even playing on it for years and never dreamed of questioning its cultural origin, until now. I felt safe and secure living down the line. My mother probably felt the same because she tried her best to restrict my movements to the *line* as much as possible when I was a boy; preventing me from venturing up the *line* and eventually ending up in the *road;* the only real street in Roebuck.

The line was not a true street in the real sense of the word. Cars didn't drive on the line. Not that there were cars in Roebuck to venture up or down it. It was rocky and uneven, and to be quite honest, downright dangerous to one's bare feet if they happened to be foreign to the place. One had to know its contours very well while traveling by foot, especially at a high rate of speed, and especially at night, or some unfortunate toes would have an unpleasant meeting with the *rock stones* that always lie in wait. That being said, I knew the topography of the line expertly. Even when moving at top speed, I was able to maneuver around its most dangerous stones at dusk and even in the darkness of night. Speaking of dusk, I always thought people were saying *dust*. I am positive that others my age thought the same thing. I learned the difference between dusk and *dust* as time went on, and as I matured into a more enlightened person.

Obviously, there were no street lights down the *line,* and the dull light coming from the *kersene* oil lamps of the houses that lined the *line* did little to improve on the darkness that always scared me as a boy. Consequently, I tried my best not to let the darkness of night catch me out of my house. Even at the height of my expertise, I would sometimes *stump* my toe on one of those *rock stones* and had to get a piece of *plaster* from the shop to cover the cut before it turned into a *lame foot* and begin to *fester* before a *scab* formed on it. Neither band aid nor *stubbed* was a part of the lexicon of the Roebuck culture. We didn't stub our toes in Roebuck. We *stumped* them, and when we did, we went to Mr. Scantlebury's shop to buy a piece of reddish plaster to put on it. Besides, in Roebuck we could not decide if they were rocks or stones, so we solved the dilemma by naming them *rock stones.* In either case, they were very handy weapons that were always available for *pelting* dogs; for pelting one another when coming home from school; or for bringing down breadfruit and coconuts. Although we said pelt when I was growing up, I always thought that pelt was another of those cultural inventions that the people of Roebuck created for their private use.

In spite of the *line's* precarious topographical landscape, children living down there were clever enough to discover a small semi grassy area of the terrain on which to *skip* and play games that did not require uniforms or equipment; only ingenuity and an abundance of youthful creativity. We never said jump rope in Roebuck. The Roebuck name for jump rope was *skipping.* What's more, an actual rope was not utilized in the *down-the-line* version of jump rope; for that would involve spending money; a resource that was not readily available for such ancillary items. Our jump rope was a *wild wist*; a *wist* being a wild and sturdy vine that grew in the bushes everywhere in Roebuck for such childhood purposes, and was easily replaced as fast as one was worn out. While searching for the best one, we often encountered the dreaded *god horse.* We were scared of them as children because it was rumored that they could crawl into our ears, even though I never heard of a single case in which a praying mantis, or walking stick, ever found its way into somebody's *earhole*, as we said in Roebuck. This was probably one of those Roebuck fables for which there was no authenticity. At times we even disturbed the occasional frog; a *crapoe,* as we called it in Roebuck.

The only use we had for a rope in Roebuck was to tie it in a noose around our sheep's necks when we took them out to graze in the mornings. The free end of the rope was then tied to a tree or to an iron stake in the ground to prevent them from wandering away until we went back to *move* them around midday and then going back again to bring them home in the evening. Hence the term *tying out the sheep*. Sometimes my mother would say to me "Go and tie out the sheep" Or "Go and bring in the *stocks*." Not that we had stocks or shares in anything, but I knew exactly what she meant. She meant for me to go and bring in the sheep for the evening after they had spent all day grazing in Sedgepond. Speaking of shares, my friend Floyd, who now resides in Washington, was telling me just recently that he was at a friend's house for lunch one Saturday after church. He said that the food was so good that he had two *shares*. I had a hearty laugh while reminding him that they don't say two *shares* in the US when it comes to food. Americans say they are having seconds. *Share*s is a Roebuck term, so named because of the process our parents, or whoever the cook was, used for taking the food from the big pot in which it was cooked and putting it on individual plates or in bowls for each member of the family. We always spoke of this as *sharing* the food, or *dishing out* the food.

As a matter of fact, the *line* was not restricted to Roebuck. There was also a *line* or two in Indian Ground. There was one by Indian Ground School, appropriately called the *school line*. This one was a lot better than my *line* in Roebuck. It was a *tar road,* probably the only reason being that it led to the *nursery* where Aunt Gloria and Ms. Holder took care of little babies. In Roebuck we never said that a road was paved. It was a tar road. But the school line was not a tar road all the way. As soon as it passed the *nursery*, it began to turn into a *cart road* that ran between two cane fields.

I also remember there being another *line* in Indian Ground, where Doriel Best and her sister, Alvean, better known as Avvy, and a brother, Lessloyd, lived. Brother Nick and his wife, Viterose, and their children, Leila, Marita, and Carl, nicknamed Nippy, also lived up that line. It was not a tar road so it became very muddy when it rained. Like my *line* in Roebuck, this one did not have a name; just the *line*. And like my *line* in Roebuck, the houses on this *line* had no numbers, like #3 School Line, or #19 Roebuck Line. Numbers on the houses were not needed. Still, Mr. Belgrave, the mailman, knew exactly where to find my house down the *line*. The only difference is that we didn't say mailman in Roebuck. Mr. Belgrave was the *postman*.

However, since beginning this chapter of the book, I have given constant and deep study as to the origin of the *line*, relying on the experiences and the exposure I managed to have gleaned as I broadened my horizon outside of Roebuck, to help me settle, once and for all, on a logical reason why my street was called the *line*. And after a careful look at the names of established streets in other parts of Barbados, and even making closer observations of street names in the US and beyond, I eventually came to a final conclusion that the *line* is simply another name for the lane. Like Jemmotts Lane, or Synagogue Lane, or Jessamy Lane, or Jordan Lane, all located in St. Michael in Barbados. Here in Ringgold, Georgia, where I now reside, I have come across Hope Lane, Haven Lane, and Evitt Lane. Even down the street from my house in my very own neighborhood is Eagle Lane. Strangely, I have noticed the street sign many times while on my walk around the block but only recently did I make the connection and decided once and for all that our *line* in Roebuck was definitely a lane. I even extended my research to include the UK since Barbados was once a colony of Great Britain, and was able to come up with Love Lane and Park Lane. *The line* was just Roebuck's unique way of putting its own stamp on our culture.

Instead of avenues, boulevards, circles, ways, gaps and streets, Roebuck had *the line*.

However, I did not reach this conclusion unilaterally. I intentionally engaged my sisters. Not even Elaine, through whom much of the family culture usually filtered down to the rest of us, had a credible explanation as to why it was called *the line* but she and my other siblings weighed in on the issue with vigor. It was that important to them. By the way, we never said siblings in Roebuck; just sisters and brothers. In either case Elaine, Yvonne, Cheryl and Heather were eager to add their contribution to this very crucial matter. As a matter of fact, I think I am correct in concluding that as far as the book is concerned, we have had the most spirited collaboration on the topic of *the line*. In a recent telephone conversation with Heather, who now lives in California, she tentatively subscribed to my original idea that *the line* was so named because the houses down *the line* were built in a straight line. Later, Cheryl, who also lives in California, completely agreed with my conclusion that *the line* was the Roebuck name for the lane, even mentioning the colonial connection to the UK.

Incidentally, the *line* of today is in deep contrast to the *line* I grew up knowing. Hortense and I were back in Roebuck three years ago, and again recently when we visited with my sisters, and were amazed to see the new and improved *line* with the remaining houses either having undergone extensive renovations, or built anew from the ground up. Cars moved freely on a paved street, completely removing the history and the familiarity of the past. Even after such massive changes, it was interesting to hear people still talking of going up or down the *line*. By the way, legend has it that the improvement to the *line* was brought about by political connections — my late first cousin, Golda, who lived down the *line*, having worked for Prime Minister, Owen Arthur. It now looks like a real lane with a new and updated name, Roebuck Lane is appropriate. But I very much doubt that the people of Roebuck would be willing to give up a piece of history and an ingrained item of the culture that has been a staple for such a long time.

Whatever the situation, *line* or lane, I grew up knowing everybody that lived up or down the *line*; and knowing everybody in Roebuck, for that matter. And everybody knew me. As a lad I felt as if all the adults living down the *line* served as extensions of my parents, with an unspoken duty to protect us; as if they claimed an assumed authority to keep us in line. Ms. Rhoda thought it was within her realm of authority to correct us if a fight was about to break out down *the line,* and Ms. Martin thought it her civic duty to tell our parents if we did not say good morning or good night. Ms. Morris thought it was the right thing to do to *dish out* a *share* of food for us when she cooked for her own children. Down the *line* in Roebuck was a shining example of community spirit and pride, and the perfect fulfillment of "It takes a village..." As a result, I always had a feeling of full protection and security, and was able to establish a degree of personal self-assurance and a confidence that powered my belief that I was loved and appreciated, and could grow into a respectable and successful young man.

With such a vast exposure to the array of rich community and supportive experiences I enjoyed in Roebuck, I expected to find a similar situation, even if on a smaller scale, when I came to live in America. To my dismay, I discovered that in some neighborhoods, neighbors are completely independent and isolated, and appear quite satisfied not knowing the name of the family living next door, far less down the street. The Roebuck culture strictly forbade this code of behavior and vigorously promoted the values and worth associated with knowing everyone in the *district*. Granted, Roebuck is much smaller than many places in America but the attempt to know one's neighbors, if only casually, definitely has its merits. Consequently, since moving to America I have always intentionally sought to exploit the culture of my Roebuck upbringing to accomplish just that.

Leopold's house was at the top of *the line*; the first one going down *the line*. Lepold, as he was so called in Roebuck, lived there with Lease, his wife. Knowing the history of Roebuck and how famous it had become for adding its own flavor to names and words, it is understandable that Lease may not have been her real name at all. It might have been Elise, but we called her Lease. Their children were Alvin, Michael and Patsy. Michael, nicknamed Hope, and I, were buddies before his parents left Roebuck for England, and sent for the children later. In Roebuck, we never said that somebody migrated. They were always *sent for*, or they went away, or they went overseas. The next house, Rita's house, was separated from Leoplod's house by the main road, the only paved street or *tar road*, in Roebuck. The Roebuck Bank was the intersection where the road intersected with the line and it was a popular meeting for some adults as they sat and socialized on the natural *bank* that was formed when the main road was cut.

Although Rita's mother, Mildred, lived there as well, I always called it Rita's house, which she shared with her sisters Eris and Doriel, known to all as Lil (Little) Girl, probably because she was always quite small. Her brothers were Anthony, popularly known as Minnie, Valda, and Emerson, nicknamed Cheek. Cheek had a dog name Tom. Carl was another brother, except that hardly anyone knew him as Carl. His nickname was Boy Blue. Nicknames were common in Roebuck, even among older people, and in some cases the spelling of some nicknames was never officially established or certified. Rita had three children of her own, Ambrose, who would become Roebuck's first medical doctor, Franceine, and Shelley. On our recent visit we stopped by to see Rita and Shelley, and also worshipped with them at the Pentecost Church, and stopped by again to see them before we left to return to the US. Rita still has that infectious smile. We also ran into Anthony at a picnic in the park.

Unlike the U.S, Roebuck nicknames, in many cases, were

unusual and strange; of the kind you will find only in Roebuck's culture; the type that was sometimes harsh and even severe. Even with real names, there is a marked difference between Roebuck names and those in the U.S. Whereas Roebuck's names were longer, as in Livingstone, Alphonsa, Charleston and Sylvester, U.S names are usually shorter, as in Dick, Bob, Drew and Bill, even though they may be abbreviated forms of the given names. When I went to college in Jamaica, my roommates Garford and Trevor, nicknamed me John, claiming that Sylvester was too long. Quite recently, Garford's brother Whitty, greeted me as John when we were talking on the telephone. We had a hearty laugh as I reminded him that "nobody calls me John any more." And just the other day I received a Dear John letter in the mail from Garford's sister Pearly. She was writing to me all the way from Jamaica, and after forty years, she is still calling me John.

As far as Carl is concerned, I did not even know his name was Carl until I was doing the research for this chapter of the book. All of the brothers, with the exception of Anthony, were much older than I was, and still living at home, even though they were old enough to live on their own. But that's how it was done in Roebuck. Older children lived with their parents for as long as they could. I remember admiring Valda and Boy Blue as they dressed up on Sunday afternoons to walk to Walkers, St. Andrew, where they had girlfriends.

Rita was always a jolly woman with a pretty smile. She and my mother were good friends and often sat on the Roebuck Bank at the top of *the line*, to socialize with other women in Roebuck. She was slightly overweight, which could not be said of many people, men or women in Roebuck. Working hard in the fields on Sedgepond Plantation was exercise enough to keep the residents of Roebuck and the line slim and trim. But Rita wore her weight well. Very well I might add. One day my mother announced that Rita was in the *family way*. My mother never said that a woman was pregnant. She was in *the family way*. Sometimes she was *expecting* but usually, a woman was in *the family way*. I always wondered why my mother was always so proper and formal in this regard. Now I wonder what she would have said if she knew that a man's wife or girlfriend was pregnant with a child that was not his. She was too formal and proper in this regard to say that he had a *ready-made shirt*.

My reaction to my mother's announcement concerning Rita was one of complete surprise, as I displayed my ignorance about her condition, and the fact that she was able to hide her pregnancy so well. I stopped by to see Rita when I visited Roebuck a few years ago, after having been gone for close to forty years. When I knocked on her door, she greeted me with the same old trademark smile, inviting me in with "Come in Syl." She had not *fallen away* much. In Roebuck we didn't say that someone had lost weight; they simply *fell away*, or that they *came down*, as my friend, Floyd, said to me one day. He told me that his wife, Shirley, was on a diet and that she was *coming down*. I had not heard it put like that in years, so it was time for a hearty laugh. Many people in Roebuck did not have to *come down* because most were skinny.

Actually, Leopold's house was not the first house in Roebuck. Slightly off the line were two houses that were in all actuality, the first houses in Roebuck. Not necessarily first in age but first as far as their locations were concerned. Norma Marshall and her husband, Otis St. Hill, lived in one of the houses, and Erla and her boys Hartley, Everton and Tony lived in the other.

One house stood out in stark contrast to the others in Roebuck, not only because it was not in line with the others but more importantly, because it was noticeably different. Situated directly across from Rita's was this small structure made of a blackish kind of large stone blocks. It was not a *board house* like the others in Roebuck. It was a *wall* house. In Roebuck we never said brick house; only *wall house*, if the house was made of bricks. Not that there were brick houses in Roebuck; only this one across from Rita.

As a boy growing up, I knew that this house looked different but never questioned why the obvious difference, and was quite ignorant and unaware of its historical significance in Roebuck. All of this changed when I was back in Roebuck for a visit in 2010 and was having a chat with Mrs. Watson, who had the distinction of being close to the oldest person in Roebuck. She had become the unofficial resident historian, a title I bestowed on her, primarily because she had answers to all my questions and could tell me anything about everything and about everyone I had not seen in years.

I remember asking Mrs. Watson about the wall house because it was not where it had been when I left back in 1973. She causally informed me that this particular structure had been a slave house a long time ago and that it was *pushed down* some time after I left Roebuck. For all the time I had lived in Roebuck I had never known that this particular and strange-looking building had been slave quarters. What was more astonishing was my complete ignorance of the fact that slavery had at one time directly touched my beloved Roebuck. I was more than grateful for the education I received that day from Mrs. Watson. The house is not there any more, neither are Aury and her children that lived in it when I was growing up. The children were Myrtene, Eversley, nicknamed Pepper; George, nicknamed Fibber, pronounced Fibba by everyone, Whitfield, Elaine, whom everyone called Lainey; and Biggy- not her official name. It now boggles my mind as to how so many people actually lived in such a small house.

Mr. Worrell lived *below* Rita. In Roebuck, living below someone meant that your house was situated next to theirs on the western side. If you lived *above* someone, it meant that your house was immediately to the east of theirs. Above and below were simply directional terms and did not mean that the homes in Roebuck were of the multi-level type. There were no *upstairs* houses in Roebuck.

Mr. Worrell's full name was Ashton Worrell. His house, which was always in very good condition, was painted in a grey color and was the only house in Roebuck with a name. Even now I can see in my mind's eye the name plate *Ashford* displayed over the front door. His sister was Ms. Malik. She was very proper and always spoke with an accent as if she had once lived in a foreign country. Mr. Worrell's wife died when I was still a small boy, leaving two sons, Goldbourne, who was known to everyone in Roebuck as Goalie, and DeCourcey, who was Courcey to all. Mr. Worrell was a *driver*, meaning that he worked for the plantation in a supervisory capacity, watching over the workers as they labored in the fields. While back in Roebuck recently, Doyle, nicknamed Duffy, had us cracking up with laughter one day when we were taking a trip around the island and while we were *rambling* to find his brother, Wayne's house. Wayne's nick name was Hardy when we were growing up. Duffy told us the story of how Goalie had built a *donkey cart* in the middle of the house, for his donkey, and only found out after it was finished that he could not get it out of the house because it was too big to get through the door.

The Martins lived below Mr. Worrell. I never knew their Christian names, as we said in Roebuck but was definitely certain that their surname was Martin. I knew them as Mr. Martin and Ms. Martin. Even if I knew their first names, I dared not address them in that way. This level of familiarity and disrespect towards our elders was never welcomed in Roebuck. It was acceptable to address them as Mr. and Ms. Martin. The Martins were not husband and wife but mother and son, even though a father or husband was not in the home. I discovered only recently while talking with my sister, Yvonne, that Mr. Martin did have a wife at one time, a union that resulted in a son, Melvin. One thing of which I was absolutely certain was that this was one couple I had to speak to as I passed by, morning and evening, saying their names out loudly. Good morning, or good evening, was not always a requirement. As long as I said Mr. Martin or Ms. Martin loud enough for them to hear me, as they both peered from the small front window, I was safe, and my parents would not receive a complaint that I did not speak to them.

That's how we were trained growing up in Roebuck. We had to have manners, and a part of having manners was speaking to the older people. Unmannerly children were not tolerated in Roebuck. Mr. Martin had one distinguishing physical feature, however. Apart from his permanent serious facial appearance, one of his arms was severed just below the elbow, leaving him with only one hand, which undoubtedly earned him the nickname Bob. Bob Martin. To me, he was Mr. Martin. I could not be so bold as to call him Bob Martin.

Even though he was Bob I am almost certain that he was not so called as a pet name or as a nickname for Robert. In either case, I still can't figure out how Robert becomes Bob in America, or how William becomes Bill, or Richard, Dick. I had a confusing first-hand encounter with this cultural difference one day, even after I was well established in the US. I was working as an assistant principal and I had reason to look in the school's records for a file belonging to a student everyone called Drew. After experiencing difficulty locating the file I found out that I was supposed to be looking for a file belonging to Andrew.

Quite coincidentally, I was reading only recently of the passing of Sir Richard Haynes from Barbados, one of my favorite politicians when I was growing up in Roebuck. He was appropriately known as Richie Haynes. In the US he would have been Dick Haynes. Go figure. Personally, I am slowly getting used to Sylvester becoming Sly, as in Sly Stallone. To this day, Debbie Bearden, the food service manager at one of the schools where I worked, still hails me as Sly whenever she sees me. I still get caught off guard at times but I am slowly growing into my new name. I have always been Syl in Roebuck. Not Sly.

Ms. Baby's house was below The Martins going down *the line*.

I never knew if Baby was her real name and I never questioned the reasoning for calling a grown woman Ms. Baby. Everyone called her Ms. Baby, and I did the same. Ms. Baby had babies of her own; grown children, to be more accurate, though I never knew of a father figure in the home. The girls were Carmen and Eugene. Carmen had a son, Levere, whom everyone called Ecaf because, as Charleston joked, he looked like the man on the Ecaf coffee box. Eugene loved to run. She ran everywhere. Her nickname was Rajack, or Raja, the origin or the meaning, or the spelling of which I never knew or understood. It was another of those nicknames that Roebuck assigned without providing the correct way to write or spell it. Richard and Roderick were Eugene's two sons. Hugh was Ms. Baby's one boy. He was nicknamed Can Can and was sometimes called Melody. On our recent visit to Roebuck, Charleston had an explanation as to why Hugh was called Can Can. He had bow legs and looked like the girls in their short and wide can-can skirts.

Ms. Aileen lived below Ms. Baby. She lived alone, and kept mostly to herself, which was unheard of in Roebuck. Although she lived above us, I never knew much about her, except that she was strangely weird and sometimes scary. I can't recall having a real conversation with her in all the years she lived above us. I can't even recall her having said much to my mother, although my mother was known for having a good relationship with everybody in Roebuck.

Our house was next on the line, below Ms. Aileen's. Seven of us shared that house until my father went to England, leaving my mother, my sisters Elaine, Yvonne, Cheryl, Heather and me, the only boy. Actually, our home would have been a lot more crowded, had it not been for the death of three brothers who did not survive beyond infancy. David, Floyd, and an unnamed baby died quite early. Our house was much like the others in Roebuck, but it had one distinguishing feature that many others did not have. It had a *cellar* underneath; something like a basement that some American houses have, but not quite. It was not a living space where we went to relax; nor did it have a pool table, or a table tennis table; nor was it a man cave that is a popular space in many new US homes of late.

Our cellar could not be accessed by stairs from inside the house. We had to go outside and open a small door to get inside the dark space under the house where we stored food like yam until we needed it for cooking. We used to talk about going under the cellar to get yam to cook when in actuality what we really meant was that we were going under the house. My house in Ringgold has such a space — the crawl space; a space that functions as a storage area for much of the stuff I really don't need but refuse to dispose of. When the yam remained in our cellar for a long time, it would begin to sprout new leaves around the head which my mother would cut off and plant. In retrospect, I now believe that to be the chief function of the cellar: to provide the yams with the right environment to ensure new growth, so that my mother would have a supply to plant in our *ground* in Sedgepond once the planting season rolled around. However, Floyd informed me only recently that the cellar at his house in Benny Hall had an additional purpose. His cellar doubled as a goat pen. Interestingly enough, when I was principal in Dalton, Georgia, I was invited to a function at one of the city's most prestigious restaurants, The Cellar. Needless to say, it was a vast difference from the cellar I knew back in Roebuck.

Nicknames did not stick to my siblings as permanently as they did to others in Roebuck. My father, Fred, was not so fortunate however. He was nicknamed Fred Goat. I am not sure how that name came about but he seemed to have accepted it and wore it without visible objections or embarrassment. It was not uncommon for some people to identify me as Fred Goat's son. My sister, Elaine, earned a nickname for a short time — Tar Baby. Tar Baby, because she was so *dark skinned*; a lot darker than the rest of us. We joked about the nickname recently while we were having a conversation concerning my progress with the book. She even joked that the name probably would have stuck had she remained in Roebuck. We never described a person's skin as being black in Roebuck; always as being dark or clear.

My other sisters grew up free of nicknames as far as I can remember. As for me, I seemed to have followed in my father's footsteps, if only but for a very brief time, when I too had a nickname from the animal kingdom. Peacock. Peacock did not stick, mainly because not many of my friends ever knew that it had been assigned to me. Just like Uncle Wilfred, my mother's brother. He too had a nickname of the animal type. He was nicknamed Pig. Elaine and I would also joke about this during one of our conversations. Wilfred's nickname was one which did not fit and I don't know how, or why his nickname came about because he was a very gentle and handsome man. Or why I was compared to a peacock, since I was never known to be proud or haughty. However, the name never gained much traction, and I was able to escape it, along with the stigma it could have carried. Today, I would be totally surprised if anyone in Roebuck remembers Peacock as being my nickname. Probably, Michael would, but he is now living in England, along with Don and Henson, who might have been the only ones privy to the secret. But the subject never came up when I visited with Henson and Don in London several years ago.

As luck would have it, Peacock would come back to haunt me a few years ago under the strangest of circumstances and in the most unlikely of places. One Friday night a group of us met at the Orchard Park Seventh-day Adventist Church in Chattanooga, Tennessee. Carlton, Earle, Robert, Maleek and I were rehearsing a song to sing in church the following day. I remember them getting on my case, poking fun at me, encouraging me to sing louder, something I rarely do, when Robert lightheartedly said something to the effect "Open your mouth and sing and stop acting like a peacock." I chuckled inside, remembering the old nickname and knowing how accurate Robert had been.

Obviously, I didn't comment on the situation, but wondered many times since that night if there had been something in my behavior since my childhood in Roebuck that would cause others to view me as strutting like a peacock; especially since my friend Bill has more than once mentioned that I am stuck up. In contrast, my uncles on my mother's side, Wilfred, Perceval, nicknamed Brown Boy, and James, nicknamed Son, all called me Chubby at one time or another when I was growing up; a name I accepted without question but later wondered why, since I was always a *poor* kid. Or, maybe they likened me to Chubby Checker, a comparison I find difficult to understand since I was not known for my singing, or to have performed the twist to a degree close to mastery that would have attracted the admiration of others.

Brother Mayers lived immediately below us. His name was Reginald, but we all called him Brother Mayers, a title he probably earned due to his consistency in church attendance at the Pentecost Church, the only church in Roebuck. He was at every Sunday school and church service every Sunday, as well as Sunday night *meetings*, Tuesday's Y.P.E (Young People Endeavour) meetings, and Friday night prayer meetings. In Roebuck, night services were called meetings, as opposed to church. Brother Mayers lived alone in a house that was usually dark and unkempt. He never married or had children and became well known for his miserly way of existing. He would drop by our house to borrow a little sugar or salt from time to time. This practice of borrowing from neighbors was not restricted to Brother Mayers. It was a common every day habit that the people of Roebuck perfected when they were in need, or did not have the money to buy necessities from the shop. Still, they had an unwritten agreement that borrowing did not mean that repayment would ever happen. Like Brother Mayers, people showed up at their neighbors or sent their small children with a cup or bowl in hand to borrow a little sugar, a little flour or a little salt. Brother Mayers and my father, Fred, were first cousins, the sons of two sisters. Although that closely related, I have nothing to prove that they were really very close.

Probably the only level spot down the *line* was in front of Brother Mayers' house, and it was used to capacity, especially during the summer months when school was out from June to September. This little spot became the sports arena for the small children living *down the line*. Hide and seek was a popular pastime. In Roebuck, the game was *hide and seek*; not *hide and go seek* as is the case in America. Both down-the-line boys and girls played endless games of mixed-team hopscotch and *rounders*, a simplified version of baseball, in which we would round the bases, without calling them bases, or mentioning anything about hits, double plays, strikes or home runs. The night of the fifth of November was Guy Fawlkes Night. The occasion was celebrated with boys and girls running up and down the *line* with *starlights*, yelling "hip hip, the fifth of November." Burning *tyres* and setting off *bombs* were also popular down-the-line activities that were enjoyed by all as we celebrated Guy Fawlkes Night.

Games of cricket were very popular as well. Down the line, these cricket contests between boys and girls on mixed teams were known as *bat and ball*. The only difference was that an actual ball was hardly used in any of the games and the makeshift bat was generally fashioned from a piece of board, or carved from a branch of a coconut tree. The ball was a used condensed milk can, or an evaporated milk can. If we were lucky, we would have the pleasure of playing with a *wind ball*. But that was on rare occasions. Both girls and boys played endless games of *pickups;* a name that suddenly changed to jacks and balls once I moved to the US. *Pitching*, however, was an all-male down-the-line sport in Roebuck; an activity that evoked a hearty laugh from one of my eighth grade boys when I tried to demonstrate pitching marbles in my office one day. Of course, he could not resist the opportunity to inform me that pitching is a baseball term.

Another popular down-the-line game we played was simply called Mother and Father. We never had an official name for it but the name alone gives a clear picture into how the game was played. I guess it was our way of preparing ourselves for adulthood. One boy would be chosen to play the role of the father and a girl was the mother. Those not lucky to be selected for parental roles had to settle for the part as children in the family. Sometimes the game promoted marriage. Weddings were celebrated, with the cake being a rather large white tiered blossom from the wild pine plant.

Ms. Rhoda lived below Brother Mayers. I can't remember much about her, except that she was old. She was one of those old people I had to speak to, or my parents would hear about it. I don't remember her going to church like Brother Mayers did, or associating to any degree with others, except Mrs. Griffith, who lived a little further down the line. In 1955 when I was only six, I remember my father working to repair her *house top* that had been damaged during Hurricane Janet.

Some time later, when were still kids, a new family moved down the line. The Gilkes' moved from Welch Town and built a house on the *house spot* that was once occupied by Ms. Rhoda's house. He was James, nicknamed Blind James because he was blind in one eye. His wife was Muriel and the children were Maureen, better known as Tiny, Melissa, Yourlene, Marcia, Lystra, and Rosie. The boys were Reuben, nicknamed Bimbles, and Theodore, better known as Sweet Boy. Mr. Gilkes rode a bicycle and was very skillful in maneuvering it around and between the rocks down the line, even though he ran into our front step at one time. Later he replaced the bicycle with a Vespa motor cycle. When I went to see The Gilkes on my recent visit to Roebuck, I found them in great spirits but it was obvious that many of the complications that accompany old age were evident. They lived alone but Ms. Watson made regular visits and house calls. Before I left, Mr. Gilkes found it necessary to share that he was ninety-six and his wife was ninety-four, and that they were married in 1949, the year I was born.

A little further down the line was The Morris' house spot. In Roebuck a house spot was the space on which a house was built. We never called it a lot in Roebuck. It was always a house spot. The house spot did not belong to the homeowners, even though they built their houses on it. They owned the house but not the house spot. The spot was owned by Sedgepond Plantation, and the people of Roebuck rented the spot to build on. The Morris family and my family were related; my father, Fred, and Hatton Morris being brothers. Like my father, Hatton went to England to find work, leaving his wife Sylvie, and my cousins Keith, Charleston, Henson, Claudette, Golda, and Genlyn, popularly known as Jenny. Cheddi would come much later. Keith had a son, Norris, nicknamed Fiddlers, with Marlene. Charleston later married his longtime girlfriend Glendeen from Walkers, St. Andrew and started a family that included daughters Sonia, Suzette and Natalie. Marvalene was a daughter from a previous relationship with Mia Gibbs from nearby Indian Ground. Eventually, the family built a house on the spot where Ms. Baby once lived. There was a very tall almond tree below Ms. Morris's house. I remember us pelting rocks at the almonds to bring them down to the ground. We would eat the skin off the hard nut before we opened it with a rock to get at the almond inside.

Hatton did send for Ms. Morris later. Keith and Henson also went to England but I am not sure if Hatton sent for them, or if they went on their own. Keith was always a neat dresser who, like Valda and Boy Blue, made trips to St. Andrew, especially on Sunday afternoons, probably looking for girls. I remember Keith dancing with Elaine my sister, in the summer time to the music of the sixties coming from our little hi-fi turn table. I don't recall him, or Golda, or Claudette having a nickname as did Charleston. Incidentally, I always thought his name was Carson but found out while researching for the book that Charleston is his correct name; Charleston Cumberbatch. It so happens that he grew up thinking that his name was Carson, not knowing all that time that he was Charleston instead. The scoop I received from Jenny quite recently is that he had a rude awakening, when not very long ago, he went to apply for a passport, only to discover that his real name was Charleston. But he added to the confusion surrounding his name when we stopped by to see him on our recent visit to Roebuck. He told Hortense, Cheryl, Neats and me that his mother, Ms. Morris, has never called him Carson, as we all did. She always called him Carston, and still does today.

Charleston, like Keith, was born before Hatton married Sylvie; hence the surname Cumberbatch. He talked so much that I once thought his nickname was Talkie. Recently I was told that he was Tucky. The verdict is still out as to which one is correct. As far as his sister Jenny is concerned, I am told that she did have the nickname Parker, because she used to eat Parker soap. Jenny's two children are Vickie and Jason, who later moved to New York. The late Golda later married Shurlan and they produced Gabrielle, Tiffany and Clintross. It was a delight to meet the kids for the first time when I was in Barbados on a recent visit, since they were born after I left Roebuck way back in 1973.

Without a doubt, Henson did have a nickname and everybody in Roebuck knew it. He was Ice Pick, appropriately named because he was so skinny. Not because he was *starve out* but because in Roebuck we never described somebody as being skinny, or even thin. Ice Pick was *poor*, or *raky*, or lanky. He was my good friend even though he was my first cousin. He went everywhere with me: to take out the sheep; to *pick meat* for the sheep; to catch *crayfish* in the river, and was always around for dinner. We were expert *pot timers*; popping up at the exact time food was being dished out from the neighbor's pot.

I was back in Roebuck recently to participate in the celebration of Ms. Morris' ninetieth birthday, an event organized by Jenny, and reveled in the opportunity to toast her and thank her for her friendship and the support she gave to my mother in so many personal and difficult situations; how she was always close by when my mother lost three sons in infancy; how they appeared to have grown closer as they both were forced into raising their families on their own after their husbands migrated to England; how she would always call out to my mother, whether she was going up or down the line; and how we were always welcome to stay and eat at her house when she was *dishing out* food for her family.

The Rudders' house was the last house going down the *line*, and unlike many of the houses there was a rather large space between The Rudders' house and Ms. Morris' house. They lived a long way down the *line*, close to the end, and close to the *gulley* through which we regularly walked when we went to Four Hill to visit our paternal grandmother. I remember how we used to go to the gulley to wash our clothes in the pond a very long time ago. A long time before there was running water in Roebuck. Much later, we made a cricket pitch close to the end of the gulley and spent many a Sunday afternoon enjoying the game. I can't remember much about the Rudders except that she rode a bicycle and where they lived was a scary place, especially when it got dark.

Coming back up the *line* after leaving the Rudders, the first house on the other side belonged to Mr. and Mrs. Griffith; The Griffuts was the Roebuck name for the couple. They had a donkey they named Nellie. Nellie pulled a *donkey cart* up and down the *line*, transporting food and other stuff for her masters. When Dorcas was visiting me in Ringgold recently, she told me that she used to get a ride in the donkey cart pulled by Nellie when she was on her way from *lessons*. The Griffiths raised a girl, Colleen. The connection, or relationship between Colleen and the Griffiths is not fully known but it was widely accepted that they were not her parents. She may have been a distant relative who was unofficially adopted. Adoption was not a term used in Roebuck and the relationship between the Griffiths and Colleen may have been just that; an unofficial adoption. However, Colleen left Roebuck and went to live in England, just as many others did in those days.

The Cadogans lived above The Griffiths. He was Cecil but everyone called him Cadogan. I never knew her name. She died when I was but a small boy and as usual, and like other kids in Roebuck, I was scared to leave the house or go to sleep at night when she died. As mentioned earlier, we had the saying that a *duppie* would come back to get us during the night. Nothing was more frightening than a hearse. I remember the hearse bringing the dead person back to his or her house and the *turnout man* putting the *box* in the front house to spend some time before taking the body to the church for the funeral service, or to the grave yard at All Saints Church for burial. We did not use the term lying in state in Roebuck but my guess is that bringing the body back to the house was the closest thing to it.

The Cadogans had four children in Mayfield, Vernese, nicknamed Nonedo, Selvin and Seymour. Vernese loved to sing as much as her father loved to whistle. From our house we could hear her sing, day and night. He was always whistling a happy tune. Seymour, on the other hand was somewhat weird, and was thought to engage in some devilish behavior. Mr. Cadogan was my family's unofficial herbalist, gathering all kinds of bush from which my mother brewed *bush tea* for us to gulp down whenever the first signs of a cold or sickness was coming on; or when school was about to begin after the long summer vacation, or whenever she felt we needed a *wash out*. Her bitter brews kept us in such excellent health, so much so that we rarely took *phensic* tablets, or hardly had to go to Speighstown to buy medicine from Noel Roach *drug store*. Muddah did her best to maintain our robust health, so much so that we were never very seriously ill, requiring us to go to the hospital to *get cut*.

We did occasionally have *bad feels* but by and large, we were a healthy family, as was the case with many of the families in Roebuck. And it was strongly felt back then that the regular doses of bush tea were responsible to a large degree for keeping Roebuck's residents in good health. In Roebuck we never spoke of herbal tea, only *bush tea* that was boiled down from all kinds of leaves and vines that proved to be very effective medicine. Sour Sop leaves, pear (avocado) tree leaves, lime tree leaves and cerasee were some of the ingredients Mr. Cadogan provided my mother when she often asked. It was as if he was too eager to go on a hunt to bring back the ingredients to my pharmacist mother. We knew to expect the stuff when we saw Cadogan gathering the greens. Even now I can see my mother standing over me with a raised threatening right hand. "Drink it," she would demand. And when the medicine reached my throat and was experiencing much difficulty going any farther she would bark one final command. "Swallow it."

Sometimes, as if bush tea was not enough, and if my mother thought that the *washout* was not as thorough as it ought to have been, she would order a dose of castor oil, which was sure to cause the *purging*. We never said diarrhea in Roebuck. It was always the purging, which at that time I did not know was a real word. I thought it was another of those Roebuck words. Only recently, as I was watching the news on television, I saw a news item that gave new meaning to purging. It said that Florida was purging its voter registration rolls in preparation for the upcoming presidential elections between President Obama and Mitt Romney. I could only smile inside as I reminisced on a different kind of purging at the hands of my mother, while growing up in Roebuck.

An interesting, humorous, and related incident happened when we were in Barbados recently. We had made a stop on our tour of the island and happened upon a guava tree that was full of the young fruit, which some of us began picking. Out of the blue, someone in the group sounded the reminder that eating too many young guavas was sure to *bound* us. The comment caused a stir in the group and started a discussion on what our parents used to do to us when they thought we were *bound,* and how the bush tea, the castor oil and the cod liver oil they made us swallow, gave us *the bowels, the purging,* and a well-deserved *wash out.*

But while Cadogan picked the leaves from almost every kind of tree, there was one from which he did not pick — the *dog dumpling tree.* I am not sure if he was counseled against doing so. For to him, the leaves of every tree were good for medicine, except the dog dumpling tree. Sounds kind of biblical, doesn't it? Maybe he thought it was poisonous and we would have surely died if we drank of it. And what's more telling, we ate the fruit from a variety of trees in Roebuck — the sour sop tree; the sugar apple tree; the golden apple tree; the guava tree; the fat pork tree; but never from the dog dumpling tree. Having said all of that, I have quite an amusing story to share concerning the dog dumpling fruit.

I was traveling cross country on an airplane one day. This was quite a while ago but the story is still as fresh in my mind today as if it had happened only recently. After reaching cruising speed and the desired altitude I began to relax with one of the travel magazines from the seat ahead of me. After only a few minutes of browsing I suddenly came face to face with a picture that caused me to exclaim loud enough to catch the attention of the passenger beside me, who probably thought that I was crazy. "Dog Dumpling," I had quietly yelled. "That's dog dumpling." Staring at me was a picture of the dog dumpling fruit, only this time it was captioned the Noni fruit. I continued to stare at it in amazement, while explaining to the gentleman beside me that we called this fruit dog dumpling in Barbados, and how we never even touched it, far less ate it. We ended our conversation by agreeing that many in the USA had made small fortunes in multilevel marketing by selling others on the health benefits of the Noni juice. We also concluded that Americans had an appetite for all things foreign; like Tahitian Noni. Had we known of the health benefits of the dog dumpling, we could have been rich selling Roebuck Noni to Americans when they visited as tourists.

Muddah

The Line as it is today with Charleston's house and our house in the foreground.

The pipe

A patch of khus khus grass.

The mile tree

The Pentecost Church

Da Da

Ms. Walker lived above the Cadogans, if one was going up the *line*. She was nicknamed Jamaican, and lived alone. I was never able to determine the reason for the nickname, or if she actually came from Jamaica or even visited Jamaica. But my cousin Dorcas confirmed that she was actually from Jamaica, when she recently came from Roebuck to spend some time with Hortense and me. Ms. Walker was a smoker, which was a kind of a novelty behavior for a woman, and even for men in Roebuck. I don't think that the habit actually killed her but I remember when they found her dead in her house one morning. She probably had a stroke. The only thing is that nobody in Roebuck called it a stroke when I was growing up. They said that it was a *passover*.

Leaving Ms. Walker, the next house belonged to The Blackmans — Levis and Deany Blackman. She was Deany Ramsay before she married Levis Blackman; Deany was probably one of those made-up names for which Roebuck was famous. Levis and Deany had several children, a family that was by far the largest one down the line, and without question, one of the largest in Roebuck. The children were Sheila, DeCoursey, whom everyone called Coursey, and who was nicknamed Sun Dick. Sheila was married to Kid Roy and their children were Horace and Delores, Loreese for short. Both Sun Dick and Sheila went to live in England. Then there was Thelma. Telma, we all called her. Thelma had a weird nickname, Rack-a-Like; one of those Roebuck nicknames for which there was no official spelling. Her children were Jefferson, Sonica and Brenda.

Other Blackman siblings included Shirley, who later became a teacher and headmistress at Indian Ground School. She had a son, Desmond. Gwen was next in line after Shirley. I vividly recall having an altercation with Gwen that did not turn out in my favor. We had a light hearted moment about the incident when I went to see her and her family when I was in Roebuck recently. Then there was Livingstone, whom everyone called Livie. Livie was my friend. We took out our sheep together in the morning and brought them in together in the evening. His nickname, Robin Hood, Robin for short, really stuck. I wish I could relate with some degree of accuracy how the name came about but I am positive that it was a name Livie was glad to have, even though I never witnessed him at any time take from the rich to give to the poor. Surprisingly, Robin and I would *butt up* on each other in a supermarket in Speighstown on the same day I landed in Barbados on my most recent visit. The other children in the Blackman clan were Dennis, nicknamed Brooks, Mavis, Pearline, Sandra and Virene. Deany's sister, Bellamy, lived with the family for a while.

A *cane piece* belonging to Brother Mayers separated The Blackmans' from the next house going up the line. Even the sugar cane field had a nickname in Roebuck; a *cane piece*. Ms. Leetha's house was next in line after the cane piece. Ms. Leetha may have been one of those Roebuck inventions, or it might have been her actual name. However, she lived with her son Osbourne, whom everybody in Roebuck called Osbun, and his daughter Joycelyn. Osbourne was paralyzed from injuries he received in a car accident. Ms. Leetha's sister, Ms. Eva, also lived at the house. One thing I remember about her is that she wore some very thick glasses, and thick stockings as well. My sister, Yvonne, recently reminded me that Ms. Eva spoke very proper, as if she had once lived overseas. Joycelyn later bought Leopold's house after he left Roebuck for England. She lived there with her children Shurlan, Everton, Cathy, Rhonda and Verneta. Shurlan eventually married Golda, my first cousin, and the family lived in the house Ms. Morris left to Golda when she left Roebuck to live in England. As mentioned earlier, the couple produced Clintross, Gabrielle and Tiffany. Gabrielle would eventually become Roebuck's second medical doctor; second to Ambrose. Both of them from down the line.

Ms. Leetha's house was the last one on the line and directly across the road, Roebuck's only tar road, was Darling's house. Darling was Mr. Lowe's daughter, and Bentley, Mr. Lowe's grandson, lived with her. Bently had one of those invented nicknames for which there was no official spelling — Buhjum.

The other houses in Roebuck that were built along Roebuck's only road were not built in a line that was as clearly defined as those that were built on my line. Just beyond Darling's house on the left side of the road was a short line, much shorter that mine. It was so short that only one house was on it, and the residents there never spoke of going up or down the line like we did on our line. Siah, whose real name was either Joseph, or Josiah, lived on this short line with Bay, his common law wife. Nobody in Roebuck ever used the term common law. They just lived together. As for Bay, that was the only name I knew for her. Together they had about ten children; six sons in Charles, Victor, Vincent, nicknamed Hopper Dollar, because he walked with a slight hop and a limp after an accident. Charleston recapped the entire incident for us when were back in Roebuck on our visit. He had us laughing when he said that Hopper was *licked down* by a car, or a truck, and has walked with a slight hop ever since. Hence the nickname Hopper Dollar; Hopper for short. I made a special effort to look up Hopper while I was visiting and the joy and excitement were mutual and understandable after forty years. He recognized me immediately when he hobbled to the door, explaining that he was just getting ready for a visit to the hospital for treatment for the cancer in his back.

Joseph, nicknamed Son; probably named after his father was another of Siah's sons but he was never called Joseph Jr. In Roebuck, fathers did not typically name their sons after themselves. There were two other boys, Wendell and Lloyd, nicknamed Snuffy. Nola, the first girl, was the only person in Roebuck that I knew of that used the word *shove* correctly. I remember her saying that somebody had shoved somebody. Everybody else in Roebuck said *shub*. Not shove. Other sisters were Wendy and Marlene. Marlene was nicknamed Bid Dove. Legend has it that her father brought home a corned beef and she called it bid dove. I can't follow the logic as far as this nick name is concerned, but logic was hard to follow in Roebuck when most nicknames were assigned. Pauline was the last girl.

The Headley's house was just off Roebuck's main road on the left and just after the entrance to that short line where Siah and Bay lived. He was Arnold and she was Ermina. The Headley family was nine strong with Ken being the oldest child. Ken and I were pretty good friends. He was clear skin, like the rest of his family, the coloring which they got from their mother. Other sons were Coursey, nicknamed Fowl, and Greg. Serita, the oldest girl, was commonly known as Reet Reet. Then there were Yvette, Jennifer and Nadine. Jennifer was back in Roebuck visiting from New York at the same time we were there and hung out with us quite a bit.

A little distance down the road on the left was the Marshall's home, the first *flat top house* in Roebuck. For a long time all the houses in Roebuck sported an A frame roof until the Marshalls converted theirs to a flat top house. Everyone seemed to follow suit, including us. In those days there were few *house tops* made from shingle; the majority being made of galvanize. We often said that the house top was made of *tennin*. The rain beating down on the *tennin* house top at night was a sure way to put one to sleep.

Rixford was the only boy of the eight Marshall children. He became a policeman and a lot of us looked up to him; he being the first professional person to come from Roebuck. The girls were Norma, Melda, and Gweneth, who told me once that I was very handsome, especially when I was dressed for church and my father *parted* my hair on the left. Then there were Clovene Melvenna, my very first girlfriend, Angela, and Junnie, all of whom went to live in Canada. I dated Clovene for a while, except that in Roebuck we never used the word date, or going out with in this context. She was simply my girlfriend.

The road in front of the Marshalls quickly became a popular spot for cricket. Consequently, the house suffered its share of broken

windows and bounces from the flying balls. The game took on a
more sophisticated approach at that venue, as a real ball made from
cloth held together by bands of rubber replaced the milk cans from
the down-the-line games. The Marshall's home was always well
kept, and like Mr. Worrell's, it was a pattern for other houses in
Roebuck to emulate. However, in spite of their remarkable condition none of these two houses had a *gallery*.

The shop belonging to Mr. and Mrs. Scantlebury was on the
other side of the road. He was McCleod. She was Ethlyn. It was the
only shop in Roebuck, and they owned Roebuck's only car as well;
a Ford Falcon *marked* E 310. The shop sold everything from *sweet-
ies* to *cutters* to flour and *lard oil*. In Roebuck we never said candy.
Candy was *sweetie*. Cutters were made by cutting a salt bread loaf
in half and inserting a slice of cheese or ham, creating a cheese cutter or a ham cutter. I never launched an investigation into the reasoning behind calling it a cutter as opposed to a *sangridge* until I
began writing the current chapter. The only plausible conclusion is
that the name cutter is appropriate only because the bread had to
be cut in half, whereas with a sandwich, the bread was already
sliced. What was even more fascinating was that a *butter bread* was
made using the same method as a ham cutter or a cheese cutter but
it was never called a butter cutter; always a butter bread.

So it was with *lard oil*. In Roebuck we never said cooking oil;
always lard oil. I remember going to the shop to buy some lard oil
for my mother and deciding to take a mouth full of the thing,
hoping that it would taste as delicious as it smelled when frying
flying fish or chicken. Needless to say, I learned instantly that it
didn't. The Scantleburys would allow us to *trust* from the shop if
we could not pay upfront when we ran home from school at lunch
time. They wrote down the amount trusted in an oversized dog
eared note book and crossed it out only after my mother had paid
the bill.

I mentioned above that the Scantleburys had the only car in

Roebuck — E 310. But there were two *lorries* in nearby Sedgepond Plantation, down Sedge Pond Hill from Roebuck. A115 was Bedford lorry and A 33 was the Austin lorry. We didn't call them trucks in Roebuck. They were lorries. As boys we used to have serious arguments as to which lorry was the faster of the two as they hauled loads of sugar cane up Sedgepond Hill to either Haymans or Porters sugar factory. I was an Austin guy and from my house I could tell when A 33 was climbing Sedgepond Hill with a load of cane. I could tell the difference in the Austin sound from the Bedford sound. One thing I have not yet told is the significance of the A or the E that was part of the license plates mentioned above. The A meant that A 115, A 33 as well as A 85, an Austin car belonging to Mr. Vaughn, the headmaster at All Saints Boys School, were from the parish of St. Andrew, whereas the E in E 310 meant that the Roebuck car belonging to the Scantleburys was from the parish of Saint Peter; Saint Peter having to take the E only because the P was already taken by the parish of Saint Phillip.

Cars from the parish of Saint Michael were marked M, as in M 5339, a Rover belonging to Mr. Lynch, my high school headmaster, and one of the most respected men that influenced my life. I am smiling as I write this, recalling that when he, or our teachers, entered the classroom, the students would stand and would be allowed sit only when the teachers were satisfied that they had our full attention. Such was the level of respect. Interestingly, I was watching Pastor Randy Roberts from the Loma Linda Church on television recently and he told of a similar experience when he was a young student in Haiti. I wonder if this aspect of our Barbados culture has survived.

Cars and lorries from Saint James were marked with S due to the process of elimination, since the J was already taken by the parish of Saint John. Those from the parish of Saint Joseph were marked O, only because the J was already taken by the parish of Saint John, while those from Saint Thomas had no competition for the T. The same was true for the parishes of Saint George and Saint Lucy as they were marked with G and L respectively. Somehow, those cars from Christ Church, like one marked X1103, a Toyata Cressida belonging to Hillary Pilgrim, an Erdiston College classmate of mine; and another one marked X 1146, belonging to Seymour Nurse, my favorite cricketer, were uncharacteristically marked with an X instead of C.

Another Scantlebury family lived below the shop. Sonny Scantlebury, the *shopkeeper's* brother, was better known as Pappy, especially to his children. His wife was Mammy and together they had many children, some of whom went to live in England. The boys were Alvin, nicknamed Hun; Eversley, better known as Brothers, Colvin known as Raw Pork, Graham, who passed away while the book was being written, and Andrew, nicknamed Foot Pad. Andrew had a dog name Butter Tot. Butter Tot chased me one night but gave up the chase as I made my left turn by Osbourne's house at the top of the line. It now appears that Butter Tot had a history of chasing, and even biting Roebuck's residents. While we were in Roebuck recently, Jenny told the story of being chased, and even being bitten by Butter Tot. She said she has the marks on her behind to prove it. And Dorcas also reported that Butter Tot had nipped her on the leg one night. Foot Pad dropped by to see me after he heard that I was visiting. I had not seen him since I left Roebuck in 1973 to attend college in Jamaica.

The Scantlebury girls were Lyrill, Gladwin, who had a son name Lennox, Beverly, Glendeen, Waveny, better known as Avvy, Denise, and Ethna, nicknamed Doll Dinks. It so happened that Glendeen was visiting Roebuck from England at the same time we were there recently. She hung out with us quite a bit. It was so good to see her again after so many years. It was also exciting to see Denise and Waveny after such a long time.

The *stand pipe* was on the same side of the road just after The Marshall's house, under a rather large and wide-spreading breadfruit tree owned by the same family. The *pipe,* as it was commonly known, was the central venue where all of Roebuck gathered to *catch* water, and since none of the houses in Roebuck had the luxury of having a *tap* in the kitchen or in the toilet, the pipe was a popular location for people to assemble to talk and gossip while waiting their turn to catch buckets or pans of water. I remember making a *pad,* using a towel or some other material, to put on my bare head to cushion the weight of a heavy bucket of cold water. Sometimes I would carry a container larger than the standard bucket to the pipe to fetch water. Under those circumstances when the load was too heavy for me to hoist to my head all by myself, I would ask another person to give me a *lift.* I would head home to empty the contents into a large barrel, repeating the process until the barrel was full of cool water for the family to use for drinking and to cooking.

I was terribly excited to discover on my recent trip back home, that the pipe was still standing and still producing water. As I stopped to turn it on I smiled to myself, remembering the times spent at the pipe waiting my turn to catch my bucket or pan full of water. At the same time I also recalled with a smile how the *zeplen,* as we called it in Roebuck, would come around to deliver water when there was none coming out of the pipe, and how we would all get in line to fill our buckets. The *zeplen* was what I heard it being called in Roebuck when I was a boy and I had no reason to check on the meaning or the spelling, until now. I am not too surprised at discovering that *zeplen* turns out to be one of those Roebuck inventions that comes very close to zeppelin that has nothing to do with a water delivery truck but everything to do with a type of rigid airship pioneered by the German Count Zeppelin in the early 20th century.

On immediately leaving the pipe, there was another line on the left hand side. It was rather short so we didn't even call it a line. It branched off to the left and led to a *gulley* through which we walked to get to Rock Hall. Along the way, my mother, along with others from Roebuck, had a *cane piece* and a *ground* with some rather tall breadfruit trees and *pear* trees. *Tumbric* flourished in the shade created by these spreading trees. *Tumbric* came up in a conversation with Hal the other day and we both had a rather hearty laugh about how we substituted *tumbric* for tumeric when we were boys. Before we hung up, he advised that I take some *tumbric* often because "it is good for blood pressure."

The second branch of that short line led to a not-so-steep hill, and we always said that the people whose houses were up there lived *up on the hill.* Another Scantlebury family lived up on the hill. This time it was Alphonsa Scantlebury, better known as Brother Scant, and his wife Rita. Some tried to make a nickname, Tina, stick to Brother Scant but he was too respected and no one was bold enough to call him Tina to his face. He was held in high esteem by all and it was evident by the level of respect we all gave him. Brother Scant and Sonny were brothers, and Rita was my father's sister, which meant that their children were my first cousins. Hugh was the oldest and he and Nazerite, better known as Nazie, went to England earlier on, leaving Dorcas and Sherrod up on the hill with their parents. Sherrod's nickname was D'Oliveira, Dolly for short; a name he got because of his ability to produce movement and swing to a cricket ball, just like Basil D'Oliveira, the swing bowler that played cricket for England when we were growing up in Roebuck in the sixties. For a long time Sherrod was the only person I knew with that name until I heard about Senator Sherrod Brown, a Democrat from Ohio. It was also quite interesting to see the name Sherrod as a brand name for a conversion van.

The recent visit to Roebuck was an unplanned and unofficial family reunion. Nevertheless, it turned into a very exciting time for all of us who had not seen each other in years. I was happy to see Sherrod and Nazie again but was disappointed that Hugh had finished his visit just before I and the rest of the family from New

York and California arrived on the island for our visit. The last time I saw Hugh was in 2001 when I was in London. However, we spent a lot of time with Dorcas, first at the Pentecost Church in Roebuck, where she preached a rousing sermon in celebration of Ms. Morris' ninetieth birthday. And secondly, at her house late one night, where my sisters, Jenny, and I, sat around feasting on fried flying fish, sweet bread and tea, while laughing and talking about growing up in Roebuck and the people like Bro. Scant, Ms. Watson, Pastor and Sister Sobers and the others that helped shaped our lives. I still rate that evening's get-together very highly among the other exciting times we experienced on our visit. I still reminisce on the lighthearted and cheerful nature of our party that evening, especially when we talked at length about how we used to eat at each other's house; how Christmastime was so special; which dog belonged to whom when we were growing up; and which dog chased and bit whom. Dorcas had us literally hysterical when she confirmed Charleston's account on how Hopper Dollar was *licked down* one day and how he eventually got the nickname that would define him forever.

Another Worrell family lived up on the hill. Mr. Worrell's Christian name was Ivan but he was nicknamed Duck Eye because he had a funny-looking eye. He had a son we called Sonna. Mr. Worrell's wife, Ida, was Roebuck's resident midwife, delivering many of the babies that were born at home in Roebuck. Not that she had official training in midwifery or nursing; she simply perfected her craft with regular practice. In Roebuck, women *in the family way* did not go to the hospital to give birth. They had their babies at home with a midwife, the likes of Ida Worrell officiating. Ida herself had several children that included Mildred, Rita's mother, Deany Blackman, Leopold, and Daphne. Daphne had a son we all called Bounce, a nickname that substituted for his real name. She was also mother to Valery, Jeffrey and Gay Boy. For sure, Gay Boy was not his real name but that was the only name we had for him. The

Lowes also lived up on the hill. Mr. Lowe was Darling's father and he also had a son, Connell.

Just as *down the line* and *up on the hill* were used to indicate where people lived in Roebuck, so too was *around the corner.* Around the corner from the pipe on the right hand side of the road was a little compound of three or four small houses. Ms. Nurse, whom everyone called El, lived in one of the houses with her husband, Darwin, and children Gloria and Don; Gloria being the product of a previous relationship. Ivy, El's sister, as well as Violet, Bay's daughter and her husband Norman also lived on the compound.

Ms. Millie lived by herself a little farther down the road on the *left hand side*, as we used to say in Roebuck. Her dog was Skillet. The Watsons lived below Ms. Millie. Sonny and Lillian Watson had quite a large family of their own, with some rather unique names given to their children. The girls were Ouida, who possessed the most beautiful hand writing in Indian Ground School. Her written work in her *exercise book* was always very neat, whether written in ink or with a *black lead*. Even though she, like all of us, usually kept a *rubber* handy, it was obvious that she did not *rub out* much. Her exercise book, the kind with the times tables recorded on the back cover, was a model to the whole class. Eudene, on the other hand, was as dark and lovely as her name was unusual. Then there were Dalmer, Octlyn, Rhonda, Marcell and Julie. The boys were Ralphston, the triplets Peter, James and John; and Sharron, nicknamed Biney. When the triplets came along, it caused quite a stir in Roebuck since many of us had never heard of a woman having three babies at the same time. We had all heard of women giving birth to twins. But never triplets. And amidst all the excitement surrounding Roebuck's first triplet, I knew that many, including me, were wondering about the scientific and biological possibility that made it happen. Even Mr. Watson, the district's newest celebrity, as quiet as he was tall and lanky, must have been stunned at the outcome of what had become a local sensation.

As for me, it was not until I sat in Mr. Holder's Biology class at The Modern High School, that I was able to understand the mechanism surrounding the formation of identical and fraternal twins and triplets. Later, I would teach the triplets in *standard three* at All Saints Boys School. The boys were so perfectly identical that I could not identify Peter from James or John. They relished in my confusion whenever I struggled to tell one from the other, especially at those times when discipline was to be meted out. The Watsons later moved up to the position of shopkeepers to manage the shop after McCleod and Ethlyn Scantlebury moved to the city.

I had to see Ms. Watson when I went back to visit in January of 2014. It was unthinkable to go to Roebuck and not visit Ms. Watson. It would have been like the unpardonable sin had I not gone to see her. I ran across her in church one Sunday morning, where she gave a very impressive, articulate and coherent speech as she presented a gift to Ms. Morris on the occasion of her 90th birthday. But that was not enough. I had to visit her in her home, so I intentionally stopped by her house after the service for what I had planned to be a brief visit. I found out once again that no visit with Ms. Watson is ever brief, especially when some of her children were there. I met Ouida, whom I had not seen since 1973. Among other things, we talked about her neat handwriting, which she said she still had. And I met her husband Val, my good friend from Indian Ground school days. Rhonda was there as well as the triplets, who still confused me as to who was Peter, James, or John. Quite coincidentally, Marcel was visiting from Canada at the time and it was good to see her again. I spoke with Eudene by telephone but did not keep my promise to call Octlyn. I did not get to see Ralphston, Julie or Biney. When I was finally able to pull myself away, Ms. Watson, true to form, made certain I did not leave empty handed. This time, it was a package of her frozen pigeon peas. "Take this with you," she said in the middle of a tight hug.

A few days later, my sisters and I were going down the line visiting and ran into Ms. Watson doing what she had always done. At one stop, we found the 87 year old Good Samaritan looking in on Mr. and Mrs. Gilkes, who were well into their nineties. And when we made the next stop at the 90 year old Ms. Morris, there was Ms. Watson making her rounds and house calls. Amazingly, she still considers it her duty and personal responsibility to look out for the older people in the neighborhood. Later, my sisters and I would comment on Ms. Watson's attitude, and were somewhat moved by the reality that the spirit of goodwill and community togetherness was still alive and well in Roebuck. I knew then, by their reaction that they, like me, were personally grateful for having grown up in such a caring and supportive environment. Each time I hear the statement "It takes a village…" I think of people like Ms. Watson, Ms. Morris, Rita, The Marshalls, The Scantleburys, The Sobers, The Gilkeses, and others, and how the spirit of support and friendship that was present when I was a boy is still as vibrant and common among them, and how they were the village that raised us.

My sisters, Elaine and Yvonne, told me a story after they returned to New York from Barbados following our recent visit; a story told to them by Ms. Watson that cemented the reputation that from way back, the people of Roebuck had always exemplified a spirit of caring and compassion towards each other. Apparently, they had gone to visit Ms. Watson after I had left the island to return to the US and during the visit Ms. Watson told them how helpful our mother had been to her when she was sick. I had never known Ms. Watson to be sick, so the story attracted my interest. She told them that when she was sick, Muddah would come to her house and wash, starch, and iron the family's dirty clothes, as well as do other jobs around the house until she was well again.

Apparently, my mother did a complete job where laundering the clothes was concerned. She not only washed and starched the clothes, either with cassava or Arrowroot starch. She would even *sprinkle* and iron them, so that Ms. Watson's family did not have to wear *rough dry* clothes. Ms. Watson continued by telling them that when Mr. Watson got his *back pay* from the plantation, and gave her a part of it to take care of the family's needs, she offered my mother a portion of the money as a reward for her help. My mother refused the offer and Ms. Watson insisted that she take the money, telling her that she cannot give it back to Mr. Watson. My mother's defense was that she was only performing an act of kindness, and was not working for pay.

Ms. Watson's parents, The Richards, lived close by, down a dark line on the opposite side of the road between two *cane pieces*. This particular line was a short cut that came out by The Griffiths and eventually led to the line where I lived. It was also a short cut to church. The place was scary after dark, especially when there was talk of an *out man* or *a heart man* on the loose. In Roebuck an *out man* was the name given to an outlaw, or a man that had escaped jail, was on the run, and was thought to be hiding in the cane piece. A *heart man* was a man waiting in the canes to cut out children's hearts. The Richards had two other children apart from Lilian Watson. They were Octalese and Darnley, nicknamed Dumb Boy, appropriately named because he was actually dumb and made funny noises when he wanted to communicate.

Pastor and Ms. Sobers lived below The Watsons. He was the pastor of the only church in Roebuck, The Roebuck New Testament Church of God, also known as the Pentecost Church. He was Joseph. She was Rita. And like Brother Scant, they were well respected as church leaders and examples of moral uprightness. Many mornings they would wake up the entire Roebuck preaching messages that the Lord had given to them, calling us back to follow God, to live right, and to prepare for His soon coming. The Sobers had two daughters, Valdene and Lynette. Ms. Sobers' sister, Muriel, and a nephew, Kenrick, also lived with the family. The Church was immediately below their house, and directly below the church was the last house in Roebuck, belonging to Charles Cox and his wife. Mr. Cox was a bus driver for the Transport Board. He and his wife had a daughter, Ernesta, who was mother to Eddie, Malcolm, David, Linda, and Phyllis.

My cousin, Charleston, told a story about Ms. Cox one day. According to him, she bought a newspaper and had it out on the bus and was looking at it, even though she knew that she could not read. She was apparently holding the paper upside down, looking at a picture of a group of people. After a few minutes studying the picture, she remarked that because of the prime minister's policies, things had gotten so bad in Barbados that he had the people walking on their heads. The veracity of the story has never been verified but knowing Charleston like I do, he may have made up the entire thing, or may have embellished the situation a little.

The Pentecost Church was by and large the center of community life in Roebuck. Apart from the nightly meetings and the weekly Sunday school and church services, the church organized an excursion every year in the summer. Sometimes called the *outing*, it was one of those rare occasions when we had new clothes, and the only time some of us got to leave Roebuck. We would dress up in our best clothes, which took a special shopping trip to town. We packed several large buses, rented for the day from the Transport Board. We would sing and beat *cymbals*, while on our way to Crane Beach, Fowl Bay, King's Park, or even Seawell Airport. Of course, rice and peas, chicken, mutton and beef stew, and corned beef sandwiches went with us on these annual trips.

The *outing* was one of two formal affairs in Roebuck; the Christmas day program at the Pentecost Church being the other. We called it the *outing* or the excursion back then. But I was quick to learn that the US name for the *outing* (at least in New York City) is the bus ride. I was also quick to discover that not only was the name different in both cultures but that the entire approach to the activity was as far apart as their geographical location. In Roebuck we dared not wear *dungarees*, or slippers, *pumps* or *soft shoes* to our outing. That was not the outing culture. That was too informal. It was vastly different from the jeans, tee shirt, tennis shoe culture I was to later adopt.

On a more serious note, the Pentecost Church was the center of moral and religious awareness in Roebuck. Sunday night services were evangelistic in nature and attracted several curious onlookers that crowded the steps of the church, or some took a seat on the benches in the back. We didn't call them pews in Roebuck. They were benches. Long, hard benches that held several people comfortably. Church members sang and beat cymbals and even *got in the power*. One of my American friends described a similar happening as *getting happy*. In Roebuck we said they got *in the power* or, that they had the Holy Ghost; speaking in tongues and moving about the church shaking violently, which was always a source of merriment for those looking on.

Subsequently, a sermon from Pastor Sobers, or Sister Sobers, or Brother Scant, on the coming of Christ and sinners burning in hell's fire and brimstone forever, would transform the mood to a more serious and contemplative one, and when the invitation was given, some of us would go down front and get saved and give our hearts to God, either because we were scared, or were truly convicted. I got saved a few times but ended up *backsliding* as well.

On Sunday nights at the church, the Communion service was celebrated. We didn't call it communion in Roebuck. It was the *Lord's Supper*. The women wore white and the men dressed in dark suits. It was a very solemn occasion where the members washed each other's feet and sipped wine from a single cup that was passed around among them. One had to be baptized to take part in the *Lord's Supper*. Strangely enough, if members felt that they had something questionable in their lives, even if it was a daughter that was pregnant out of wedlock, they would decide not to participate, for fear of being *rebuked*, either by Pastor Sobers, Sister Sobers, or

Brother Scant. A rebuke was very public and very humiliating, with the Pastor, Sister Sobers or Brother Scant, speaking in tongues and saying something like *sickie Messiah,* leveled in the direction of the member that was about to stand up and testify. I was saved several times at the Church but backslid before reaching the status of the rebuked. I never got up to testify. I was too scared; or never attempted to participate in the *Lord's Supper,* so I was never in line for a *rebuke.*

My friend Floyd, was the one who reminded me of *sickie Messiah.* He called one evening, laughing his head off. "Do you remember *sickie Messiah?*" he asked. I had to take a few moments of think time before answering in the affirmative. We both enjoyed a light-hearted moment, reminiscing on the *rebuking* sessions at the Church. It appears that the only time they spoke in plain English was when they yelled "Don't sip it," at the person who was about to take a sip of wine from the communion cup. I was privy to many *rebukes.* Not that any of them happened to me. But there was one *rebuke* that got a lot of attention and was the source of much talk. Legend has it that my paternal grandmother, Ethlyn Griffith, was *rebuked* one night and never recovered from the experience. Knowing my grandmother like I did, she probably deserved the *rebuke* but certainly not the consequences.

The annual revival at the Church was also a popular event that lasted for several weeks. Again, curious on-lookers packed the steps of the church to peer through the doors and the windows to catch a glimpse of people swaying and dancing and getting in the power. People came nightly from all over to Roebuck just to witness the revival; from Indian Ground and from Four Hill, and even from as far away as French Village. Guest preachers from nearby Rock Hall and from not so far away Diamond Corner, to far away Checker Hall and Crab Hill, brought in their members in buses and vans on their appointed night, and preached fiery sermons on the coming of Christ and on hell's fire and brimstone, to convict sinners and

Christians alike. Usually, some sinners were saved but some nights the invitation fell on deaf ears.

But having said all of this, to me personally, *the line* was much more than a narrow rocky path with houses on both sides. It would eventually become an important symbol and a location where a personal decision was made; a decision that was the turning point for me, and one that would shape my future. The following story is applicable and is significant in playing a major role in what and who I would become later in life. I recall the drama of the day as if it was yesterday, and I have played its scenes over and over again and again in my mind with some degree of thankfulness, as well as shame.

It was one of those mornings that I did not have to run from my house to make it to the bus stop at the top of the line in time to catch the school bus to the city of Bridgetown. Most mornings would find me scampering from my house in a state of total unreadiness; sometimes with my shirt halfway buttoned, or totally untucked. At other times my belt would be only partly through the *tabs,* or on another day, my tie in my hand would be flying like a flag in the breeze, acting as a speedometer to indicate how fast I was really moving as I raced to outrun the school bus before it got to the stop. And I could really speed it up in those days.

It was a red school bus. Not a yellow one. A big, long AEC, with Transport Board written along the length of it. Sometimes we got the more luxurious blue and white Mercedes Benz, E 442. The Mercedes crashed one afternoon, hitting Sonny Lou's guard wall in Aston Hall, while on its way back to the *bus stand* after depositing all the students home safely. But on this particular Monday morning, like most mornings, our school bus was the usual AEC, M 5721. The immaculate Mr. Altman was the driver. We all called him Altman. He was the neatest bus driver there was. Clean, thin, and well dressed. It was obvious that he went to great lengths to make sure that his appearance was unrivaled. His black tie was professionally knotted and fitted perfectly and snugly in its place under the buttoned down collar of his blue shirt with sharp seams that ran from shoulder to wrist along the length of sleeves that were starched and stiff. I stepped on to the AEC, passing the *conductor* and immediately began to meander my way around other students standing in the aisle, in order to reach the back of the bus.

I always liked to ride in the back and would have had no problem riding in the back in the days of Rosa Parks. The bus wasn't very crowded that early in the morning as it usually was during the afternoon run back to the country. So it was not the same as forcing my way through as was common during the afternoon rush. There was no *spy* on the bus that morning. *Spies* didn't board the bus that early in the day, or never in Roebuck, for that matter. It was my friend Hal that reminded me of the *spies*. One day, out of the blue, he called and asked if I remembered what a *spy* was. I wasn't thinking of the book at the time, and therefore, was not in the frame of mind to provide the answer he was looking for. "Of course I know what a spy is," I answered haltingly, thinking about the professional spies that work for the CIA or for the KGB. He came to my rescue when he asked with a chuckle, "Don't you remember the *spies* that used to board the buses in Barbados?" A moment of hearty laughter was in order.

On the morning in question I encountered Valery Waterman somewhere about midfield on the AEC and without warning, provocation, or mutual threat, we became embroiled in an altercation, a fancy name for a fight that was both vicious and dangerous. It happened so suddenly, as if spontaneous combustion had taken place. Valery was as tall as she was strong. I was lanky and athletic. Both of us characteristically quiet; both engaging in a fight for which there was no known cause. The one-rounder was short and intense with personal pain as well as life lessons that remain with me to this day. I learned never to fight with girls ever again. Not because they are good at it. The reason may be surprising.

Girls do not fight fair. They respect none of the rules that govern a civilized brawl. They fight to maim, or even to kill. They pull no punches, or should I say, they throw no punches. Valerie didn't either. She simply swung wildly with both arms like a windmill on a windy day of an approaching Barbados hurricane. She went for my eyes. I don't know why. And she grabbed for my tie. I am sure she thought of lunging for my hair but there wasn't much to grab. And she deployed the one weapon of mass destruction that all girls have in their arsenal — the dreaded fingernails that carved random and creative designs on my face and arms. She drew blood. My DNA was under her fingernails.

My attempt at a civil fight was a serious mistake; one that could have resulted in serious personal bodily harm. "Float like a butterfly, sting like a bee" was ineffective under the circumstances. Valery would have none of that refined stuff. She fought me using the same tactics as if she were fighting another female. A *cuff* here and a jab there met with limited success. In total desperation, a couple of left-right combinations connected. And it was all over. The events that followed would be the catalyst that was responsible for setting in motion the determination that would change my life forever.

Mr. Altman put me off the bus that morning. I stepped off and stepped right into it; into her, to put it more accurately. There she was, as if by miraculous design, or by divine providence; as if God had put her there *for such a time as this*. In another way of looking at it, she was my biblical Jonah, sent specifically for me, with a message and a prophecy. There she was, waiting, ready to judge and to pass sentence. She was Ms. Griffith from down the line. I was not ready for her verdict but she delivered it anyway. And it was as deliberate as it was final.

"You, Fred son," she began. "You will never amount to anything good." I was sure she didn't take the time to consider the evidence, or consult the witnesses. It obviously didn't concern her that I had suddenly become disheveled and totally humiliated and embarrassed because I had fought with a girl. I knew it was not gentlemanlike to hit girls but in a moment of weakness I had had broken a cardinal rule — the eleventh commandment. I had brought shame and reproach to my mother's name, and even at that very painful moment wondered why Mrs. Griffith addressed me as Fred's son, instead of Iola's. By this time my father had already left for England to find work to support the family and my mother was well into her role, raising the five of us on her own, working hard in the fields on Sedgepond Plantation to earn money to pay my school fees. Still, Mrs. Griffith addressed me as Fred's son. My conclusion is that she, like most in Roebuck, was very familiar with the reputation my father had made for himself as a tough father and a respectable and reputable gentleman. I am sure that she harbored no disrespect for my mother, who had also done a marvelous job of building a strong reputation in her own right. Personally, I felt that the damage I had done was to my mother because she was the one providing direct parenting and guidance at the time.

Old Mrs. Griffith had struck; striking me hard in my weakened state. That morning, I realized that she simply took one look at me in my moment of weakness and was quick to make judgments and predictions about my future. "Let her make her predictions." I spoke to myself. "Let her pontificate and play God." Quite surprisingly, I began thinking quite maturely, concluding that her prophecy was purely conditional and that it was up to me to see that it did not come to pass. It was up to me to prove her wrong; creating a false prophet out of her. But most importantly, the events of that morning were also revealing, in that they showed me in a very real way that God positions people and circumstances at opportune times, and in pivotal places, to give warning, to provide direction and to inspire a reason to think, to evaluate, and to redirect one's behavior; to listen to an inner voice and to respond to a higher calling. My time had come.

That morning as I made the trek down the line back home, I came face to face with my first serious reflection and personal introspection. "You, Fred son, you will not amount to anything good" was replayed in my head. I had walked that rocky path a million times before and knew all too well where each dangerous stone was positioned. Even in the darkest night I had safely maneuvered my way home barefoot as I tried to outrun the darkness. That morning, as I walked back down *the line* I saw the same familiar stones; this time appearing as boulders, as if I had not encountered them before. And simultaneously, I saw myself as I had not seen me before. Suddenly I began to see me the way I wanted to see me in the future. I could see the end of a journey. A new Sylvester began to emerge. And he was happy. And excited. And successful.

It had taken me only a few seconds to disgrace myself and my family, and an equally short time to decide that I would amount to something good. The rest is history. I went on to complete high school and began my teaching career immediately after in 1968, and have been teaching ever since. I completed an undergraduate degree, two graduate degrees and a doctorate in education along the way. I have taught at all levels of education in Barbados, the Virgin Islands and also in the United States, and have served as school administrator in Tennessee and Georgia. I am certain that Ms. Griffith would have agreed that I did amount to something good after all, had she lived to witness my success. Her prophecy was probably correct at the time it was delivered because it was based on the behavior presented to her by me, even though it should not have been her only frame of reference. The fact that I had a history and a reputation of being a good boy in Roebuck all those years, meant nothing to her. She determined from this one event that I would not amount to anything good. It was up to me to prevent this from coming to pass. And I did. She did her job. And I did mine. And it all began going back down *the line* in Roebuck.

My sisters and I talked about the fight with Valery when we were in Barbados recently. They updated my account with the additional details that Valery's father had come to our house that night to complain to my mother about me fighting his daughter on the school bus that morning. Apparently, he had approached my mother in a very threatening manner, throwing down his bicycle and demanding that she punish me in some way. According to them, my mother stood her ground and ordered him to take his bicycle and get off her property. I had completely forgotten about the incident and had to remark that I did not know that my mother had a feisty streak.

CHAPTER EIGHT

Bullers and Wickers

But Pastor Sobers, Sister Sobers and Brother Scant from The Roebuck Pentecost Church would definitely question if this was a winning argument that has its fundamentals firmly entrenched in biblical teaching.

Some years ago in Washington State, my friends, Floyd, Hal and I, were having a spirited conversation about some words that we used as kids while growing up in Barbados that had a completely different meaning, or no meaning at all, here in the U.S. I am not sure what was the motivation for our discussion or what one of us had said that led us into the dialogue but I began taking mental notes, knowing that the publication of the book was a major personal goal for the future.

That evening, words like *buller* and *wicker* came up in our talk, and even though *buller* is virtually non-existent in American language or folklore, the mere mention of the word on that particular day in Washington was enough to spark a lighthearted discussion. *Wicker*, on the other hand, is common to the American cultural landscape, but as we shall see later, its meaning is far removed from how it was used in Roebuck when I was a boy. The comparison, though funny to some, may appear insensitive or even offensive to others. Bear in mind however, that this chapter, or this book for that matter, is not meant to offend anyone or any group, or to criticize the personal lifestyle of those residing in Barbados, the U.S,

225

or any other culture. This work is simply a play on words and how they are used in the two cultures addressed in the book.

One aspect of cultural relevance became very clear, at least to me, during our conversation that day in Washington, back in November of 2009; the fact that cultural customs, like most anything, diminish with decreasing frequency of use. The often cited quote *if you don't use it, you'll surely lose it* is certainly applicable here. So is the case with the two Roebuck terms, *buller* and *wicker*. I had not used them in conversation in a while, so it should not be difficult to understand why their place in my cultural vocabulary had diminished almost to the point of extinction. One thing became clear that particular day; that in order for cultural norms to be strengthened and perpetuated, they have to be practiced repeatedly if they are to be passed on to succeeding generations. Cultural promulgation, to some degree, can be analogous to the development of a muscle. It becomes noticeably weaker and softer with decreased physical activity. Or it can be compared equally as well to acquiring a foreign language in which proficiency is severely hampered due to a lack of regular practice.

Personally speaking, so much of my cultural customs in the area of word usage has been lost on two fronts; the first of which, as cited above, is the lack of regular usage. There is nobody in Ringgold, Georgia, to engage me on a meaningful level, in my cultural lingo to which I had become accustomed while growing up in Roebuck. I am only able to do this on any significant level when I occasionally get together with my sisters, or when I have regular conversations on the telephone with Floyd from Washington; or with Hal, who lives in the Atlanta area; or with Kathy, Laura and Jasmine from nearby Chattanooga. Even though we may frequently indulge in our cultural way of speaking when we talk, we communicate in standard language the vast majority of the time. The same is true of my friend Randy from Maryland.

Secondly, and probably the more disturbing of the two, is the comment that I hear every once in a while. "You don't sound like a Bajan," some tell me from time to time. But while I desperately want to be identified as, and sound like I am Bajan, and from Roebuck specifically, my situation is compounded by my struggle to be politically correct. The desire to communicate effectively in Roebuck lingo is severely hindered in these parts where I now live, for I can't go around talking to my neighbors in terms such as *black lead, lorry, chinks* and *cheese cutters*, or describing people as *bullers* and *wickers*.

It is now time to end the suspense for some readers and reveal that in Roebuck, *bullers* and *wickers* were descriptive terms that identified a strange and unusual lifestyle that had a sexual designation. I say strange and unusual because that was the way the people of Roebuck would have described the lifestyle. Maybe not in so many words but their simple characterization of the behavior that it was wrong would have been just as effective. In Roebuck, a *buller* was a male that exhibited a sexual interest in other males. In Roebuck we never used the word homosexual. We never even knew that the word existed. And even if we had known of its existence in the dictionary, my intimate knowledge of my people back then, tells me that they might have never used it anyway, with the excuse that it was too sophisticated a term for a behavior so strange. It was never a part of our vocabulary.

One would think that the ultra religious of Roebuck would have at least been privileged enough to have knowledge of the word since it is a practice so pointedly mentioned in the Bible. But in their defense, the word homosexual is not recorded in the KJV, the only version we knew about in those days. So it was not ever mentioned by the spiritual elite from The Roebuck Pentecost Church, or among the laity in passing conversation, or in the exercise of their Sunday worship service. In Roebuck, the label was always *buller,* and was always looked at as being a despicable and repulsive lifestyle, even though those descriptive terms were foreign to us back then.

Needless to say, the buller behavior was non-existent in Roebuck, even though just over Penny Hill in nearby Indian Ground, rumor had it that one particular young man was so inclined. In fact, he did lend some degree of truth to the speculation, at least in my estimation. I can recall very vividly the young man in question wearing a dress one Sunday afternoon, an event that caused a stir of excitement, to put it mildly.

Surprisingly enough, we did use the word *gay* quite a bit in Roebuck but not in the context described previously. Gay was the first part of a person's name — Gay Boy, we used to call him. Gay Boy was the only white looking person in Roebuck; the alleged product of an interracial relationship between his mother Daphne and Fred Gill, a white plantation manager. I never knew Gay Boy's real name. Actually, I don't think anybody knew it but he was Gay Boy to all of us. I am positive that he was not gay, as in the gay lifestyle, and to this day I don't know why, or from where, the name originated. Oddly enough, he never lived up to the meaning of his name, as he seldom appeared gay. As in happy.

In Roebuck we also coined our own peculiar name for women that preferred other women as sexual partners. They were *wickers*. Lesbian was a word we never used in Roebuck. Like gay and homosexual, it was not a part of our cultural vernacular, and even if it was a word that was known by the people of Roebuck, I am sure they would not have utilized such a word for a lifestyle they thought was so objectionable. Like buller, the *wicker* behavior was nonexistent in Roebuck, even though in nearby Indian Ground, the sister to the young man mentioned above was said to be either a participant, or was interested in this particular sexual approach. And she had the nickname to prove it.

Unlike buller, wicker is a useable American word that has to do with a brand of furniture, or things made of twigs, canes or reeds. The first time I heard about wicker chairs was after I came to America, and I remember chuckling inside, thinking of a funny situation that could actually happen if some unsuspecting visitor from America should visit Roebuck and express the desire to purchase, or worse yet, sit on a wicker. I had an even bigger inner laugh recently when a television commercial, sponsored by a local furniture store, announced that they had a variety of wickers on hand.

On a more serious note, you may have already concluded that the people of Roebuck did not subscribe to the lifestyle of *bullers* and *wickers*. It was not a cultural conduct that was becoming of our little remote district. It wasn't viewed as normal, or proper; so much so that it was not even talked about, even in biblical or religious discourse in our Bible-toting community. And even if it was talked about among the biblically astute of the neighborhood, the language of the conversation would certainly have been be spiritually appropriate, corresponding with the seriousness of the nature of the topic. For sure, Pastor Sobers, or Sister Sobers, or Brother Scant, would have ceased and desisted from even uttering the words *buller* and *wicker*, or even homosexual, or lesbian, for that matter. They would have chosen to bathe their conversation in biblical terminology with words like sodomy; making a direct connection to the story of Sodom and Gomorrah, and the consequences they suffered for such a behavior.

But the one thing that continues to cross my mind, even as I write this particular section, is the fact that I had never heard Pastor Sobers, Sister Sobers, or Brother Scant, preach a sermon on the topic of homosexual behavior. And I have heard a lot of their preaching. Even today I continue to wonder why they never ever broached the subject. Probably, as mentioned before, it was not a timely issue that plagued Roebuck, for there was not a single person, male or female, in Roebuck that claimed to relish such activity. If the issue of homosexuality and lesbianism had been a high profile one, you can be certain that many sermons would have been delivered by the three, blasting the behavior and its participants as sinful, as an abomination, and committing both the evil and the evildoer to burn forever in hell's everlasting fire and brimstone, even if they sought refuge in the argument "We were born like this."

But without skipping a beat, Pastor Sobers, Sister Sobers and Brother Scant would have fired back with a biblical response of their own to the *born like this* argument. "We are all born in sin," they would have intoned. "Born with a sinful nature and with the propensity to sin," they would have explained. "We have a tendency and a temptation to sin," they would have preached from the *platform* of the Roebuck Pentecost Church; "be it stealing, or bearing false witness, or adultery, or murder, or even homosexuality." And the punch line of their argument would have been that having the tendency to sin is not a sin in itself. It is the yielding to the temptation that is the sin. And beyond that powerful declaration, they would have driven home the point that sinners will not enter the Promised Land as sinners; that practicing liars will not enter as liars, or practicing adulterers as such, or practicing homosexuals as homosexuals. In my own vivid imagination I can see them pounding the podium in the midst of a chorus of amens and hallelujahs as they conclude their sermon with the profound rebuttal that all of us have something in our sinful character that needs to be rectified before it is too late. They probably would not have used a term as eloquent as rectify, but would have settled for more simple diction that the people of Roebuck could understand; like change, or give up.

This brings me to a second point in the argument that usually comes up when supporters and sympathizers defend the homosexual lifestyle. This group includes religious leaders seeking ordination, as well as politicians and others from all walks of life. "What would Jesus do?" they often ask, injecting religion into the argument as a way of rationalizing their behavior. And for the answer, I again defer to the expertise of the moral and religious triumvirate from Roebuck — Pastor Sobers, Sister Sobers and Brother Scant, who in their day would have simply answered the question, which to them would have been a no-brainer. So what would Jesus do?

According to them, He would do what He has always done: condemn the behavior in the strongest terms possible, as He did in the case with the woman caught in adulterous behavior. "Neither do I condemn you. Go and sin no more," they would have quoted. "Jesus loves the sinner but hates the sin," they would have preached.

Quite coincidentally, as I write on this topic, the battle over same sex marriage is raging here in the U.S. It is as if it has become deeply ingrained into the moral fabric of the country, with men wanting the right to marry men, and women defending their constitutional right to marry other females. And I wonder, as I write, if the culture of Roebuck has changed as this particular movement is igniting across the USA. And to add fuel to the fire, President Obama has come out in favor of the right of anyone to marry whomever he or she wants to. So more and more same sex couples have been emboldened and are *coming out* and getting married in those states that allow it. By the way, we didn't say *coming out* in Roebuck unless we were talking about coming out of the house, or church, or something like that. There was no closet to come out of because there were no walk-in closets in Roebuck homes. The only closet we had in Roebuck was the toilet that was outside, and it was always a joy to come out of there.

Just suppose that Prime Ministers Errol Barrow, or Tom Adams of Barbados, like President Obama, had come out in favor of same sex marriage, giving *wickers* and *bullers* the right to marry? You would have heard Ms. Watson say he was *bewitched, cheupsing* her mouth in disgust as she said it, without fear of anyone in Roebuck protesting against her shop keeping business, as was recently done against Chick-Fil-A, when its president voiced his opposition to the gay lifestyle.

As if by some stroke of mere coincidence, as I am writing and watching the news on the television, one man is talking about himself and his male wife. It sounded so odd to me, and although I am living in the 21st century I still had to pinch myself really hard and long to prove I was actually hearing what I was hearing. Almost instantly my thoughts flashed back to Roebuck and readily entertained those obvious questions that Brother Scant, Pastor Sobers, Sister Sobers, and the residents of Roebuck would have discretely asked back in the day. "When two men are in a marriage relationship, how do they determine the one to 'play' the part of a female and the one to act the part of the male? Or in the case of two *wickers*, "Is there a designated male and a designated female prior to marriage? And they would certainly end their discussion with this rhetorical question, though phrased in simpler terms: "Do you see how many questions this lifestyle generates?"

I am very aware that what I am about to reveal can be construed as delving into the nitty-gritty of a homosexual relationship; a situation that so unnerved me when I was confronted by it some time back. But the first time I saw a man kiss another man on the lips, I was flabbergasted, to say the least. No, it was not on Brokeback Mountain. I never saw that movie. It was a long time before that. And it moved me. Not in the way you may be thinking. Certainly not in the same way as when a man kisses a woman.

It was at President Bill Clinton's second inauguration. I had taken a group of students from my school in Chattanooga, Tennessee, where I was principal at the time, to witness the inaugural proceedings. Somehow, either by accident, or by some providential directive, we ended up, not only in the freezing Washington, DC winter, but also in the immediate vicinity of a group of vociferous men, shouting their support for the president. And then out of the blue, it happened. Two of them locked lips in a real way. Not in a sexy way. At least not to me. Even though there were literally thousands of people standing around in the celebration, it appeared as if I was the only one in the vast multitude that was gazing intently on the phenomenon, which to me was as new as it was unacceptable. At the same time, it was as if everyone in the crowd that day had witnessed a similar scene some time before, and that I, from my sheltered Roebuck culture, was the only one caught off guard. For a while after that, I worried that my students from my small Christian school had witnessed my interest in the kiss. However, none of them ever mentioned it to me after we got back home, so I was able to regain my sense of naiveté.

Just after the same sex marriage issue was settled at the ballot box in the recent elections in Washington State, I sat gazing with overwhelming shock at Chase Lawrence kissing Chris Howard, and likewise Terry Gilbert, about to kiss his husband, Paul Beppler, on the day of their marriage. And the scene is just as personally unappealing today as it was so many years ago. But something struck me really heavily as I gazed on those photos via the internet; something that had never bothered me this seriously before. It was the perception that two men kissing each other, is in my estimation, more revolting and more nauseating than two women engaging in a similar act.

But the kiss mentioned above was not an end in itself as far as my education in the homosexual lifestyle was concerned. I am becoming less surprised at the tight grasp the lifestyle has on politicians and the political considerations they are forced to pay diligence to, especially in an election year. The lessons from the kiss were more of a means to an end; the end being my conviction that the gay movement was no longer a closet group on the fringe of the national scheme of things. Rather, it was one that has major foot holes internationally as well. No other event brought this reality more forcefully home to me than when I was preparing to teach a graduate class in diversity some years ago, when my background reading, research and class preparation opened up my awareness to the political power the homosexual movement wields. It speaks volumes about a culture when the rights and feelings of a sub culture, along with other social and moral issues — homosexuality, same sex marriage and abortion, highjack the political discourse during a presidential campaign, as well as in other local and political races and conversations in the off season.

When I was a boy I used to admire Frank Walcott, Burton Hinds, Asquith Phillips and Doc Husbands as they campaigned in Roebuck for a seat in The House of Assembly. They did not have to contend with the rights and wishes of gay groups. They were not forced to take a political position on either side of the issue. In the culture of the day, there were no men clamoring to marry each other; or women expressing a desire to marry women; nothing of the sort to distract them from what was culturally relevant. They were too concerned about what the people of Roebuck wanted, and they paid attention, knowing that it was the smart thing to do if they were to win the Roebuck vote: street lights; running water; that the cane factories keep producing sugar; good education for its children; maintaining the positive image that the country commanded in the estimation of those in the region and beyond; and emphases that prolonged the culture of Roebuck and the island as a whole.

As mentioned previously, the homosexual agenda usually seeks a defense in biblical, moral and Christian promises. Homosexual priests pursue ordination in their respective church affiliations, and the gay and lesbian laity believe that their sexual orientation is right on target to win them the same Christian favors to which all Christians aspire — heaven at last. But Pastor Sobers, Sister Sobers and Brother Scant from the Roebuck New Testament Church of God would have definitely questioned if this was a winning argument that had its fundamentals firmly entrenched in biblical teaching. And to ask the same question in simpler but more pointed terms, they would have questioned the possibility of an individual being simultaneously Christian and homosexual; whether the two lifestyles could safely coexist in the same body; and whether the two behaviors would war against each other. These would have been questions they, and the people of Roebuck, would have posed as a basis for attacking and denouncing a behavior so radical. They would have also extended the discussion by adding that no one spoke of a Christian thief, or a Christian liar, or a Christian adulterer, or a Christian fornicator. So why a Christian homosexual?

Still, Pastor Sobers, Sister Sobers and Brother Scant, while speaking out in opposition against gay and lesbian behavior if they had to, would have been just as adamant in their hostility towards *sin* in general. They were not respecters of wrong-doing in Roebuck, and used the pulpit at the Roebuck Church to denounce sin and sinners, with each category of sinful behavior receiving an equal opportunity attack from Roebuck's three religious and moral examples. They preached against liars, fornicators, thieves and the like, condemning them to hell if they did not repent. And one can be sure that if they had reason to preach against the gay and lesbian lifestyle, a practice that was not common in Roebuck, they would have lumped the offenders in with the other sinful behaviors mentioned above; each receiving a similar and deserving punishment.

Even though the word homosexual itself is not specifically found in the King James Version of the Bible, the version of choice of worshipers at the Pentecost Church, Pastor Sobers, Sister Sobers and Brother Scant were astute enough to know that First Corinthians, chapter 6 and verses nine and ten intentionally singled out homosexual behavior, as well as other sinful acts, identifying them as behaviors that prevent those who practice them from inheriting the kingdom of God. For sure, they would have certainly cited this specific text of scripture as the basis for their fiery sermons:

...Be not deceived: neither fornicators, nor idolaters, nor adulterers, nor effeminate, nor abusers of themselves with mankind, nor thieves, nor covetous, nor drunkards, nor revilers, nor extortioners, shall inherit the kingdom of God.

Today, they would be fortunate to have more ammunition for their argument, knowing that the New King James Version of the

Bible does mention homosexuals specifically as a category of people, who along with others, will not inherit the kingdom of God. And they certainly would have questioned the wisdom of engaging in such behaviors, knowing that they were deterrents to gaining the ultimate prize — the kingdom of God. "Why train for a marathon if you do not plan to be around at the finish?" they would have asked. Or, why enroll in college if you don't plan to graduate?

Chapter Nine

My Da Da

"You should not be using my tools. You should be reading books."

Our father was Da Da to us. Back then in Roebuck, I never heard anyone else call their father Da Da. Since then, I have lived in several places and the name Da Da has remained uniquely Roebuck, and definitely a kind of registered trademark that is owned by my sisters and me. We had, and still do, own the rights to the name. We have the monopoly, so to speak.

Because we owned the rights to Da Da, other families had to create their own names for their fathers. Da Da was already taken and we did not share the rights with anyone else. My oldest sister, Elaine, the originator of Da Da, passed it on to me and I in turn passed the Da Da culture down to Yvonne, who passed it on to Cheryl until it eventually reached Neats. My only conclusion as to why the term stuck is that as a toddler Da Da was much easier and more natural to say than anything else to describe our father. Even though it was childish and babyish language, it has stuck with us, and I am glad it did, for it has a way of distinguishing our family's culture from the others in Roebuck and beyond.

We did not share Da Da with even our closest relatives. Our first cousins, Hugh, Nazie, Dorcas and Sherrod called their father Daddy. Close, but not as unique as Da Da. And to the other Scantlebury family, their father was Pappy to them. Interestingly enough, neither Da Da, Daddy, nor Pappy is ever or hardly used as a term for father in America. Besides, I have been living in this country for quite a long time and have discovered that there is not much variety for father names as there was in Roebuck. Dad is the preferred name for father in the US. There may be others, but Dad is by far the most common. My first son, Sheldon, experimented with Pops for a short time but had to drop it for lack of traction. However, one fact cannot be denied. Whether Da Da, Daddy, Pappy, or Dad, each one generates a vast amount of emotion, respect and endearment when focused in the direction of the one we call father.

Da Da, Pappy, Daddy and Dad have the same meaning, even though the cultural names differ slightly. As was the case with Muddah in a previous chapter, I have decided to devote a major part of this chapter to reflect on my Da Da and the experiences we had with him; the impact he had as a father and the relationship we formed while growing up with him in Roebuck. As was the case with Muddah, it is impossible to weave this unique term into the narrative of the book in any meaningful way without a personal story — an account that renders this section of the book autobiographical in nature.

Like Muddah, Da Da was definitely a term of endearment. And like Muddah, Da Da was pronounced with much reverence and respect for the man to whom the honor was directed. My Da Da was held in high regards by the residents of Roebuck and the other districts around, and to be known as Fred's son was an honor, as it was a complete ratification as to the level of respect and admiration he garnered from those who knew him. It goes without saying that the same level of praise and approval that was heaped on Muddah in a previous chapter belongs to Da Da as well. He was just as involved in our training and upbringing as Muddah was. Until he left for England, theirs was a united effort that was intentionally designed to bring us up with good manners and with respect for others, as was detailed earlier.

But as united as they were in the child-training business, certain contrasting characteristics were plainly evident between Muddah and Da Da, with him being outgoing and social and she appearing shy and reserved. Secondly, my Da Da loved to sing, regarding himself as an excellent bass voice in the Roebuck Pentecost Church choir that performed during the annual Christmas day program. One of the songs performed by the choir went something like this:

Since the price you cannot pay,
In this land you cannot stay,
You must pack up one of these mornings and move...

And I can even hear and see Da Da now, twisting and contorting in enjoyment, as he responded in deep bass tones *"you must move."* I must say that his love for singing was passed down to us as we regularly engaged in singing in our home. Muddah, on the other hand, was severely tone deaf, could not carry a tune to save her life, and was regularly the subject of family jokes that were usually initiated by Da Da — jokes, which she took rather lightheartedly and in a spirit of give and take, knowing full well that she was equally comfortable at returning the favor when it was her turn. There was no way she could have survived an audition for entry in the Roebuck Pentecost Church choir. She was that bad.

Another outstanding feature of my Da Da was that he loved to dress. And he knew that he looked *smart* when he was dressed, with a swagger that drew attention to him. When dressed for church on Sunday mornings, even I have to admit that there was no match for him in all of Roebuck. And he knew that, and relished the fact. As a lad, I too was the recipient of such attention, especially on Sunday mornings, when we were on our way to Sunday school. Da Da would part my hair on the left, dress me up, and we would walk together, up the line and down the road to the Church. Those Sunday moments are forever etched in my memory and were among the experiences I anticipated each week as I walked with my Da Da to church.

I was always a happy kid and had loads of fun engaging in my share of mischief while growing up in Roebuck. But the joy I experienced from walking to church with Da Da on Sunday mornings was one of the highlights of my young life. As I grew older, and regularly remembered those Sunday morning walks, I often wondered if the feelings of joy and happiness were mutual; if he nurtured the same sentiments from walking with me, his son. Da Da treasured a white bible which he dared not handle with his bare hands. It was too precious a possession, and had to be handled with care. A handkerchief was used for that purpose.

Da Da was a good father and for the most part we were happy children that thoroughly enjoyed having him as our father, even after he dispensed his brand of corporal punishment, which he did with authority and severity. But the good times outnumbered those painful experiences by far. By the way, Roebuck culture did not make mention of corporal punishment. That was not a term used in reference to punishment. It was a description that was too foreign for Roebuck and was only a milder name for the harshness of the punishment we received at the hands of, not only Da Da, but from Muddah as well. *Licks*, and even *beatings* were Roebuck terms that we understood only too well.

At the same time, it was as if Da Da knew what made us happy and excited and he was intentional from time to time at providing those experiences that evoked a chorus of unsaid 'thank yous' and appreciation. At random times and without warning, Da Da would come home with a can or two of Exeter corned beef, fix it up with onion, black pepper and a little lard oil, and readied it to be served with Eclipse biscuits before the feast was called to order.

In light of the events mentioned above, I never had the slightest trace of doubt concerning Da Da's wish for me, even though I never heard him articulate his personal desire for me in lengthy detail.

Even though little was said, at least to me, on the subject of my future, it was those snippets of his actions that told me that he cared, and that he wanted the best for me, especially as far as my education was concerned, even if he only wanted to live vicariously through my impending success, since he, like Muddah, had not gone too far in school. He probably discussed his wishes for me with Ms. Parris, the headmistress of the Indian Ground School. They were very close friends and he might have confided in her.

One particular incident that proves my point that Da Da wanted me to do well still resonates with me to this day. Da Da was a carpenter by trade. He kept his collection of chisels, spirit levels, planes, hammers and saws in an old tool box in the back house; the old box specially made with a narrow outlet to accommodate the protruding end of a saw that was too long for the box. Come to think of it, there must have been a few *spanners* in the old tool box as well. My sister, Neats, reminded me of the spanner recently when she sent me a text to say that her husband, Bernard, told her that he was looking for his spanner to fix something he was working on. "Do you remember what a spanner is," she asked. I had to admit that I had forgotten all about that word because I had not used it in a very long time.

It was as if there was an unwritten rule forbidding anyone to tamper with Da Da's tool box and its contents. That was until I got brave one day and attempted to use one of his tools. I was totally unprepared for his reaction that was as startling as it was surprising. "You should not be using my tools," he told me. "You should be reading books." I am not sure if he remembers the occasion but it is an unforgettable one for me.

As simple as it was, Da Da's statement has had two divergent effects on my life; effects that are still fresh today. First and foremost, Da Da's comment told me in no uncertain terms that he wanted something better for me; that he did not want a life of carpentry or a similar profession for me. The encouragement to read books was his way of telling me that he wanted me to be a teacher, a bank worker, or some other similar civil service position with the government. This was a profound compliment thrown in my direction; more so because Roebuck was not known for producing a workforce that filled government jobs. Students from *town* and other parts of Barbados usually did that. Roebuck was a farming community, whose labor force worked on the plantation, in construction, and other similar fields of work. Da Da did not want this for me. He wanted something better; something more in line with my remarkable achievements that would happen later.

Unlike Muddah, Da Da never taught me his craft; a decision he made with one purpose in mind: to turn me into a civil servant. The encouragement to read was his way of telling me he expected more for me, and more of me. Still, Da Da's goal to steer me away from building tools and in the direction of books continues to have an unintentional consequence. He never let up about the books, and just as driven, he never allowed me to use his tools, or even thought of teaching me at least the very basics of his trade. In time, I mastered the books, though not in keeping with his time frame and personal agenda for me. But in spite of major personal academic success, to this day I am noticeably awkward, self-conscious and totally ineffective with tools. I am constantly haunted by this one lingering fact that I am severely lacking in this one vital component that makes a man a useful man. On the other hand, I admire my friends Earle, Franklin, Bill and Robert and his boys for their expertise in mastering major and minor projects around the house and at church, from start to completion. I, on the other hand, am like Bill Cosby, still trying to master the very basics of home improvement; a skill I regrettably was not able to pass on to my sons.

But mastering the books came with another personal price as well; a price that was surprising and emotionally draining for a while. Da Da had left Roebuck for England and I subsequently completed high school and Teachers' College, still aiming to please Da Da, even though my wish to study in England did not materialize. After teaching at All Saints Boys School for only a short time I decided to further my education at Erdiston Teachers College and then at West Indies College (Northern Caribbean University) in Jamaica, still pursuing the books, just as Da Da had advised many years previously. Two comments by him, one prior to my enrolling in West Indies College and the other after graduation, are unforgettable. "Be careful of those Jamaican women," he passed on indirectly. But quite unlike his advice concerning his tools, my reaction to this latest directive was one hundred percent in the opposite direction. I was not careful enough of the Jamaican women he had warned me about. I ended up marrying one of those Jamaican women; a marriage that has lasted for more than thirty-six years.

However, it was Da Da's second comment, issued three years later that inflicted a little personal pain. "He must think he is better than anybody else," he is alleged to have commented to someone on learning that I had graduated from college. What a complete turnaround from "You should not be using my tools. You should be reading books?" Since then I have gone through three graduate programs, ranging from an MA to an Ed.S to a doctorate in education and Da Da's attitude towards my success has been consistent. Never has he uttered a single congratulatory word on my academic success, or recognized my professional achievement as a teacher and principal. Looking back at my academic achievement, I now believe that some of it can be labeled as revenge education; so named because of the energy I devoted to my studies, just to prove to Da Da that I could be a success without his blessing. Without a doubt, many reading this may have lived my experience and can speak to their own personal struggles of growing up without the support of a father, and despite the lack of paternal backing and encouragement, purposed in your heart that personal success would be achieved, no matter what.

Without a doubt, my present situation with tools is exactly the same with cars, or with bicycles, for that matter. Cars were not common in Roebuck when I was growing up. Mr. Scantlebury, the shopkeeper, was the only one that had one at the time; E 310, a blue Zephyr. If Da Da did have a car, even though he drove cars off and on and was very familiar with them, his advice to me would have been the same as the one about the tools. "You don't need to be changing flat tyres, or spark plugs, or brakes. You need to read books," probably would have been his advice. In other words, don't get your hands dirty. Today, I can change a flat, check the oil and replenish the antifreeze but would be hard pressed to locate or differentiate between a transmission and a carburetor, or a four cylinder from a six. So far removed was I from cars that I only got my driver's license at the age of twenty-six or twenty-seven when I was living in the Virgin Islands.

Da Da did have an old bicycle, a Raleigh. But once again I was not allowed to fool with it, and like other boys in Roebuck, never owned one. It was not a part of the culture in Roebuck for boys, or girls for that matter, to own bikes; quite unlike the culture in the US where bikes are standard gifts at a very young age. To make up for the shortfall of real toys, boys in Roebuck were extremely good and creative at inventing their own *rollers*, scooters, *tops* and *catapults* from scraps of wood, tree parts and other bits and pieces of raw material.

I went into some detail above about Da Da's educational goals on my behalf. And I also alluded to his time frame as to when they would begin — at eleven years old, a moment of truth for every eleven year old in Roebuck and in all of Barbados. That milestone could make or break a kid. And my Da Da wanted it to make me, not break me. I was grateful for that. The dreaded eleven plus exam was given to every child in this age group and a passing score on the *screening test* determined which of the great government secondary schools one would enroll. In Roebuck culture the test did not have a fancy name or catchy acronym like the CRCT (Criterion Referenced Competency Test) that is given in Georgia or the TCAP (Tennessee Comprehensive Assessment Program) that is given in Tennessee. In Roebuck, the test was not called the EPE, for the Eleven Plus Exam, or the ST for the Screening Test. It was simply called the screening test. And that was just what it did.

Da Da would have been ecstatic if I had done well enough on the test to get into at least Colridge and Parry, or even the Alleyne School. Harrison College or even Combermere, Lodge, or Foundation would have been fantastic. To make a long story short, I fell short of Da Da's expectations. I failed the screening test and Da Da's advice to stay away from tools and read books had not delivered the results he was hoping for. He was disappointed to say the least, and when the results of the eleven plus came back I remembered crying my eleven year-old eyes out, not certain if I was crying because I was disappointed in myself, or because I disappointed Da Da.

But this disappointment appears not to have been grounded only in the present at that time so long ago. It now appears that it was the beginning of a set of disappointing circumstances that were set in motion in the years that followed. Da Da left Roebuck soon after the eleven plus disappointment to find work in England. That decision was part of the culture of Roebuck in those days. Several men, including Leopold, Sun Dick, my cousin Hugh, and Uncle Hattan, Da Da's brother, migrated to find work to provide for their families back home. Work was hard to come by for women as well and some from Roebuck as well as others from all over Barbados migrated to England in search of a better life for themselves and their families back home.

In Roebuck we never said that people migrated. They just *left for*, or *went away*. For some time we knew that Da Da would be leaving us for England. We became increasingly sad especially when we saw that certain things were being put in place for his imminent departure. His *ping pongs* were taken and his passport was ready. Even

though his going away was necessary and was an action that had
been taken by many men in Barbados to make a better life for the
families they left behind, horror stories of men forgetting their
wives and children once they got to England may not have been
uppermost in Muddah's mind at the time. Certainly not in mine. I
was too young. It would certainly not happen to us.

I remember well the day when Da Da, with his *grips* and *valise*
packed, took us to the Deep Water Harbour to see him get on the
big ship that would take him to England. It was the Deep Water
Harbour in those days; not just the harbour or the port, but the
Deep Water Harbour, as if there was a shallow water harbour as
well. The event was heartbreaking and the effects continued for
weeks until we received his first letter in a blue oddly-shaped envelope, stamped *par avion.*

It had taken the ship that long to reach England. It took him a
while to find a job and he usually complained about how cold it
was in England. Later, the British pounds, sometimes five, sometimes ten, even twenty, started coming in the mail, in a regular
airmail envelope, and we looked forward to this special envelope
arriving in the mail from time to time because more often than not,
it contained pounds. Muddah would take them to the post office
in Speighstown and exchange them for $4.80 per pound and the
money would go a long way to help Muddah take care of us and
the house.

As a boy I got used to the first kind of envelope mentioned
above; those blue oddly-shaped envelopes that came with instructions on how to fold them. I got to know them very well, even
down to the statement that was printed on them that read something to the effect that they *should not contain any enclosures or they
will be surcharged.* At that age I wondered what surcharged meant
and even wondered if the word should have been searched, instead
of surcharged. Later I understood what an enclosure was and the
reason Da Da never sent money in this kind of envelope. Even

though they did not contain money, still I looked forward to receiving them and reading what Da Da had to say. This alone should be an indication of how much attention I paid to those blue envelopes and how much I looked forward to getting mail from him. We all enjoyed reading Da Da's letters and Muddah was all for sharing them with us.

In time we got used to Da Da being gone but I lived for the future and relished the thought that one day he would send for us and that we would all leave Roebuck to live in England. Da Da did not come back to Roebuck to visit that often and during the time he was gone, two significant things happened — one, a major disappointment; the other, a signal honor. Despite failing the screening test, I enrolled in the Modern High School, one of the leading private schools on the island, since Muddah was determined that I get a good education, no matter what, even if she had to pay for it.

Somehow, I had become very interested in a British education and when Da Da left for England I began wishing and hoping that he would send for us so that I could continue my education in England. I was an avid listener to the news on the radio and often heard of the successes of scholars from Barbados attending and graduating from the University of Birmingham, or Leeds, or Essex and I so much longed for that experience. What really intrigued me at the time was someone being *called to the bar* at Gravesend. At that time I did not know what that meant and often wondered why someone would be called to a bar, knowing full well that in Roebuck a bar meant a *rum shop*. But it sounded impressive on the radio and I knew that I wanted something like that. Obviously, I never got the opportunity because Da Da never sent for us.

While in this train of thought I think it appropriate to mention the other major disappointment I suffered at the hands of Da Da while he was away. Some may think this is petty and minor but to me as a small boy, it was one more thing that told me that things were not as they should have been. I mentioned before how much

I loved Christmas time in Roebuck and how Muddah made it special for us as best she could. On Christmas day, as well as at other times during the holiday season, the Rediffusion would broadcast a special program called *Christmas from Across the Seas* (or something like that) during which time people who had left for England would send Christmas greetings back to their families in Barbados.

I remember hovering around the radio every Christmas listening to the greetings as they were read, in anticipation that Da Da would at least remember us and send us Christmas greetings. But he never did. He probably tried and was not successful, but with all those Christmases away from home, at least one greeting would have meant a lot, and hearing my name on the radio would have been a wonderful thing. But Nazie, my cousin, did come through for me one Christmas. I can't remember the exact year but I can vividly recall her greetings from London; mentioning me by name and wishing me a merry Christmas. That little sentiment made a big difference in my Christmas that year.

Secondly, as was mentioned above, Da Da rarely came back to visit us in Roebuck but we received *parcels* from him from time to time. But during the time he was gone, something significant happened that sort of pushed me into an unofficial position of role model, leader and father figure, as young as I was at the time. When he left, my sister, Heather (Neats), was but a small child and did not know him very well. For a while I was the only male presence in her young life and in time she began to refer to me as Da Da. What an honor! On one of those rare times when Da Da did return to visit, she referred to him as *dah man* (that man), a testament to how little she knew him.

Something else happened on one of Da Da's rare visits. It may have been when he did come back to attend Grandmother's funeral. I was happy to see him and remember the visit well, even though one incident in particular that told my young mind that all was not well. He had brought back a Polaroid camera and I enjoyed snapping pictures and watching them develop before my very eyes. I was the envy of every little boy in Roebuck and was of the impression that Da Da had brought the camera for me. I could not have been more mistaken. He took it back with him when he was leaving to go back to England. I never forgot that and always viewed it as a signal that something was not the way it ought to have been. In time other things happened, some of which are beyond the scope of this book. Suffice it to say, the arrival of the blue par avion envelopes as well as the regular airmail envelopes and the pounds that came with them became less frequent, and Muddah was left to raise five of us practically on her own. As described earlier, she stepped up to the plate in a big way and before she passed, was able to see all of us grow into independent and successful citizens. That's why she will always be number one in my estimation.

Though specific and personal lessons were learned from the experiences mentioned above, some questions will always linger in my mind, no matter how old I become, or how far removed the experience with Da Da has become. As mentioned earlier, he had been a good father, doing his best to provide for his family. He was not the hugging, kissing type but still we knew that he loved Muddah, and us as well. So in spite of all the singing we did as a family, walking to Sunday school on Sunday mornings, the corned beef and biscuit parties we enjoyed, and the desire that I stay away from his tools and read books, something went wrong. Why did Da Da abandon his family? I have often wondered if I, by not passing the screening test, began a series of disappointing events, even though I have made up for it in a very big way. I have an idea what the real answer is, and like I mentioned before, that matter is beyond the scope of this book. That's a story for another day and time. There is a line in *Crying Time Again,* one of Ray Charles' old songs that says:

Oh they say that absence makes the heart grow fonder,
And that tears are only rain to make love grow...

The sentiments of the lyrics seemed not to be true in Da Da's case.

But if there is some good that can emerge, or that has emerged from a bad situation, it is certainly true in this case. Personally, I have learned from the experience with Da Da, and determined a long time ago that my sons' experiences with me would be the opposite from what I personally experienced; that I would never leave them under any circumstance.

Even if I had the minutest thought of doing such a thing, my son Haniffe, would remind me of my solemn obligation to him, his brothers, and his mother. We were living in the Virgin Islands at the time and I had gone back to Michigan State University for the summer to complete the requirements for the Ed.S degree I had started a year earlier. I was only gone for a short time when I called to check on the family as I had done each day since I was gone. On this particular day, Haniffe, who was not even two at the time, passed on a personal message to me via his mother "It is time for daddy to come home now," he said. I am left to wonder if my situation with my Da Da would have turned out differently had I sent him a similar message when he left Roebuck when I was a boy.

Still, my Da Da was a good man in many ways even though his relationship with his family changed drastically after leaving Roebuck for England. In many ways, some of my basic tenets of fatherhood and values relating to good character and basic human goodness can be traced back to his early association with me, and the family in general. He worked hard to provide for his family and made the home environment comfortable and warm. He lived the culture of Roebuck at the time, believing that all that was required of fatherhood was to satisfy the financial needs of his family, and like others in Roebuck, found little or no time for extras. The fatherhood culture that existed in Roebuck at the time did not allow for father-son trips to a cricket match at Kensington Oval, or a trip down to the river in Sedgepond to catch crayfish, or working together on a dog house for Fluff, or just throwing a ball back and forth to each other, or even romping together on the floor once in a while, or setting up a tent and camping out for a night in the *grass piece*. I did not expect it from him, simply because none of the other boys in Roebuck had the luxury of spending one on one time with their fathers. It just wasn't cultural in Roebuck. Years later while raising my own children, I was quick to learn that the job of fatherhood is very inclusive and requires much more than providing for the financial needs of a family.

Da Da left for England when I was around eleven or twelve; at a time when a young boy needs his father around to provide sound leadership and to answer questions on growing up and becoming a man. Understandably so, his checking out was something he had to do. Like several others from Roebuck, he was displaying a level of responsibility; taking his commitment to fatherhood and being a good husband and provider seriously. Yet, in the years leading up to this time, eternal impressions and lasting social principles had been taught to me vicariously through Da Da by how he lived; lessons I observe to this day.

Da Da did not smoke or do drugs. Not that drugs were available in those days. And I feel confident in proclaiming that he would not have gotten involved in drugs even if they were a part of the culture back then. The story line is the same with alcohol and drinking. Da Da might have had a drink once in a while but not to the extent where he lost all sense of reality and self-control; conditions that drove others to the brink of violence, domestic abuse, as well as being a danger to themselves and to others as they stumbled all over the place and talking nonsense. But it goes without saying and without contradiction that the noblest social lesson I learned from Da Da is the respect and esteem I have for women. I have never witnessed him lay a hand on Muddah, or physically mistreat her in any way, as was the common culture back in the day. So to be fair to him, and in spite of what happened later, his examples in character building and integrity have been tutorials in the social graces that I have adopted as a way of life, and that I have hopefully passed on to my three sons.

THE EPILOGUE

What started out as a book on how two cultures use specific words and phrases to represent similar and different meanings, evolved into something more than when the idea to write the book was initially conceived. The primary plan was to draw attention to those common terms that convey a completely different meaning in each of the two cultures examined; simple words used by normal people in everyday conversation and communication. The list of words continued to grow as I engaged in conversations, especially with relatives and friends from my native Barbados, and by listening more closely to my American friends, colleagues, and the news media. Throughout the entire writing process, my listening skills became increasingly acute as I found myself paying close attention to personal conversations between others, only as a means of growing my word bank for the book.

Even though I was armed with a growing list of words, it became evident that a mere mention of those on my list and a description of how their usage was different would not have been adequate enough to produce a volume of any significant length. Hence, in the very early stages the plan was revised to include, as far as possible, a brief story around each word. Around the same time, the decision was made to change the setting of the book from a more global perspective, Barbados, to one that was specific and personal — Roebuck, the district in Barbados where I was born and raised.

As I continued writing the manuscript, other major changes were significant. First, the ideas mentioned above forced me to revise the book's initial title. Secondly, the genre, though remaining non-fiction throughout, give some evidences of being autobiographical in some areas as I delved into personal stories about my younger years in Roebuck.

Additionally, I discuss a historical accounting of some of the people and culture of Roebuck in some detail. While collecting words and formulating appropriate stories to support their meanings, it became quite clear that the book could gain the distinction as a resource document on the past, particularly for the younger generation presently living in Roebuck, while serving as a reminder of the cultural behavior of Roebuck and its people.

As a matter of fact, the book evolved in many small and specific ways; ways that kept expanding the narrative. This created the need for ongoing editing and the challenge of inserting additional material when it came in from independent sources.

One such instance happened when my friend, Floyd, called out of the blue one evening. "Do you remember *sickie messiah*," he asked with a mischievous chuckle. I honestly had to take a few seconds to think before catching my bearings. "Isn't that what they said when they rebuked people in the Roebuck Pentecost Church?" He called me again one Sunday morning, when, as far as I was concerned, the book was finished, asking if I had a *peck* he could borrow. Obviously, this new addition required me to return to the narrative to find an appropriate place in which to seamlessly insert it.

I encountered similar incidents from time to time during various stages of writing the manuscript; such as the day Hal called, just to ask me if I remembered what a *spy* was. Another time, shortly after Hal's call, my sister, Heather, fired off a text message reminding me of the *spanner*. Later, another sister, Cheryl, called to ask if I remembered what a *ping pong* was. Before hanging up, she threw in *grip* for good measure. In each of these cases, the manuscript was already in an advanced stage of development and I had to do a quick revision so as to accommodate the additions from those helpful sources. Without them, I would not have remembered the specifics they shared.

My personal observation also added to the evolution of the project in a small way. For two days I drove past a tennis ball sitting on a neighbor's perfectly manicured lawn. On the third day of my drive in from work I wondered why the ball was still there. Only then did I realize that it was there for a specific reason — to jog my memory that the ball was in fact a *wind ball.* I went home and immediately inserted wind ball into the narrative. The next day the ball was gone.

In each of the examples cited above, as well as many others, the challenge was to find appropriate places in the manuscript to insert the new ideas as they came in during my writing, or even when I thought that the writing was done. Surprisingly, it was much easier than initially thought as the task of adding them into the narrative was accomplished with a little effort and creativity. Such is the case with *bad feels.* Only very recently, even as Hortense was doing the final reading of the manuscript, I came across *bad feels* in a column by Eric Lewis in one the Barbados newspapers. Obviously, I could not resist the temptation to go back and find an appropriate place in the narrative that was naturally supported by its inclusion.

The book did take a long time to complete; a matter of years from the time the idea to write it was conceived. Still, this can be viewed in a positive light as the extra time provided opportunities for listening, observing and talking with family and friends; all proving to be helpful resources for a wider variety of words to add to my list, as well as providing ideas that shaped this work.

About the Author

Sylvester Carrington hails from Roebuck, St. Peter, a remote agricultural district located in the northern part of the Caribbean island of Barbados. He is a graduate of Erdiston Teachers College in his native Barbados, and West Indies College (Northern Caribbean University), Jamaica. He also holds graduate degrees from Andrews University, Michigan State University, and a doctorate in Education from Loma Linda University. A career educator, Dr. Carrington has taught in his native Barbados and The Virgin Islands, and has held instructional and leadership positions at all levels of education in Tennessee and Georgia, where he now resides. He and his wife, Hortense, have three grown sons and one terrific grandson, Max.

Dr. Carrington is also the author of *A Principal's Personal Journey*. He can be reached at lionel49.c@gmail.com.

Acknowledgements

This work could not have been successfully completed without the input of many. I am indebted to my friends, Floyd Marshall and Hal Griffith, for engaging me in numerous unplanned conversations that produced many of the words and terms that are unique to Roebuck (and Barbados), some of which I had long forgotten. I want to thank you guys for being excellent resources, for answering my many questions, and for your enthusiastic attitude towards the project.

My gratitude is also extended to Jasmine and Laura Goodman for serving as consultants on some of the entries that are included in the book. I also thank Joyce Franklin for sharing some key details when she visited me from New York. I extend an abundance of thanks to my cousin, Genlyn Morris, for your help with the names of some of the families in Roebuck, and for your role as the unofficial historian for the project. Your willingness to share your knowledge of Roebuck, its families and customs is truly appreciated. I also want to thank my friends, Frank and Kathy Purnell for taking the time to get the images ready for the book. Your contribution to the project is immensely appreciated.

I especially want to thank my sisters Elaine, Yvonne, Cheryl, and Heather for contributing significantly to several sections of the book, especially the chapter on the line; for refreshing my memory on the makeup of the families in Roebuck; for bringing back to memory the many nicknames, and for providing details on the customs we celebrated when we were children. I thank you for your constant encouragement while I was writing, and for gently nudging me to get the book finished. Special thanks to my aunt, Gloria Pitt, for playing a major role in one of the chapters, and for your input into the accuracy of one particular story. My cousins, Charleston Cumberbatch and Dorcas Scantlebury, also contributed to the book in a huge but unintended role. While back in Roebuck on a recent visit, your conversations with me validated many of the stories included in the book.

Major thanks to my wife, Hortense, for proof reading and editing the manuscript; for adding your suggestions and corrections based on your sound judgment, and your superb writing and literary skills. Thanks for your trust and for the volume of confidence you have always placed in me.

GLOSSARY OF TERMS

above	to the east of
air	stomach gas
arrows	sugar cane blossoms
back pay	bonus, or retroactive money paid to plantation workers
backslide	a departure from one's faith
bad feels	an ill feeling
bade	bathe
band	made by joining leafy parts of the sugar cane to hold a bundle of sugar cane together
bank holiday	a holiday
bat and ball	a street game of cricket
bedstid	bedstead
below	to the west of
bewitched	stupid
bill	a tool used in harvesting sugar cane
black lead	a pencil
boar	a male pig
board house	a house made of wood
bomb	a small device that exploded when smashed against the ground
boner	an erection

bonnet	a hat
botsie	the buttocks
bound	constipated
boxes	a mailed package containing clothing, etc.
bowels	diarrhea
breaking cane	removing sugar cane from a field
brewing	the process of cooling hot tea
buller	a homosexual male
bureau	a dresser
bush	brush
bush tea	herbal tea
bus stand	bus terminal
butt and bound	abutted; bordering another district
butt up	to run into somebody unexpectedly
cabbage tree	land rented by the plantation for farming
cabinet	a china cabinet
cane	sugar cane
cane cutters	men who harvest sugar cane
cane ground	a field of sugar cane
cane heap	a mound of sugar cane
cane piece	a sugar cane field
cane row	sugar cane planted in a long line in a field
cane top	the leafy portion of the sugar cane
cart road	a narrow unpaved path usually between two cane fields
casserina	the casuarina tree; a mile tree
cellar	the space under a house
chambers	bedrooms
cheupsing	sucking one's teeth
chink	a bed bug
clap down	clapping/jeering someone off the stage
class three	grade three
clear skin	of light complexion

cock	a rooster; a male fowl
cockaroach	a cockroach
cold	the mucus-like material in the corners of one's eyes on waking in the morning
conductor	the person responsible for collecting fares on a bus
cou cou	a Barbadian dish made of cornmeal and okra
cou cou stick	a flat wooden instrument for stirring cou cou
coming down	losing weight
constitution	the immune system
coolie man	Indian salesman on foot
cork hat	a type of hat worn by a plantation driver
cotton	thread
cracker	a biscuit
crapoe	a frog; crapaud
crayfish	shrimp caught from the river in Sedgepond
crop time	season for harvesting sugar cane
cuff	hitting someone with a closed fist
cuss cuss	khus khus grass
cutter	a sandwich
cutting canes	harvesting sugar cane
cymbal	a tambourine
Da Da	daddy; dad
darn	a patch on clothing to close a hole
dear	expensive; costly
deaths	obituaries
dickey	penis
disgusting	disobedient
district	a small village
dog dumpling	the noni fruit
doggie	a small boy's penis

domestic science	home economics
donkey cart	a donkey-drawn carriage for carrying goods
down	dung
drake	a male duck
draw up under	snuggle
dribble	dried up saliva around the mouth on waking from sleep
driver	a supervisor watching workers on a plantation
drug store	a pharmacy
dungarees	jeans
duppie	a ghost
dust	dusk
emp out	to empty a container of its contents
exercise book	a student notebook
fall away	losing weight
family way	pregnant
Father Christmas	Santa Claus
feel up	petting; necking
feeling the fowls	inserting a finger in the behind of a hen to feel for the presence of an egg
fester	formation pus in a wound
fifth form	12th grade
fireplace	an outdoor or indoor cooking area
fixing to	getting ready to do something
flat top house	a house with a flat roof
fly stick	a trap used to catch birds
fob	a small pocket in the front of a pair of pants
food	a meal
fowl	a hen; chicken
fowl down	fowl dung
fowl house	chicken pen; a chicken run; a chicken coop
frenchie	a condom

full stop	punctuation mark at the end of a statement
gallery	a porch
games	P.E; gym
gipsy	minding another person's business
god horse	a praying mantis; walking stick
grabble urn	a long iron tool for digging limestone
grace	a prayer before meals
grass piece	a field of grass; a pasture
grip	a suitcase; a valise
grits	roadside gravel
ground	a large field of sugar cane; corn, etc.
ground provisions	food grown in a field or garden; produce
gulley	a ravine
half bath	washing only some parts of the body: face, legs, arms, etc.
hand	money invested in an investment project called a meeting
hand work	arts and craft
hard ears	being disobedient
heading canes	carrying a bundle of sugar cane on the head
heart man	an outlaw hiding a cane field
hen	a female fowl
horning	a move to take away someone's girl friend or boyfriend
horsepital	a hospital
hot water tea	tea made from hot water and sugar
house spot	a lot; the space on which a house is built
house top	the roof of a house
infants A	kindergarten
jelly	the soft white substance in a coconut before it turns hard
jew	dew
kersene oil	kerosene oil

jooking	to stab with a sharp object
jooking board	a special board used in washing clothes
khus khus grass	a special grass used in making beds
kimber	a cucumber
knock off	the time to leave work on the plantation at the end of the work day
knotty hair	nappy hair; kinky hair
lame foot	a sore or a cut on one's foot
larder	a pantry
lard oil	cooking oil
lark	a slat
lash	to strike someone or something
lessons	private tutoring
licked down	knocked down by a car
lift	help hoisting a load to one's head
liming	hanging out with friends
line	a lane; narrow street
look for the sheep	visiting the sheep in the field around the middle of the day
look out	heads up
Lord's Supper	the Communion service
lorry	a truck
major stop	a stop sign
marked	a license plate on a car
marks	grades on a report card
marl	limestone
mash up	to destroy something
mauby	a bitter drink made from the bark of a special tree
meeting	an investment organization that returns large lump sums of money to the investors
mist	fog
mock sport	making fun at another person

monkey	a pottery vessel for keeping drinking water cool
mouth organ	a harmonica
moving sheep	moving the sheep to a new graving area around midday
muddah	mother; mom
multiplication tables	multiplication facts
musketeers	mosquitoes
musty	a bad body odor
oat flakes	oatmeal
ortaman	an ottoman
outing	a bus ride sponsored by the church
pad	insulation made from cloth or similar material to place on the head to cushion a heavy load
parcel	a package containing clothing, etc.
passover	a stroke; rupture of a blood vessel in the brain
pear	avocado
peck	a tool used to remove tree stumps, stones, etc.
phensic	aspirin
picking meat	gathering specific grasses/vines for sheep to eat
picking rice	removing bad grains of rice before cooking.
pickups	a game similar to Jacks and balls
pine	a type of wood used in building houses
ping pong	passport pictures
pissy	smelling of stale urine
pitching	a marble game
plaster	a band aid
platform	the church pulpit
please for a pass	excuse me; may I have a pass?

pokey	vagina; jail
pooch	the buttocks
poor	thin; skinny
poor great	proud, self-important
poorly	being sick unto death
postman	mailman
post mortem	autopsy
pot timer	one who pops up just in time for dinner at a neighbor's
pound	British currency
pounkin	pumpkin
power	having the Holy Ghost
pram	a stroller
pressing	ironing clothing
prong	prawn; crayfish
pumps	a tennis-like shoe
purging	diarrhea
pushed down	demolished
rabbit meat	a special kind of grass fed to sheep
raky	skinny; thin
rambling	difficulty finding a specific location while walking or driving
rank	smelling of stale urine; pissy
ready-made shirt	a pregnancy resulting from an affair with a man that is not the woman's husband
rebuke	to prevent someone from participating in a religious service
red herring	smoked herring
Rediffusion	radio
road	the street
rock stone	a small rock; a stone
roller	a toy made from bicycle tire rim and propelled by a narrow piece of wood

roti	a pancake-like Caribbean pastry usually stuffed with curry
rough dry	wrinkled clothes
rounders	a street game similar to baseball
rubber	a pencil eraser
rub out	to erase with an eraser
rum shop	a bar
run	to chase someone
rusty	ashy
salt fish	cod fish
sangridge	a sandwich
santapee	a centipede
scab	hardened blood covering a wound
scotch	limping along in tight shoes
set	an erection
setting up	getting ready to rain
share	a serving of food
shub	a shove
sickie messiah	term used in Roebuck Pentecost Church when rebuking a member
six	six runs in cricket
skipping	a game of jump rope
sky lark	joking around
sleeping policemen	speed bumps
smart	looking good when dressed up
soft shoes	tennis shoes; sneakers
sow	a female pig
spanner	a wrench
sprinkle	damping clothes before ironing
spy	a Transport Board employee that checked on the record-keeping of bus conductors
skin out	the name given to the action of emptying a drawer, etc.

stand pipe	a public tap or a spicket connected to the main water supply to provide water for the public
starlights	sparkles
starve out	starving
steppers	chicken feet
stick	a cane
stocks	a flock of sheep (or cows)
stump toe	a stubbed toe
surname	a person's last name
sweet drink	a drink similar to soda pop
sweetie	a candy
sweet water	a drink made of sugar and water
tab	a belt loop on a pair of pants
tap	a faucet
taking out sheep	taking the sheep out to graze in the morning
tar road	a paved road
teefing	stealing
tenin	tin
timble	a thimble
time	thyme
tink	think
topsie	vessel kept under the bed during the night to hold urine
tot	a drinking utensil made from a tin/aluminum can
town	the city
trembling	shaking
trunk	a chest for storing clothes
truss (trust)	a purchase made on credit
tumbric	tumeric
turn out	the handling of a funeral by an undertaker
undertaker	funeral home director
tyre	an automobile tire

upstairs house	a house with stairs
valise	a piece of luggage
vest	an undershirt
wall house	a brick house
wares	dishes
water closet	a toilet or bathroom with running water
west cut	a waist coat; the vest to a three-piece suit
wicker	a lesbian
wild wist	a vine used as a jump rope
wind ball	a tennis ball
zed	the letter zee
zeplen	a water delivery truck

Review Requested:

If you loved this book, would you please provide a review at Amazon.com?